Agriculture and the
Industrial Revolution

Agriculture and the Industrial Revolution

E. L. JONES

Professor of Economics
Northwestern University

With a Foreword by R. M. Hartwell

BASIL BLACKWELL · OXFORD

ISBN 0 631 15370 5

Printed in Great Britain
by Western Printing Services Ltd, Bristol
set in Linotype Times
and bound by the Kemp Hall Bindery, Oxford

To the Warden and Fellows
of Nuffield College, Oxford

Contents

Acknowledgements   ix
Foreword by R. M. Hartwell   x
Introduction   1

ONE: Agricultural Change
and the Process of Industrialization

1. Eighteenth-Century Changes
   in Hampshire Farming   23
2. Agricultural Conditions
   and Changes
   in Herefordshire, 1600–1815   41
3. Agriculture and Economic
   Growth in England, 1660–1750:
   Agricultural Change   67
4. Agriculture and Economic
   Growth in England, 1650–1815:
   Economic Change   85
5. Agricultural
   Origins of Industry   128

TWO: Agriculture
in the Urban-Industrial Economy

6. Hereford Cattle and Ryeland
   Sheep: Economic Aspects
   of Breed Changes, 1780–1870   145

7. Industrial Capital and
   Landed Investment: the Arkwrights
   in Herefordshire, 1809–43   160
8. Wheat Yields
   in England, 1815–59   184
9. The Changing Basis of English
   Agricultural Prosperity, 1853–73   191
10. The Agricultural Labour
    Market in England, 1793–1872   211

Acknowledgements

The author and publishers wish to thank the following for permission to reproduce the articles listed below:

The British Agricultural History Society for 'Eighteenth-Century Changes in Hampshire Chalkland Farming' and 'The Changing Basis of English Agricultural Prosperity, 1853–73' (*Agricultural History Review*, Vols. VIII and X, 1960 and 1962); Methuen & Company Ltd. for 'Editor's Introduction', *Agriculture and Economic Growth in England, 1650–1815* (London, 1967); the Economic History Association for 'Agriculture and Economic Growth in England, 1660–1750: Agricultural Change' (*Journal of Economic History*, Vol. XXV, 1965); *Past & Present* for 'Agricultural Origins of Industry' from Number 40, 1968; Edward Arnold Ltd. for 'Industrial Capital and Landed Investment: the Arkwrights in Herefordshire, 1809–43' from E. L. Jones and G. E. Mingay (eds.), *Land, Labour, and Population in the Industrial Revolution: Essays Presented to J. D. Chambers* (London, 1967); the Royal Statistical Society and Mr. M. J. R. Healy for 'Wheat Yields in England, 1815–1859' (*Journal of the Royal Statistical Society*, Series A, Vol. CXXV, 1962); the Economic History Society for 'The Agricultural Labour Market in England, 1793–1872' (*Economic History Review*, 2nd ser., Vol. XVII, 1964); and Miss Meryl Jancey for 'Agricultural Conditions and Changes in Herefordshire, 1660–1815' and 'Hereford Cattle and Ryeland Sheep: Economic Aspects of Breed Changes, 1780–1870' (*Transactions of the Woolhope Club*, Vols. XXXVII and XXXVIII, 1961 and 1964).

Foreword

For most of history, most of mankind have been 'agriculturalists' —hunters, fishers, food-gatherers, food-growers, animal-breeders, timber-fellers—yet the study of economic history is now dominated by the problems of industrialization. Economic historians devote their efforts increasingly to the analysis of industrialization and modern economic growth, yet this great phenomenon is only one of three in the long-term economic history of world population: two, the agricultural revolution and the industrial revolution, were the great discontinuities of history, but there was also that very long, very slow, economic growth which, over some ten thousand years or more after the agricultural revolution, raised man from illiterate and subsistence barbarism to the economic, social, political and cultural sophistication of an eighteenth-century France or England. France and England in 1700 were not 'advanced economies'— neither were they 'underdeveloped' in the modern sense—but they were certainly 'advanced civilizations'. Indeed the great civilizations of history, it is important to emphasize, were agriculturally based, even though they produced great urban cultures. Modern civilization, however, is urban and industrial, and predominantly urban, in contrast with older civilizations; and agriculture has been seen, usually, as economically less important and less efficient than industry, as well as being politically more conservative. In the history of modern Europe agriculture's role has often been 'unprogressive', *Junkers* and peasants resisting economic change and market economy, as well as opposing political change and democracy. But much of the world today, outside of Europe and European societies overseas, is still agricultural, and so the relationship between agriculture and economic growth is probably the most important contemporary problem. These modern agricultural economies are finding it difficult to industrialize and grow.

What, then, is the lesson of history? How did England and the other developed economies progress in the past from their agricultural base? Economic historians and economists both show that industrialization and economic growth are not possible without agricultural change, without an increase in agricultural productivity; and, obviously, that the sustained population increase that invariably accompanies growth is not possible without an increase in the supply of food. But what is the relationship between these? Which is cause, and which effect? Does (did) an agricultural revolution produce an industrial revolution or vice versa? Does (did) more people produce more food, or more food more people? Does (did) an agricultural surplus allow the growth of industry, or does (did) industrial change induce agricultural change? What is (was) the relationship of an agricultural revolution to an industrial revolution and a population explosion? These are the sort of questions to which Eric Jones has devoted so much effort and ingenuity, with so much enlightenment for other economic historians.

The empirical evidence about the relationship between agriculture and industry is suggestive but not conclusive. There are no examples of industrialization and growth in any of the major economies of the world which were not preceded or accompanied by an agricultural transformation. On the other hand, as Eric Jones points out: 'One of the less palatable lessons of history is that technically advanced or physically productive agricultures do not inevitably bring about a sustained growth of *per capita* real income, much less promote industrialization.' In an obvious sense, since all industrialized economies were preceded by agricultural economies, the origins of industrialization must be sought in an agricultural society. But where? Under what circumstances? Why do some agricultural economies grow, and not others? In recent years the spate of literature on the history of English agriculture has done little to elucidate these problems. Eric Jones, however, has made explicit, with historical and theoretical underpinning, the essential relationship between agriculture and the industrial revolution. In a series of articles—of which the best known is probably 'Agriculture and Economic Growth in England, 1650–1815: Economic Change' (reprinted in this volume)—he has shown just how 'agriculture . . . contributed in real if complicated ways to the emergence of industrialism in England'. This he has done by putting theory into the analysis of past agricultural change, thus lifting the level of discourse from casual empiricism to a scientific analysis of the transformation of a traditional agriculture. In particular he has made clearer two great problems: the longer-term causes of agricultural change in the centuries before the industrial revolution; agriculture's role in the industrial revolution through such activities as capital formation, the release of productive factors and demand expansion.

A foreword to another man's book is not a place in which to parade one's own ideas, but let me be self-indulgent. There is a widespread disease which T. W. Schutz has called 'agricultural fundamentalism', which affects not only nations but historians. Why, for example, is an 'agricultural historian' so much more common than an 'industrial historian'? Why has agriculture its own specialized historical profession? Agricultural fundamentalism leads inevitably, as did the theories of the Physiocrats, to a belief that agriculture is different, is more important, is fundamental. Agricultural fundamentalism is a universal phenomenon, and stems not only from the basic importance of agriculture's role in food production, but also to the extraordinary strength everywhere of the agricultural lobby. Agriculture once dominated the world both economically and politically; what is interesting, and what is not adequately explained by the historians, is that the political importance of agriculture survived its economic decline. Indeed, the conservatism and strength of agriculture everywhere would suggest that industrialization occurred in spite of agriculture. No consideration of modern history can ignore the continuing strength of the agricultural lobby; it has been, and often still is, a massive immobility in the economy and politics of most advanced nations. Yet there have been occasions when, as in England, a progressive agriculture and an agricultural revolution were intimately associated with industrialization and growth. In other countries, as in southern Italy, the character of agriculture in the nineteenth century was such as to produce almost total *immobilismo*.

Agriculture, also, has played an important role in the development of economic theory and in the formulation of economic policy, especially because it has provided the main examples of two important economic 'laws': the law of diminishing returns and Engel's law. Historically the law of diminishing returns was formulated in the first place on the basis of agricultural experience (or alleged agricultural experience); it was a necessary part of the Malthusian law of population, and was, in consequence, influential in the formation of nineteenth-century economic policy; it justified the New Poor Law and the repeal of the Corn Laws. In the long run it proved difficult to sustain the theory in agriculture, where it is doubtful that the marginal product ever fell towards zero in the advanced economies. Indeed the increasing productivity of agriculture over the last two centuries has been a matter of wonder and relief. Engel's law, then, is more important? Engel's law states that as incomes rise, less is spent on food, and there is long-standing empirical support for the proposition that as *per capita* income rises, the demand for food rises relatively more in low-income than in high-income economies. Because of this, the trend away from agriculture in growing economies is universal, whether measured in terms of occupational distribution or of the commodity distribution of output; the higher the level of income in an economy, the smaller the agricultural sector. It is in these characteristics of agriculture that part of the explanation of the structural changes in economy—from agriculture to industry and services—is to be found.

Let me admit, in conclusion, that agriculture is different and is important, and that understanding pre-industrial agriculture in England is a prerequisite to understanding the industrial revolution. In aiding this understanding nobody has done more than Eric Jones, and this collection of essays will add significantly to that growing body of literature on the industrial revolution.

R. M. HARTWELL

Footnotes are to be found at the end of each chapter.

Introduction

Until our Philosophers and Heroes of Science and Art, handle the Plough and Spade, and undertake the more plenary discovery and description of these Rustick operations ... I hope this indigested Piece may find a place in our Rural Libraries, and then I shall willingly be the first that shall commit this to the Flames to give way for a better.

John Worlidge, preface to *Systema Agriculturae*, 1669

Demography and agriculture and urbanization are fundamentals of man's past, so much so that their comparative neglect by professional historians is surely an odd historiographical sport or paradox. Nevertheless, despite relative neglect in favour of political subjects or the history of ideas, the absolute number of scholars concerned with these three topics grew sufficiently during the 1960s for the mere job of scanning the output of secondary literature to have become a daunting exercise—given our limited individual capacity to monitor the work of others.[1] In the course of this growth the quality of the best of the literature has improved almost out of recognition. It is my opinion that the very best work on the economic history of English agriculture is now being done by some of the Americans who bring the tools of economic theory to bear on the 'Rustick Operations' of old England.[2] The subject has become one with a quite numerous and lively body of students among economic historians.

This was not the case during the second half of the 1950s, when my own interest in the subject was emerging. At that time interest in the 'Agricultural Revolution' and its links with the 'Industrial Revolution' seemed to be displayed as much by agricultural scientists and development economists as by general economic historians. The attention was gratifying rather than illuminating, scientists and development economists both being capable of useful insights into the processes of change but being about equally prone to draw on stale secondary histories and inclined to trample rough-shod over the tender plants of historical evidence. The specialist investigation of agricultural history was a solitary pursuit, openly regarded by some political historians and publishers as nasty, brutish, and from the career point-of-view likely to be short. In the late 1950s and early 1960s it was the writing of nine or ten scholars, the late J. D. Chambers, the late T. W. Fletcher, W. G. Hoskins, A. H. John, Eric Kerridge, G. E. Mingay, Joan Thirsk, F. M. L. Thompson, E. H. Whetham, and I hope myself, that brought the agricultural sector to the attention of all economic historians interested in the last four centuries or thereabouts, and kept the flame burning so that the topic received its share of students and funds when economic history took its place in the general expansion of universities and colleges. This group did not operate as a caucus—the individuals named do not find the same sort of questions interesting nor address them with the same tone or techniques—but their collective influence on the study of economic and social history and historical geography, and to a lesser extent economic development and adjacent subjects, has been considerable. Certainly my own pen has been aimed at the general economic historian rather than at readers interested purely in the history of farming.

What the source was of my interest in this branch of economic history I cannot say, although clearly it had something to do with the love for the English countryside that I had developed as a schoolboy naturalist. There were economies of sorts to be reaped from looking at survivals of older agricultural landscapes and at the birdlife 'in the field' on week-ends. It is easier to be sure that my teachers at Nottingham encouraged my leaning, notably David Chambers of course, though his own work was turning towards demography, but also, and to a much greater extent than they would avow, Bob Ashton and Bob Coats. Hence as an under-graduate I took to reading agricultural history with the absorptive capacity, and no doubt in some measure with the analytical powers, of a sponge. I have a particularly vivid memory of reading Joan Thirsk's *English Peasant Farming* and W. G. Hoskins's *The Midland Peasant* on the diesel train which sped me, on Saturday mornings, across Lincolnshire to Boston, to go bird-watching on the Wash, and looking up from time to time to catch sight of a skein of Pinkfooted Geese against those wide Fenland skies. The train, had I known it, was rushing me into a future which would include a decade at Oxford, where the ten papers reprinted here were written, and on one later occasion a visit to the derivative Boston for a conference on the European peasant economy at Endicott House, which, by no very great coincidence, Dr. Thirsk was also attending. The cab driver insisted on my marking the steeple where the Liberty Bell had hung, the Bunker Hill monument, and *Old Ironsides* in perpetual drydock. My interests were for a time moving away from agriculture, and Boston to Boston seemed to draw a symbolic line under a long excursion into the English rural past.

The interim, then, saw the writing of these essays. They have appeared before, but in widely separated and not always very accessible places. While they report inquiries into a rather wide range of topics in agricultural change and its relation to the early industrial economy, they do fall into two distinct groups by both theme and period. Because the essays do form these two sequences which reflect the evolution of my thought and the progressive widening of my interests, and because the second sequence follows the first quite naturally, it has seemed reasonable to collect them in the present volume. With hindsight I would not tackle the topics in quite the same way, but neither would I select radically different foci than the configurations of change within agriculture and the consequences of a freer agricultural supply response for economic growth (Part One), and the moulding of agricultural activity by the market forces of the very first urban–industrial country (Part Two). The pieces are reprinted here in their original form, apart from the correction of a thin spatter of typographical errors and the deletion of a very few sentences or phrases which affixed the essays too firmly into their previous publishing contexts.

I

Part One, 'Agricultural Change and the Process of Industrialization', deals with the twin themes of change in agriculture and its economic implications over the period from the middle of the seventeenth century to the end of the Napoleonic wars. The opening two papers treat change—primarily technical change—in a local or regional context. The first has the setting of the Hampshire chalklands. These are my native heath, or rather downs, and my first research concerned them. The second is a parallel study of the state of agriculture in the beautiful, secluded county of Hereford and was written as background and introduction to the analysis of post-1815 trends there which formed part of my doctoral thesis. Herefordshire's agricultural products were and are exceptionally varied, and much of the farming is on heavy, clayey soil quite unlike most of that on the Hampshire chalk. The two studies are intended thereby to complement one another in building up a picture of the eighteenth-century scene.

Chapter 3 is a much broader attempt to generalize about the supply response of English farming between the mid-seventeenth and mid-eighteenth centuries. Again, the emphasis is on technical change and its implications for regional and edaphic shifts in the location (and hence cost and profit levels) of farming systems. Some mention is made of the significance for aggregate agricultural investment of the landlord and tenant system. That system was peculiarly benign in England in this period and was surely a crucial element in England's agricultural progress, helping to differentiate English experience in recent centuries from that of medieval times, and to differentiate modern English and mainland European experiences. Elsewhere, notably in Chapter 4, the role of institutional change is somewhat consciously played down. This should be taken as the combined result of two opinions: a feeling that the difficulties which non-specialists seem to encounter when discussing the somewhat elusive changes in farming systems, where even the terminology has an indefinite quality about it, constantly tend to sweep these technical matters out of sight; and a tongue-in-cheek daring of the institutionalists to spell out, instead of interminably asserting, say, the productivity rather than the welfare effects of the enclosure movement. I tossed down that glove again elsewhere and it was then quickly picked up by Professor McCloskey, who selected English Parliamentary enclosure as a suitable subject for work in 'neo-institutional' economics.[3] This is all to the good, though it will be unfortunate in my eyes if the very genuine excitement which work on institutional change is generating deflects more than half the available research effort away from the development of farming techniques.

Chapter 3 therefore deals with what, to judge from most of the recent literature, must be regarded as an intermediate period in agricultural development. Furthermore it deals with the achievements of that period (1660–1750) in an intermediate way—making claims for their importance but decidedly not setting out to label the period as one of (or worse, as *the* period of) 'agricultural revolution'. A gentler, more gradual view of the chronology, course and consequences of progress is taken than in the polarized views which are at the moment dominant. Firstly, the case which is made is not congruent with the position that to all intents and purposes English agricultural methods had been thoroughly and utterly transformed before the eighteenth century. Undoubtedly there were many earlier introductions of crops and practices than was once thought or than is still admitted by proponents of a late eighteenth-century 'agricultural revolution'. But many of these early innovations were tentative and incomplete. The eighteenth-century record, especially as revealed by farmers' own account books and diaries, is that 'new' crops and ways of doing things were often kept on with in a small way for decade after decade; for example, turnips might be grown in some small field for years without becoming a full course which went round the farm. Perhaps farmers aimed to offset the risk of seasonal failure in some other fodder crop without irretrievably committing many of their resources to growing such a laborious and somewhat unreliable crop. Some alert farmers of the eighteenth century tried innovations like turnip growing only to reject them and take them up again at a later date. The didactic writers of the late eighteenth century, Arthur Young, William Marshall and the rest, do describe farming systems the individual components of which (the range of crops for instance) had indeed been used for up to a couple of centuries; but their descriptions do not constitute evidence that even rather a large number of innovations added up to a 'revolution' in which integrated, working systems of mixed farming (mutually dependent crop and animal production) replaced medieval or Tudor ways before the eighteenth century.

Neither is the case which is outlined in Chapter 3 fully compatible with the opposing point-of-view, which holds that before the middle of the eighteenth century innovation in farming was the exception rather than the rule, and not of major economic importance. This position seems to rest in large part on the assumption that because it was only after about 1750 that farming was required to supply a fast-growing population, there cannot have been an enormously important earlier increase of supply. Neither this view of a very late, nor the view of a very early, transformation of agriculture, need be correct. As Chapter 3 suggests, changes in agricultural production before 1750—though not necessarily more than a couple of generations before—introduced slack capacity into the economy: witness England's large and rising export of grain during the first half of the eighteenth century, the low and comparatively stable prices on the home market, London's growth, and the signs of industrial expansion.

However, it is wise not to be emphatic. There is ample evidence available about changes on the supply side of agriculture, but their effects are easier to deduce than to document. Too little is known about changes on the demand side, though they may (for example) share an equivalent responsibility for the unprecedentedly relaxed attitude of post-Restoration governments towards enclosure and the price of foodstuffs. What does seem to have occurred between the Restoration, or a little earlier, and the middle of the eighteenth century was the trial-and-error welding of new crops and practices into novel farming systems. The essence of these systems was that they made possible the replenishment and upgrading of soil fertility. 'This great revolution', wrote an early historian outstanding for his grasp of ecological realities, 'was the introduction of grass-seed and of the "great trefoils", of the various clovers, including later on Lucerne or alfalfa.'[4] This reduced the limitations on soil fertility and crop yields imposed by relying for manure on livestock fed from a restricted acreage of not very good grass. One does not have to be a coprophile to see the central importance of farmyard manure. FYM was a scarce resource, used in the early seventeenth century for fuel as well as fertilizer, sparsely produced in the winter when animal feed was short, and difficult to collect from the expanses of common in the summer. Consider the value of organic manure implied by a case at Swindon, Wiltshire, in 1656, when John Ruddle, Jr., was fined ten shillings because he had, ' "fed and depastured his sheep in this manor and in certain fields called West Swindon fields, and lodged them in the fields within the tything of Eastcott, it being chasing and rechasing, which tends much to the impoverishing of this manor and improving of the other" '.[5] The case was not of an uncommon kind; even the taking of turves from the common fields to use as firing was punishable.[6] In other words, one must not remove or transfer the means of maintaining the fertility of the land.[7]

A tussle over the competing demands on organic materials for fuel and fertilizer persisted where there was any common left, and was perhaps intensified in such localities by the growth of rural population in the early nineteenth century. However, in the agricultural economy as a whole the 'new' fodder crops had essentially tipped the balance long before then. Regional readjustments in agricultural distributions had followed. These offer an ordering device whereby a mass of descriptive evidence about local farming may be merged into nation-wide patterns of economic change. The processes became known even across the Atlantic when Richard Jackson's account of Norfolk agriculture in 1751 was smuggled to Franklin, Bartram and Jared Eliot, and published anonymously by Eliot among his *Essays Upon Field Husbandry*. Jackson declared that the 'artificial grasses' enabled soil fertility to be restored, so that wheat was being grown on thousands of acres throughout England once thought to be too infertile, with massive feedback effects on hitherto rich parts of the country. The rents of 'natural Pasture, and that formerly called Wheat Land, are *fallen in Value*, while the Price of most other Things are rising'.[8] The earlier years of the textbook 'agricultural revolution'—the later of the two chronologies now so widely espoused—from say 1760–90, probably saw a lull in cropping innovation. Thereafter, the systems of production put together in the late seventeenth and early eighteenth centuries were developed a little, but much more to the point were replicated widely to cash in on the high prices of the French wars.

The two remaining chapters in Part One turn to the results of these developments. Chapter 4 lists the major economic effects and discusses the evidence about them at some length. A discussion of this kind is necessarily inconclusive, since it is extraordinarily hazardous to try to assess the total impact of agricultural changes by tracing individual links between that sector and the whole economy. The intention is merely to arrange the evidence according to simple categories—by putting it into economic boxes. As more research is done it will be possible to make these boxes a little fuller, but hard data on the exchanges of factors of production and of goods between farming and manufacturing are scattered and are often specific to individual years and small localities. Although there is a great deal of such material about the flows of goods and services through the markets of the eighteenth-century economy, the prospects of summing it into a single satisfactory conclusion about the 'role of agriculture' are not over-encouraging. Further advance will probably have to be by way of deduction from economic principles, though if this approach is to account for the evidence in any detailed fashion it really must be made by someone who is master of at least the secondary rural literature. Were I to repeat the more elementary exercise of categorizing the interactions of agriculture and industry, one other matter would come to mind —the inadvertent effect of the competition for land between farmers and the growers of wood fuel. Given the inefficient farming methods of the early seventeenth century, the demand for additional arable land was such as to bite into the area available for growing wood, thus intensifying the 'timber famine'. Fortunately an alternative to wood for domestic heating and industrial uses was available in the shallow, coastal coal deposits of the north-east. Although a few decades later the improvements in farming method discussed above did increase per acre output and reduce the pressure on a finite land area, it seems to have been basically sheer good fortune that prevented a food/fuel stalemate serious enough, perhaps, to have impeded the growth of London. 'England's a perfect World! has Indies too!' an eighteenth-century versifier declared, 'correct your Maps! Newcastle is Peru.'

The fifth chapter moves on to structural changes in the economy which were induced by a more responsive agricultural supply in the context of markedly different, and changing, regional comparative advantage. One possible explanation is put forward for the timing with which expansions of rural domestic industry took place in a number of other early advanced economies, as well as England, and some attention is paid to the advantages of active cottage manufacturing for the ensuing emergence of factory industry. My interest in industrial development was first engaged by observing two sets of more-or-less simultaneous phenomena, the dieback of old industries in south-eastern and south-central England (and the torpor which overcame old textile centres in the south-west)[9] and the contrasting growth of industries in northern England and the north and west Midlands. A possible link with the predominantly southern innovations in crop-growing crossed my mind. The extent of the divergence and the quite different agricultural settings of industry in southern and northern England can be illustrated by two quotations, which must stand proxy here for all the evidence of redistributions in economic activity. The former is from Joseph Massie, *Observations on the New Cyder-Tax* (1764):

> when making due Inquiry into the former and present State of our Woollen Trading Towns, I believe it will be found that the Southern ones, comprehending those in the Cyder-Counties, have had a much less than proportional Share of those vast Advantages which have resulted from a Threefold Increase in the yearly Exports of English Woollen Manufactures, since the Accession of King William.[10]

The latter is from a nineteenth-century observer:

> From almost any manufacturing town in England, a country as

barren and wild as the backwoods of America can be reached in a short walk. The grouse crows almost within hearing of the inhabitants of the outskirts of Sheffield; wild Yorkshire moors come up close to the busy towns of Halifax and Bradford; bleak Cheshire and Derbyshire hills look down upon the smoke of Manchester; it would be hard to find farming, properly so called, of any kind in the coal district of Birmingham. It is only towards Leicester that manufactories and farming seem to approach each other; but there it is caused by the rich green pastures of the county.[11]

These environmental observations are in themselves hardly the prime concern of the economic historian. On reflection they do however seem to act as signals to key processes in the transformation of agriculture and industry. Chapter 5 attempts to relate these features to one another by focusing on vigorous phases in the emergence of industry in the countryside which coincided with marked improvements in agricultural supply. As mentioned, this discussion ranges much farther afield than England. Indeed, the wave of interest in rural domestic industry which has become apparent during the past three or four years is more evident among scholars concerned with continental Europe than those solely concerned with England. It seems necessary to add only that where Chapter 5 extended previous work on the subject was in its insistence on the importance of reciprocal markets for the goods of agriculture and cottage industry.

An important strand in the causality of economic change in the developed countries thus seems to have run from agriculture to industry. It ran from a loosening of supply constraints in agriculture, through the evolution of clusters of cottage industries in areas poorly suited to cereal-growing, to the rise (often within these clusters) of steam-powered factory industry. In pursuing this line of thought I have never intended to appear, so to speak, an agrarian monocausalist. But economies are such complicated systems that in delimiting a field of inquiry within them and tracing one set of relationships it is easy to give that impression. While sectoral studies may not be the best place to begin the examination of whole economies, they nevertheless have the advantage over more general approaches of obliging the student to come to grips with primary evidence on the processes of production and exchange. And when all is said and done, the size of the agricultural sector during this period must make it a topic of first-rank importance. That would have been so had the entire agricultural system been nothing more than a gigantic treadmill worked by peasant dullards. In England, at any rate, such was far from the case. There is a lotting book of 1778 for Sulhampstead, Berkshire, which describes the procedure for allocating communal haying rights under the head, '*each lot returns and is the same as it was five years before and so continues changing for ever*'.[12] Within thirty years this arrangement at Sulhampstead was done away with for good, as it was in so very many other parishes. English agriculture proved not to be a repetitive cycle; its active responses to the market were absolutely essential in the creation of eighteenth-century industrialism.

II

The essays in Part Two, 'Agriculture in the Urban-Industrial Economy', do not form quite such a connected sequence as those in the first Part. Instead, they examine various aspects of agriculture's response to the urban-industrial setting in which it was placed from the end of the eighteenth century to the withering of the Victorian 'Golden Age'. Throughout those years agriculture was adjusting to the advantages and penalties of operating within an industrial economy—farmers bought more and more industrial inputs; manufacturers spent industrial profits on the purchase and reconstruction of landed estates; urban markets for farm products expanded; eventually the industrial sector came to compete with agriculture for resources, notably labour. The abundance of the harvest was to become of less moment than the fluctuations of the trade cycle. Some earlier economies, including that of England herself, had been comparatively urban, but had neither possessed the metallurgical and chemical industries to provide agriculture with quantities of producer goods—tools, machines, artificial fertilizers—nor marshalled anything approaching the same tonnage of shipping to import oil-cake and fertilizers. With perhaps the exception of the United Provinces, earlier economies had also spared their farmers the massive challenge which English farmers ultimately had to face in the nineteenth century—competition from imported grain that could be sold at the farmer's gate at prices lower than he must ask for the crops of his own fields.

The difficulties of entering a world of international trade and the need to adjust to marked international differences in comparative advantage took many decades to wreak full havoc among English grain-growers. With hindsight the condition of agriculture by the 1880s has an atmosphere of inevitability about it. Modern scholars are more familiar with the cold passion of the classical economists (embodied in great books) than with the grass-roots economic thought of farmers (embodied only in an obscure farming press). As a result, they find it hard to grasp how reluctantly, how incredulously, English agriculture faced the final swamping import of cheap grain. Nevertheless many farmers had been making some changes in the mix of their products to conform with earlier, more gradual shifts in the relative prices of grain and livestock. Chapter 11 recounts this process, while acknowledging that the full extent of the required adaptation escaped almost everyone. The economic virtue of the mixed farming systems so widely practised in mid-Victorian arable areas was a capacity to offset a fall in the prices of either livestock or cereals. The integrated production of grain and livestock, with an extensive on-farm use of all by-products, was its own insurance policy. That is, unless relative product prices went right out of kilter, which they finally did at the end of the 1870s.

In the late eighteenth century the opportunities and not the disadvantages of a new economic order were more readily perceived. The potential of rapidly widening urban and industrial markets for livestock and livestock products, especially beef, mutton and wool, was most astutely understood. Landowners as well as working farmers took an eager, sometimes faddish, interest in the breeding of fat cattle and fat sheep. High prices were paid for fashionable breeding stock. The remarkably confident aristocracy of Farmer George's England mixed the stall and the salon. Southey might sneer at the equation of the Venus de Milo and a picture of a prize Dishley ram, but oil paintings of gross animals adorned the great houses of the land. The paintings may exaggerate the attainment of the breeders—Thomas Bewick declined to paint animal contours as a patron desired to see them—but livestock really were inflated to meet the needs of the meat market almost as a child models clay.

Chapter 6, the first of this section, describes the efforts and achievements of sheep and cattle breeders in Hereford, a foremost shire for livestock production. The great English sheep and cattle breeds date very largely from the last decades of the eighteenth century and the first decades of the nineteenth century. That was the epoch when the malleable genetic clay was hardened. County breeds became recognizable at a glance. Before long the advertisement value of particular colour types and body shapes, enshrined in long pedigrees in breed society registers, seemed to become of greater worth than further improvements in real performance, for example in feed conversion. If physical efficiency could only be advanced by diluting the visible, registered characteristics of the breed, it would probably not take place. Breeds became gentically isolated and 'real' changes apparently slowed down. Once breed identity became commercially valuable there was no easy way to amend the established breeds. Competition became restricted to the relative status of prize beasts within known breeds or to the relative merits of the various breeds. Non-pedigree blood was excluded and the creation of entirely new breeds by selecting from the whole range of available animals slowed right down. The remarkable resorting of livestock breeds over the turn of the century quickly became a barrier to further changes directed at improved performance.[13]

One wonders how far the trade-mark of the dominant Hereford colour pattern—the Oxo bull of the advertisements—helped the export trade for breeding stock, and thus compensated the leading breeders of the herd book for any drawbacks imposed by a limited genetic pool. Of course, that pool did serve them well. Hereford cattle spread to the pampas, the range and the outback, after some setbacks in regions subject to diseases against which they had no resistance.[14] In any event, judges at nineteenth-century agricultural shows found it easier to award on the basis of conformity and colour than to assemble hard data on growth rates or feed conversion. There were, it is true, plenty of performance challenges issued in the farming press, but the experiments seem to have been poorly designed and for all its verbosity the reporting of the results was not conclusive. However, while the dis-economies of locking British livestock into a narrow range of breeds need to be investigated, Chapter 6 considers only one county and recounts the rapid adjustment to the urban-industrial market that Hereford livestock breeders did succeed in making.

Another essay in Part Two also deals with an aspect of increased agricultural output (Chapter 8), this time in the arable sector. The results of a remarkable crop census carried out at the behest of a firm of Liverpool corn merchants are presented. The series of wheat yields graphed and tabulated here are the best ones available for the first half of the nineteenth century—the sampling technique used to acquire the data was astonishingly advanced. Presumably the firm found it profitable to have accurate advance predictions of the size of the domestic harvest, and to judge from William Cobbett's fulminations against them in *Rural Rides* as Quaker speculators, they no doubt translated their knowledge into pricing and purchasing behaviour. Other firms perhaps followed their lead. Nineteenth-century man was entirely capable of prodigious efforts at data-collecting to no very obvious effect—witness, as a single instance, Cornelius Walford's 280-page article on 'The Famines of the World: Past and Present' in the *Journal of the Statistical Society,* volumes XLI and XLII, 1878 and 1879—but with the Cropper Benson-Sandars wheat census we see the beginnings of a new tradition of assembling agricultural statistics. The figures were usable; they were of a scope and precision beyond anything that had gone before and much that was to follow. It is unfortunate that the agricultural statistics available from 1867 did not follow this lead, and tabulated crop acreages and livestock numbers in a manner suitable for mapping but not for the calculation of output. Scholars have understandably swum to the island of the Agricultural Census as firm ground in a sea of literary impressions, but it would have been a more inhabitable island had it contained yield figures.

The wheat yield series presented here have been commented on in various places, sometimes as though no *caveat* about the high absolute level of the raw data had been entered in the original essay. So far as I am aware the only published use that has been made of them in a manner both satisfactory and complete is that by Dr. G. R. Hawke.[15] In themselves the yield figures, though possibly deriving from more than averagely prosperous farms, are a fair indication of the results of early Victorian agricultural improvement. One need only make weak assumptions about the trends of sown acreages to see this. Such a substantial collection of quantitative evidence, gathered at the time, together with the very fact that it was gathered, differentiates nineteenth-century agriculture from that of previous centuries. We are introduced to the age of sophisters, economists and calculators which in 1792 Burke cried had dawned.

That is not to imply that numerical data of any comprehensiveness or exactitude exist to denote many trends in the nineteenth-century agricultural economy. These lacunae may in part be responsible for the continued relative inattention to the 'Golden Age' of English agriculture which followed the Repeal of the Corn Laws, despite the gloomy forebodings of cereal growers. The agricultural basis of the 'Golden Age' has remained a hiatus in the literature between the dangerous excitements of the post-Napoleonic deflation and the 'Great Arable Depression' of the 1870s and after. In absolute terms there has certainly been more written on the interim period than was available when the essays offered here as

Chapters 9 and 10 were written, but the period has still not attracted the proportionate attention devoted to the slumps. The reason may not be far to seek if one agrees with Marc Bloch's dictum that, 'just as the progress of a disease shows a doctor the secret life of the body, so to the historian the progress of a great calamity yields valuable information about the nature of the society so stricken'. Although earlier authors exaggerated the damage in the nineteenth-century farming recessions, there was very painful sectional distress, a major problem of readjustment, and a sharp upturn in the collection and publication of material on agriculture. Comparatively speaking the 'Golden Age' *was* gilded and less introspective; but if it is the base line against which the structural changes of the last quarter of the century are to be measured, there is cause enough to scrutinize it closely. Before doing so, however, let us return to the opening years of the century and the brave days when industrial (rather than mercantile) capital first began to flow into landed property on a vast scale.

This access of industrial funds swelled investment in agriculture above what the percentage return on the money would lead one to expect. Chapter 7 starts with a case study of an early example of this process. Agriculture could command such resources because it seemed secure, because it was carried on in the enviable environment of landed property, and because it led to social prestige and political power. Manufacturers seem to have seen industry as the means to maximize personal wealth, and the land as the means to maximize personal welfare; the great hero figures of the 'Industrial Revolution' opted for the latter almost to a man. The particular case examined here throws light from an unexpected angle on a matter about which little is known—the business behaviour of Richard Arkwright, Jr., cotton-spinner. This shaft of illumination is provided by the record of Arkwright's manœuvrings to buy a large landed estate in Herefordshire. From the purely agricultural standpoint the study is less informative than estate studies can be, owing to Richard Arkwright's frequent pauses in investing in the land after 1815 and his son's (the occupier's) belated discovery that superintending an estate could be enjoyable.[16] Chapter 7 is therefore more an exercise in business history than in agricultural history, though by suggesting some generalizations about the industrial effects of the flow of money into land it is somewhat more than a case study.

The estate system—the 'superfirm' conjunction of a landowner and tenant decision-makers—helped to maintain a high level of investment in mid-Victorian agriculture and to promote some impressive technical developments. It had little impact on the product mix within the mixed-farming systems discussed above. Conceivably its own disarticulated investment structure, though so successful in offsetting a fall in tenant expenditures during earlier short spells of depression, was—like mixed farming—incapable of reorientating to cope with the market collapse of the seventies. Most mid-Victorians were apparently, astonishingly, unprepared for that culminating shock. Very many more of the farmers kept accounts than is still sometimes admitted; it is no very hard job to find examples rotting in farmhouse attics or estate offices to this day. However these accounts seldom distinguished crop and livestock profitability within mixed farming. Both sets of enterprises were continued as long as the total system paid—the shift in relative profitability was almost certainly disguised. Chapter 9 discusses this situation.

The final chapter turns to the topic of farm labour. In particular it deals with the trend of rewards for farm hands over the years from the start of the French wars to the arrival on the scene of Joseph Arch's national union of agricultural workers. The aims at the time of writing were to disengage the attention of scholars from isolated incidents of oppression or the supposedly crucial role of labour organization in raising the total return to the workforce, and to focus on the gradual amelioration of the labourers' lot during the third quarter of the century. At that period urban and industrial competition really began to eat into the labour supply. Farm labour was seemingly becoming scarce relative to capital, and there were indeed substitutions of machinery for hand work, though they were not universal.

Whatever preconceptions it offends, the evidence in Chapter 10 indicates that farm workers by and large became better off during the 1850s and 1860s. Further, this was mainly due to market forces and not to bloody riot, rick-burning,[17] machinery-breaking, labour combination, or the like. These propositions, of course, are not at all the same as asserting that the mid-Victorian farm hand was satisfactorily treated by later, modern, or even some 'ideal' standards. Since the essay was written there has been good work done on farm labour as a factor of production, as the piece urged there should be, and detailed research into early union activity. But the reaction from labour historians to the evidence of an improvement in workers' rewards has been glum. This, coupled with occasional remarks by reviewers about my views on the social effects of eighteenth-century enclosure, and a misuse of the wheat yield statistics, alerted me to the extent of the intrusion of politics and ideology into this field of scholarship.

In the opening paragraph of this Introduction I referred to the increased volume and improved quality of the work now being done. These are features of the study of economic history in general. There is another, less welcome, feature. With increased numbers of scholars has come the wherewithal for sub-division into semi-formal groups in whose membership political views play a part, at times quite explicitly. There are books, articles, and book reviews where an ideological leaning, to left or right, now occupies the forefront of the scene. This is especially true concerning the economic and social history of the period of English industrialization, though it is by no means confined there.

> It should be the business of teachers to stand outside the strife of parties and endeavour to instill into the young the habit of impartial inquiry, leading them to judge issues on their merits and to be on their guard against accepting *ex parte* statements at their face value. The teacher should not be expected to flatter the prejudices either of the mob or of officials. His professional virtue should consist in a readiness to do justice to all sides, and in an endeavour to rise above controversy into a region of dispassionate scientific investigation.[18]

A programme like this is hard, very hard, to live up to. Nevertheless, though objectivity may be as unattainable as infinity, a frictionless motor, or absolute zero, collective action to avoid seeking it is downright unscholarly. The proper end of economic history is not to reinforce current prejudices but to depict the past and find ways of understanding the processes of economic and societal change that led to the present. There is already too much dispute in academic life without adding the dimension of ideology. To return to the particular case, if the total return to farm labour as a factor of production did not rise over the 1850s and 1860s, let this be demonstrated from the evidence... 'and then I shall willingly be the first that shall commit this to the Flames'.

III

Before the period with which this volume is concerned, agriculture was primitive, local, and subject to a great buffeting as a result of its ecological abnormality. The English environment was not a harsh one, indeed it was one of the most favourable in the world, yet farming it provided plenty of upsets. As Professor Postan has shown, the yields of late medieval crops were abysmally low by nineteenth-century standards and a small livestock population did not produce enough organic fertilizer to raise them. Farming systems were quite neatly adjusted to individual localities because there was no technology adequate to reshaping local conditions. Bad weather inflicted immediate damage. Plant and animal disease, insect pests, weeds, none of them could be controlled; cultivations were shallow and the soil structure had to be accepted as given; the seed varieties available were poor. Conceivably the open field strips were a means of distributing risk, in which each family could hope to minimize loss by holding lands scattered across different types of soil, any one of which might fail to produce a harvest if the weather did not suit it. One has only to read Shakespeare with the appropriate antiquarian eye to detect an agriculture in which output remained low and uncertain through natural causes—the condition, as a wag observed, from which more people die than from any other.

The power of natural depressants on farm output in days when there were only folk remedies to combat them has been hard for modern students of western economic history to recognize. In England the problems were already being eased by the technical advances of the seventeenth and eighteenth centuries. With a greater area under cultivation and more powerful methods new ecological imbalances were brought about, but richer, better-informed agriculturists usually managed to cope with them—though sometimes only by self-denying ordinances against desirable but risky intensities of production. In this respect it may be that growing a variety of crops, and thus losing potential economies of scale in production, was the individual farmer's way of insuring against the loss of any particular one to pests or bad weather.

By the mid-nineteenth century control over the environment was of quite a different order from three or four centuries earlier. Artificial fertilizers, underdrainage, machines, and seed selection, gave the farmer a mastery over the elements and competing species (pests: pathogens, predators, weeds) that had never before been known. Industrial inputs made this mastery possible. Yet agriculturists were still riding a tiger. The drenching year of 1879—which left an indelible impression among the childhood memories of elderly farmers I have talked to—revealed all too clearly man's ecological complacency. The wheat was brought home 'sopping wet like manure', and a massive sheep rot began to spread. The rains of that season screened many men from a clear vision of the long-foreboded impact of international trade in cereals. They took the spell of bad weather, which had reduced the volume of products they had to sell, rather than the enormous imports, which had reduced the prices, as the underlying cause of their falling incomes. Their will to adjust was sapped; bad weather must surely pass. It did, but low prices did not. Ever after, though the arable sector of English agriculture was puffed up in wartime, the old sense of security was gone. Farmers had to relinquish their belief that agriculture was the basis on which the economy rested. The time when that was so had gone.

NOTES TO INTRODUCTION

1. Derek J. de S. Price suggests that each individual scientist may monitor the work of about 100 others. *Little Science, Big Science* (Columbia U.P., New York and London, 1965), pp. 71–2.
2. I am thinking especially of the work of Paul David and Donald McCloskey. Probably the worst work on the subject is also being done by other American economics students, judging from manuscripts I see: Robert Clower is surely right in arguing that bad theory and bad scholarship are not additive but multiplicative. See 'Snarks, Quarks, and other Fictions', in L. P. Cain and P. J. Uselding (eds.), *Business Enterprise and Economic Change* (Kent State U.P., 1973).
3. See e.g. my review of W. E. Tate, *The English Village Community and the Enclosure Movements* (London: Victor Gollancz Ltd., 1967), in *Economic History Review*, 2nd ser., xxi (1968), pp. 168–9, and Donald N. McCloskey, 'The Enclosure of Open Fields: Preface to a Study of Its Impact on the Efficiency of English Agriculture in the Eighteenth Century', *Journal of Economic History*, xxxii (1972), pp. 15–35.
4. V. G. Simhkovitch, 'Hay and History', *Political Science Quarterly*, xxviii (1913), p. 393.
5. Various authors, *Studies in the History of Swindon* (Swindon, 1950), pp. 71–2.
6. See e.g. T. J. Goddard-Fenwick, *Stanton Harcourt* [Oxon.]: *A Short History* (privately printed, 1962 edn.), p. 16.
7. See e.g. Sir E. John Russell, *A History of Agricultural Science in Great Britain 1620–1954* (London: George Allen and Unwin, 1966), pp. 38–9. The long-run effects of fertility transfers which did take place in English parishes are discussed in Sir Joseph Hutchinson, *Farming and Food Supply* (C.U.P., 1972), pp. 46–7, and a lucid section on the problem of manureless cultivation appears in M. M. Postan, *The Medieval Economy and Society* (Berkeley and Los Angeles, 1972), chapter IV.
8. In Jared Eliot, *Essays Upon Field Husbandry in New England* (H. J. Carmen and R. G. Tugwell, eds.), New York: Columbia U.P., 1934, pp. 86–7.
9. See E. L. Jones, 'The Constraints on Economic Growth in Southern England, 1600–1850', in *Contributions*, iiiᵉ International Conference of Economic History, Munich 1965 (forthcoming).
10. Quoted by D. B. Horn and M. Ransome (eds.), *English Historical Documents, X, 1714–1783* (London, 1957), p. 454.
11. G. G. Richardson, *The Corn and Cattle Producing Districts of France* [c. 1887], p. 485.
12. M. Sharp and W. O. Clinton, *A Record of the Parish of Padworth and its Inhabitants* (Reading, 1911), pp. 161–2.

C

13. We have been reminded of the dis-economies inherent in this process by Sir Joseph Hutchinson, *op. cit.*

14. Early imports of Hereford and Durham (Shorthorn) cattle in Georgia, for instance, were eliminated by disease. James C. Bonner, *A History of Georgia Agriculture, 1732–1860* (Athens, Ga.: University of Georgia Press, 1964), p. 135.

15. G. R. Hawke, *Railways and Economic Growth in England and Wales 1840–1870* (Oxford: Clarendon Press, 1970), pp. 110–12, 119–20.

16. The records of the estate under the regime of John Hungerford Arkwright in the second half of the nineteenth century are of peculiar agricultural interest. I would like to record my double good fortune in discovering the Arkwright letters: the late T. S. Ashton once told me that he was apprised of the existence of the Herefordshire Arkwright material by an excited American visitor in the 1920s but never found time to follow the lead; and when I came upon the letters independently they were in the hands of Mr. David Arkwright, whose notions of the proper conditions for scholarship proved agreeably lavish.

17. Ironically, rick burning was likely to have been arson by farmers whenever there was a slight downturn in prices. See the evidence to the Select Committee of 1867 quoted in Cornelius Walford, 'Fires and Fire Insurance Considered', *Journal of the Statistical Society*, XL (1877), pp. 372–3.

18. Bertrand Russell, *Unpopular Essays* (New York: Simon and Schuster, 1950), pp. 116–17. The partisanship for which Russell himself was notorious was surely in his capacity as citizen, not scholar.

*ONE: Agricultural Change
and the Process of Industrialization*

1. Eighteenth-Century Changes in Hampshire Chalkland Farming

The past farming systems of light-soiled districts are often described as 'sheep-and-corn'. The term does not reveal the changes which took place at various times in the exact objects of sheep and grain production and in the relative importance of the two groups of products. This chapter describes some agricultural developments in the Hampshire Chalklands, traditionally a 'sheep-and-corn' area, in order to show how greatly the emphasis on certain products changed between the early eighteenth and early nineteenth centuries. The evidence so far available permits no final conclusions on the evolution of Chalkland agriculture, but the sequence suggested here may provide a framework for more exhaustive studies, and should stress the inadequacy of 'sheep-and-corn' for describing farming systems which changed in essentials over time.

The early decades of the eighteenth century may only be taken as the base period for a discussion of the whole century if it is recognised that they themselves were times of agricultural transition. In the Hampshire Chalklands the agricultural advances of the late seventeenth and early eighteenth centuries were towards increasing the supplies of sheep feed. The greater provision of artificial fodder crops and irrigated grass for the flock made the cultivation of more and more sheep-walks possible, and this continued during the late eighteenth century under the impetus of rising prices for grain. The increase of fodder supplies, the extension of tillage, and the changes in farm production and costs which they helped to bring about are considered here.

I

The sheep flock was the pivot of Chalkland husbandry. From the later seventeenth century demand for local wool was falling, but ewe flocks remained of central importance for breeding stores and fertilizing the ploughland. The large, lanky downland sheep were admirably suited to a routine in which daylight was spent grazing the downs and darkness folding on the arable. On the other hand they gave only a small fleece, although of good quality, and the culled ewes fattened only slowly.[1] The grassland flocks were limited in size by the shortage of fodder in winter and at lambing. Supplementary supplies would mean that more sheep could be stocked; these in turn would promote higher crop yields and permit the permanent cultivation of the thinner chalk soils.

These desiderata became attainable from the latter half of the seventeenth century with the spread of water-meadows and 'new' crops. In 1669 John Worlidge of Petersfield recommended sowing turnips and 'several new Species of Hay or Grass', and floating water-meadows.[2] Thirty years later sainfoin, ryegrass, clover, and turnips had been established widely, as the work of Edward Lisle clearly reveals.[3] These crops alone, however, were of great but not inestimable importance, as was emphasized by Lisle's difficulties in overwintering cattle on the high downs.[4] At Crux Easton even sheep pressed hard on resources of fodder. 'It is a hard matter', lamented the would-be grazier, 'tho' one have a good stock of that grass, to get the shepherd's leave to hayn it from the sheep for that end [to feed cattle], he stands so much in need of the hop-clover grass from the middle of March to the beginning of May.'[5] Lisle was unfortunate in that Crux Easton lies far from a river valley. In the common type of Chalkland parish abutting on to a stream forced grass from floated meadows was at this time being added to the 'new' crops, effecting an unprecedented improvement in the fodder situation.

It has been stated that 'during the eighteenth century in particular, water-meadows must have been pushed to the limits of areas where it was possible to construct them'.[6] This accords with the visible remains of irrigation systems on the valley bottoms and with contemporary documents. For instance, on the Compton reaches of the Test payments for irrigation are recorded from 1714, when it was patently routine and had induced three men to specialize in the work; they charged by the acre for drowning meadows and piece rates for such tasks as 'Shutting ye hatches Down'.[7] In the Park meadows fifty-one acres were drowned regularly. These meadows were maintained partly for dairy cattle, and in accordance with local practice herds and pasture rights were let annually at Pittleworth, Compton, and Brook. Sheep were also kept and other flocks agisted for the lambing season. Despite some use for dairying (later in the century possibly releasing some parish cow downs for tillage) the improvement of sheep husbandry was doubtless the main aim in watering meadows.[8]

Incidental light on the extent of water-meadows in the mid-Test valley is shed by the proprietors' disputes with a downstream miller. In 1713 thirty-eight acres of Pittleworth Farm were watered, while in 1743 'Mr Gatehouse   waters by his carriage that has been cut time out of mind, flood mead about 35 Acres   he waters by the carryer that has been cut about 30 Years, about 30 Acres   he waters by Sir William's Wire [weir] about 13 Acres, & carry the Waters intirely from Mottisfont Mill.'[9]

On the Itchen there were attempts to float common meadows, the improvement of which presumably tended to lag behind that of meadows belonging to single proprietors. In 1704 a contractor was required to water Otterbourne common meadow for the mutual benefit of the proprietors through 'the greatest Increase of Grass & Hay as the sd Land is Capable of in respect of the Sd improvement by watering'.[10] This scheme failed, for the meadow became badly flooded from the attempted Itchen Navigation. From 1724 John White, Sir William Heathcote's agent, took an interest in the problem and by 1731 had secured the proprietors' assent to a scheme for which he had prepared estimates: 'It is to be considered, that it must be first layn dry, & afterwards improved by drowning'. That year a surveyor began work and thenceforth annual levies were raised to meet the cost of improvement, but the physical difficulties were not overcome. By 1740 the meadow 'hath for some time Past been overflowed with Water and lain in a Ruinous Condition', and in 1746 another estimate for draining, partly by 'Lowering the Carryage', was submitted. John White also suggested watering forty acres of common meadow at Compton on the Itchen in 1728. This was successful; his proposal is endorsed in another hand, 'NB the pasture ground was watered, in the year 1730 & it proved beyond expectation.'[11]

The examples given, which might be extended, indicate the scale on which meadows were floated. The expenditure and exertion involved suggest the large return expected and further that there was no cessation of 'improving' activity during the depression of 1730–1750. Floated meadows, Dr. Kerridge concludes, 'made possible earlier lambing and increased sheep stocking, ensured a supply of hay in drought, and by integration with the sheep-and-corn husbandry of the district, promoted increased yields of corn, especially of barley, thus constituting an improvement of the first order'.[12]

II

The improved fodder supplies made possible the folding and thus the cultivation of thinner soils, this being 'the feature that impressed most travellers' in the Chalklands in the late seventeenth and early eighteenth centuries.[13] In 1724, for example, Defoe noted the recent extension of tillage by the sheep-fold system on the chalk of Hampshire, Wiltshire, and Dorset. Although he observed prodigious sheep-flocks it was already apparent that 'the number of sheep fed on these downs is lessened, rather than increased, because of the many thousand acres of the carpet ground being, of late years, turned into arable land, and sowed with wheat'.[14] Lisle was interested in the costs of cultivating marginal soils, and recommended 'gentlemen who have great downs, to plough a furrow across them in some places, that they may turn the best of such lands into arable'.[15]

Incentive for the general cultivation of downland was nevertheless lacking before mid-century. Until then a farming system was evolving in which the degree of sheep-folding dictated the relatively slow rate at which fresh land could be brought and kept under the plough. With the lessening return to wool production, sheep became increasingly the tool of arable husbandry. Water-meadows and 'new' crops provided the means of multiplying the tools. The inextricable bond between the folding flock and grain production was thus explained to Lisle by Mr. Hawkins, 'the great Hampshire farmer': 'If a bane fell on sheep, corn would be dear, because there could not be a fifth part of the folding that otherwise there would be, and consequently a deficiency of the crop.'[16]

The integral role of the sheep-fold in the production of the cash crops, wheat and barley, was accentuated during the depression of 1730–50. This depression has been described by Professor Mingay from the rentals of the Duke of Kingston.[17] An examination of the rentals for Broughton Manor, part of the only Kingston estate containing Hampshire lands, between 1722 and '39, supports the general thesis.[18] Arrears occurred in 1728 and in all years from 1730, by far the heaviest in those ending at Michaelmas 1735 and '37. Yet in those years there were estate outgoings which cannot be attributed entirely to the landlord's desire to prevent farms falling into hand. Forty pounds were 'Allowed towards building a New Rick-house 1738 as per Agreement on Farmer Morgans taking an advanced Rent', and elsewhere smaller sums were spent on improvements, notably in 1735 and '36 on breaking up Broughton Common Down.

During this depression there were other attempts to increase production. The floating of some water-meadows has been noticed. In 1745 a Stoke Charity farmer whose affairs were in straits considered planting 500 acres of 'Cinque Foyle' and the quite exceptional area of 100 acres of hops.[19] Some sheep stints (but not those of great cattle) were raised far beyond the accepted carrying capacity of the common downs. For instance, Barton Farm, Weston Patrick, carried a stint of 160 sheep on Broad Down from 1719, but a 'concealed' increase in folding was achieved by temporarily reducing the farm's acreage, between 1733 and '47, from sixty to forty-five acres.[20] At King's Somborne the Court Baron raised the long-standing stint of forty sheep per yardland to forty-four in April and fifty-two in October 1735. This was reduced to fifty in May 1736, but the level of forty was not regained until 1741.[21] This abrupt raising of stints acknowledged the vital influence of the flock on the harvest, perhaps of wool as well as of grain, since the prices of both were low in the 1730s. It is possible that all these examples were attempts to combat ruinously low prices by increasing production. The response of the supply curve of aggregate agricultural output to falling demand is slow even today. In the first half of the eighteenth century labour would account for the largest share of farm production costs; it would be largely family labour, the 'opportunity costs' of which would be effectively nil in times of depression and unemployment. As purchased inputs would be few, and in any case cheaper at such times, and as fundamental shifts in demand might be masked at first by unfavourable weather, efforts to offset lower prices by actually expanding output might not have seemed irrational.[22]

At the end of the eighteenth century agriculturists still claimed to be convinced of the necessity of the sheep-fold. Much of this acclaim was retrospective and was prompted by the decline in the old folding system brought about by the vast conversion of sheep-walk to tillage. This extension of cultivation was the result of private rather than parliamentary enclosure. Of the total county area only 6 per cent was affected by Acts enclosing open field and only a further 5 per cent by those concerning the 'waste'.[23]

The aim of those who financed parliamentary enclosure in chalk Hampshire was less the taking-in of new ploughland than the creation of compact and private holdings from common field strips. On this the Articles of Agreement for an enclosure in the Chalkland edge parish of East Dean in 1809 are especially clear. 'The Parts and Pieces of Individuals in the ... Fields lye so dispersed & intermixed with the lands of others as not only to render the same inconvenient to the sev. Prop^{rs} & Occupiers thōf but Detrimental to good Husbandry & in their present Situation are incapable of any Improvem^t & there are also within the s^d Parish of East Dean some old Inclosures & the dividing & lay^g the Old Inclosures near would be a considerable Advantage to all the Proprietors interested therein.'[24] The proprietors at another enclosure went so far as to enter into a bond for £200 to allot one of their number his new enclosure next to his existing closes.[25]

On the enlarged and private farms which parliamentary enclosure thus tended to form the trends of the market for farm products could be followed more nearly than on the jumbles of closes and open-field strips which they superseded. In the late eighteenth century this implied a shift towards grain production, as Arthur Young's 'Minutes of Inclosures' in Hampshire suggest. After the enclosure at Monk Sherborne Young noted, 'Corn. Has not increased much', whereas sheep had decreased. At Up Nately corn had increased while sheep had merely 'not lessened', and at Basingstoke corn had 'Very greatly increased', but sheep, Young was obliged to hedge, 'The number, probably, lessened; but the produce in value being so, is questionable.'[26]

The effects of parliamentary enclosure on agricultural production were therefore of a similiar quality to those of the contemporaneous private enclosure of sheep-walk. It is, however, in the latter, affecting so much greater an area, that the major changes of the century must be sought. Nevertheless, the numbers of Enclosure Acts do provide a rough index to the rate of all enclosure, for some downland was included in many Acts aimed more specifically at open-field. Under the same market influences a broadly similar rate of progress must be assumed for public and private enclosure, although difficulties of administration probably retarded the former a little by comparison. The increase of enclosure is shown by the passing of nine Acts relating to parishes wholly or partly on the chalk from 1709 to 1773 inclusive, fourteeen from 1774 to 1792, and twenty-five from 1793 to 1815. This acceleration is not altered by the inclusion of formal private enclosure agreements. The ultimate direction of the movement is evident in that five of the eight Acts passed in 1809–12 dealt exclusively with the 'waste'.

The crucial importance of the large-scale cultivation of sheep-down hinged on the land-utilization balance of many Chalkland parishes and farms. Like the attenuated parishes, many farms held in severalty stretched from narrow valley to untilled hill pasture. It was 'the favourite idea among the down farmers, that no farm can be advantageously disposed for the general circumstances of that country, unless it has water-meadow at one end, and maiden down at the other'.[27] This ideal balance was to be upset, as the profitability of grain farming grew, by the piecemeal conversion of sheep-down to tillage on individual farms. The shift is symbolized on Lord Bolton's estates by the contrast between 1660, when permission was granted to make a rabbit warren, and some year between 1783 and 1799, when a 285-acre warren was destroyed to make an arable farm.[28] Enclosure of downland for permanent arable cultivation was taking place in the late seventeenth century,[29] more rapidly from the mid-eighteenth, and fastest during the Napoleonic wars. Enclosure for other purposes—to carve pasture from the Clay-with-Flints scrub which was nearest to true waste, to protect coppice, or to impark—was by comparison insignificant.

Compared with the evidence for parliamentary enclosure, that for the enclosure and cultivation of downland is fragmentary, but its sum is impressive. The commonest clues are incidental notes that certain parcels of arable were formerly downland, for example, '2 acres of arable at Old Down',[30] or 'New Down—arable',[31] or 'The two(?) meadows . . . That next Stockbridge is now plowed.'[32] Isolated references in modern works are not infrequent, for instance to the 'field, known as Breachfield, situated on a hill about a quarter of a mile north-east of the village of St. Mary Bourne; the field having formed part of Eggbury down till 1772, when it was broken up'.[33] This example shows the elements of the process—the first cultivation of an elevated down in the late eighteenth century giving rise to a field-name typically associated with the ploughing of virgin land. A complete survey of literary evidence would be a considerable task, although a useful chronology of the movement might be obtained by its collection for selected groups of parishes.[34] To demonstrate the occurrence of the process in the eighteenth century ample references are to be found in leases, farm accounts, and estate records. Leases are especially useful. They may reveal indirectly the spread of cultivation, as at Hurstbourne

Tarrant, where four hundred acres of woodland and a similar acreage of furze and heath were tilled between 1778 and 1816. Alternatively, they may specify parcels of sheep-down which tenants might plough without penalty—e.g. part of Northbrook Down, Micheldever, in 1737, common down attached to Compton Farm in 1745, and forty acres of Pearch Down, Kingsclere, in 1809.[35]

Actual proposals and agreements to break up downland are direct evidence. An incomplete, probably late seventeenth-century, paper endorsed 'Nether Wallop—about breaking up th Downs', states that 'The Tenants of Wallop would break up 50[(½?)] acres of the Downs & pay my Lord an acknoledgemt for it, it is the Course pt of the Down lying beyond the Salsbury road   other lords doe permit the same thing & have some . . .'[36] A 1740 proposal 'relating to the breaking up & inclosing part of Compton Down' concerns four hundred acres leased by various persons from the Dean and Chapter of Winchester, who asked £1 per acre to license tillage. At this price the Compton tenants were licensed in 1741, when they also agreed to enclose the common fields, 'to burn, bake, plough, and convert to tillage 21 acres of downland'. The new fields were called 'Bakelands'.[37]

A detailed scheme for cultivating sheep-downs on Chalton Manor was advanced in 1756.[38] The Duke of Beaufort's tenants at Blendworth petitioned for further licence to plough Blendworth Down, on which they claimed 'an immemorial customary Stinted Right of Common of Sheep', for 742 animals on 304 acres. Permission was requested to cultivate 209 acres; the remaining 95 acres were hangers, the steepest slopes, which the margin of cultivation had not reached, and were deliberately excepted. Agreement was forthcoming. Of the tenants on the manor, those at Catherington and Blendworth who had 'lately' received licence to break up common downs were to be indulged in a forty-two-year repetition. Tenants at Clanville and Chalton were to be granted similar rights if they desired them—at Clanville for 400 acres and at Chalton, 'such a Quantity as they shall judge convenient and beneficial to be broke up'. This points to the final approval of permanent cultivation after a trial period, and shows the tenantry unanimously willing to sacrifice grazing rights to the plough in a year when wheat prices were rising steeply.

The inducement to sow wheat on maiden downland was considerable, despite the high initial cost of paring and burning the sward. No reliable yield figures are available, but crops were certainly far above the average on the chalk hills at first, although dropping subsequently. All the signs point to an expansion of the arable acreage in this way as the eighteenth century advanced. It is not suggested that this took the form of a smooth upward curve, but much detailed evidence is required before short-term variations in the rate of progress are distinguished.

So marked a shift in the balance of land utilization had serious repercussions throughout the farm economy. The especial fears of contemporaries were that successive grain crops would exhaust the poorer soils and that the shrinkage of downland would mean fewer sheep to be folded on a growing arable acreage. The former apprehension proved in the event unjustified, but the literature to which it gave rise indicates the new emphasis on grain production. This swing to arable farming may be related reasonably to the late eighteenth-century rise in the price for wheat, since wheat was usually the first and often the subsequent crop on freshly broken land. Provident farmers followed with barley, oats, and two seasons' ryegrass before reverting to wheat, but opportunists sowed as many 'white straw' crops as the land would bear. Particularly during the Napoleonic wars, wheat prices were sufficiently high to induce the most cautious to crop hard and to encourage the profiteering, the reckless, or those whose tenancies were running out to take all from the land. This was reflected in the contemporary concern, although there is no evidence of widespread or persisting soil-exhaustion. Temporary local conditions made the threat seem real, and even Young, who approved the cultivation of downland, was angered by fields reduced to 'a wretched state', where, tempted by 'a great sudden fertility' to be 'bad farmers for present profit', some 'bad managers have, on first breaking up the down, taken more than three crops, sowing as long as the land would yield'.[39]

As grain prices soared, so observers became more disquieted. An estate agent noted of New Down Farm at Stratton in 1799, 'the tenant is too much disposed to sow the land in a greater proportion than it ought to be; it would pay her better if less of the Down land were in tillage and more of the poorest parts of the farm either in sainfoin or laid down with artificial grasses. Some limit to the cropping upon this estate in general, as well as here, would be highly proper and useful.'[40] Another agent, valuing Gerrard's Farm, Nether Wallop, in 1803, claimed that it had been 'like most others in that country . . . rather improperly treated by the practice of burning the Land, and sowing too many Crops in succession'. He considered much of the farm's down too shallow to sustain burning and cropping, which was 'only a present advantage, with certain ruin in future'.[41] By 1810 Charles Vancouver, the Board of Agriculture surveyor, was outspokenly criticizing the 'madness, extravagance, and folly' of all who broke up downland.[42] Nevertheless, the more extensive system of grain-growing spread. It was made possible by the use of various rotations akin to the Norfolk four-course and by resting the land with sainfoin and clover leys. Buildings for threshing and manure storing were erected at the down ends of the elongated farms, thus saving journeys from the main farmstead by labourers and by the flock, which could be concentrated to fold the better 'home' arable.[43] Ultimately, the success of the general cultivation of the downs was sealed by establishing on them entirely new farms, named Down or Warren or New Barn. The physical enclosure of the downs, albeit in huge fields, by quickset hawthorn hedges and beech shelter-belts marks this agricultural expansion as a most significant stage in the development of the Chalkland landscape.

III

The other fear provoked by the extension of tillage—a decreased number of folding sheep—was better founded. Awareness of the trend was shown in a query circulated in 1785 by the Odiham Agricultural Society, asking anxiously or hopefully, 'How far can a Tillage System by means of artificial Grasses and Roots be made to support a Flock without natural Pastures or Sheep-Walk?'[44] Another sign of the growing need for an alternative to natural pasture may be seen in the 'boom' in water-meadow construction between 1780 and 1830.[45] It might be expected that turnips and ley grasses would have offset the shrinkage of downland, but in practice they did not completely compensate. Sheep had been fattened on turnips for the London market well before the improvement in the Southdown and other mutton breeds, but the old breeds were nevertheless primarily grassland animals. The numerical drop in these sheep has been overlooked, partly because the total in the county was always impressive (for the Southdown spread during the horned breed's swiftest decline), and partly because Hampshire sheep fairs remained in the forefront, although largely as entrepôts for western-bred lambs bound for fattening pastures in the home counties. Yet in 1794 a decline of one-third in the county's sheep population was estimated and was attributed to the enclosure and ploughing of sheep-walks.[46] At this date Young, who thought

Hampshire better sheep country than Norfolk or Suffolk, claimed the county was understocked. In 1798 Marshall said, 'the long-established breed of Wiltshire and Hampshire are routed, in every quarter; and may soon be extinct'.[47] As late as 1810 the ubiquitous rotations involving turnips and green crops, the recently introduced swedes, and the 'still partial' introduction of Southdowns had not compensated for 'the great deficiency of sheep stock' arising from 'the improvident destruction of the former sheep-walks'.[48]

Although extensions of grain production characterize the Napoleonic war period, there was some redress in a similar expansion of store and mutton production. Growing demand for mutton prompted Hampshire farmers to adopt the Southdown sheep in the 1790s. A flock was purchased in 1792 by W. P. Powlett of King's Somborne, a member of the Board of Agriculture, on Young's recommendation. By 1795 both men were convinced that the experiment had demonstrated the breed's superiority, and Young was able to support this conclusion—which he had embraced in advance—by calculating that at best horned sheep gave only the profit of the fold. Southdowns, he admitted, were dear to buy, but three, he claimed, could be run for two of the old breed. Vancouver observed the ratio as five to four.[49]

Early mentions of Southdowns in Hampshire come from the south-eastern parishes flanking the South Down Hills—from Soberton in 1799, from Hambledon and Buriton in 1801.[50] In the former year, with the main spread beginning, Thomas Edwards of Hunton bought two Southdown rams and two hundred ewes locally and one ram from nearby Longparish. Edwards was soon buying Southdown rams in south-east Hampshire and Sussex and selling them in his native north-western corner of Hampshire.[51] In 1801 Thomas Terry, squire of Dummer, bought 300 Southdown ewes at Lewes, with 'more than a proportionate number of rams' to cross with his Hampshire ewes.[52] Terry and his son faced ridicule at local markets, but within seven years opinion completely changed in their favour. By 1815 the Southdown, or its cross on the Hampshire ewe from which the Hampshire Down derives, was the dominant Chalkland strain.

The spread of swedes followed that of Southdowns. At Buriton in 1801, 'Swedish turnips have been introduced and highly approved of.'[53] They were introduced at Dummer in 1802 and at Hunton in 1803.[54] There was a causal connection between the two innovations. Southdowns were admirably suitable for a period of contracting grassland since they were folded and fattened on arable crops. Their successful overwintering thus demanded a fodder crop which would bridge the 'hungry gap' between the last turnips, which kept badly during frost, and the first bite of watered grass. Swedes filled this gap, since they kept better than turnips and could be reserved until these had been fed off. It may be suggested that the nation-wide spread of swedes, which has been described as only occurring in the first decade of the nineteenth century although their properties had been known for years,[55] was much influenced by the wide substitution of arable for grass sheep.

The grass flocks of the horned breed had been suited above all else for the fold. The lambs were forced for sale at Weyhill Fair at Michaelmas, but otherwise mutton and wool production left ample room for improvement. Southdowns, by contrast, were fatter, producing more lambs, better carcases, and more, shorter-stapled, wool. Their disadvantages arose from the higher costs of managing and feeding arable sheep, especially the great expense of growing roots. Shepherding costs rose, since fewer sheep could be tended when permanently folded than when loose on the downs. Shepherds commanded wages higher by half than labourers, with still higher rates at lambing. The capital cost of the Southdown flock was high, and altogether sheep became an expensive item in farm budgets. Probably only the example of the large class of squires and wealthy tenants, the overall profitability of wartime farming, and the growing demand for mutton made feasible so quick and complete an introduction of Southdowns. The cost of their maintenance was to become a matter of moment after 1815.[56]

IV

Another change in the cost structure of Chalkland farming during the Napoleonic wars was due to difficulties of labour supply. Wages were raised early, as provision prices mounted and the lot of the private soldier, which it was thought advisable to equal, improved.[57] Attitudes towards labour were noticeably less benevolent after the failure of the Peace of Amiens, when military requirements and war-work at high piece rates (notably in Portsmouth dockyard) depleted the agricultural labour force and left the remainder discontented.[58] Between 1801 and 1811 the proportion of Hampshire's population engaged in farming fell, precisely when efforts to expand production might have absorbed an increase. The total population of the 148 Chalkland parishes increased by only 2,740 (compared with

8,724 between 1811 and 1821) and the population in 49 parishes actually decreased.[59] The farm labourer's weekly wage rose by three or four shillings. With the expensive parochial administration and the current provision prices the £50,000 which the Chalklands population of nearly 60,000 spent on poor relief in 1809 may have gone to support only the transient, the unemployable, and those who were jobless in winter.

Hands were at a premium for harvest, and from 1802 Thomas Edwards of Hunton was glad to engage soldiers to help reap his wheat.[60] As Southey explained, 'the country is mostly down, recently enclosed, and of wonderfully thin population in comparison of the culture. Indeed harvest here depends upon a temporary emigration of the western clothiers.'[61] Another farmer, James Edwards of Horsebridge, was troubled by the restlessness and unreliability of labour; he began to board out his men, acting on a clear intention of avoiding the direct impact of rising provision costs.[62] The increasing cost of labour, as much as the growing profitability of grain production, must have induced the investment in threshing machines, which by 1808 had 'been erected of late years, and at a very heavy expense, in many parts of this county'.[63] Thereafter labour for threshing by flail, the main winter occupation, became increasingly redundant.

V

Hampshire Chalkland farming evinced many signs of a boom between 1793 and 1815. Farmers needed little urging to expand their businesses and may have borrowed heavily on the expectation of continuing high prices for farm products.[64] The Hampshire Agricultural Society grew from the annual wool exhibition at Magdalen Fair, Winchester, and local societies multiplied. The true boom was probably short-lived, as costs soared and the burden of taxation became weightier. There was no rebuilding to match those which locally characterize the mid-eighteenth- and mid-nineteenth-century agricultural expansions. Real profits were doubtless smaller than wheat prices, farm turnovers, or the alleged appearance of a claret-drinking, fox-hunting tenantry might suggest.

Yet, although insubstantial, the boom carried to a hasty conclusion the gradual developments of a half-century. The plough made immense inroads into the downland and grassland flocks dwindled. Sheep began to contribute more than the benefit of the fold and

D

store animals—more mutton, wool, and store lambs. A labour-saving machine of general application was introduced. Last, but not necessarily least, a new acceptance of progressive change and rising living standards was born in the farming community. The superstructure of Chalkland agriculture came by 1815 to rest on sky-high prices for wheat and mutton. This transition and increase in scale had been bought only at high and sometimes continuing cost. The shifts in the relationships between farm enterprises were fraught with significance for the coming depression.

In contrast to 1715, the accent in 1815 was on the greater sale of sheep products and a more extensive grain production. Changes in techniques and costs had been wrought and could not be easily reversed. Thus, although 'sheep-and-corn' certainly applies to Chalkland farming at both dates, it neglects the essential economic and technical distinctions between them.[65] Similarly, its use to describe farming on the 'good sands' of Norfolk, the 'Ryelands' of Herefordshire, and the chalk of the southern counties, fails to draw the necessary distinctions between dissimilar system.[66] It may be urged that the acceptance of popular descriptions of farming systems should be replaced by scrutiny of their economic features in each locality and at every period. From this an appropriate terminology for the phases of change should emerge.

NOTES TO CHAPTER 1

1. Edward Lisle, who farmed at Crux Easton from 1693 or 1694 until 1722, did not regard Hampshire Chalkland sheep as abundant wool bearers, and contemporary farm accounts record less valuable sales of wool than of sheep on the hoof.—E. Lisle, *Observations in Husbandry* (1757), *passim*; Farming and Domestic Account Book for Property at Compton and Somborne, H[ampshire] R[ecord] O[ffice]: 2M37/148; Accounts of Mr. Rumbold's executors 1707–21, HRO: 2M37/153. The sale of stores is stressed in Defoe's *Tour* of 1724, Everyman edn., p. 289.
2. J. Worlidge, *Systema Agriculturae*, 1681 (1st edn., 1669), pp. 11, 17, 46.
3. Lisle, *op. cit.*, *passim*. (Contemporary farm accounts refer to Rye Grass, Sainfoin, Hop Clover, and Broad Clover.—HRO: 2M37/148, 153.)
4. *Ibid.*, pp. 229–33, 263.
5. *Ibid.*, p. 217.
6. H. P. Moon & F. H. W. Green, *Land Utilisation Survey*, Hampshire, ed. L. D. Stamp (1940), p. 377.
7. HRO: 2M37/148, 149, 150.
8. Incidental advantages of water-meadows included the control of drainage, which lessened the risk of sheep-rot, and the release of a surplus of hay for sale.—Papers relating to Pittleworth Farm, HRO: 18M54/Box G, pkts. A, C; Edwards's Collection: Farm Accounts, HRO: 2M37/148–53.
9. HRO: 2M37/149. See also Papers relating to watering of meadows of Pittleworth and mill at Mottisfont, HRO: 18M54/Box G.B., 1–10, and Particulars of Pittleworth Farm, HRO: 18M54/Box G.C., 12.
10. Draft Articles of Agreement, HRO: 18M54/1 pkt. I. Subsequent schemes are detailed in the same bundle.
11. Documents relating to Compton Estate, HRO: 18M54/1 pkt. F, No. 1.
12. E. Kerridge, 'The Sheepfold in Wiltshire and the Floating of Watermeadows', *Econ. Hist Rev.*, 2nd ser., VI (1954), p. 289.
13. A. H. Fry, *Land Utilisation Survey*, Wiltshire, ed. L. D. Stamp (1940), p. 236.
14. D. Defoe, *Tours*, Everyman edn., I, p. 282; see also pp. 187, 285.
15. Lisle, *op. cit.*, pp. 3–4, 266.
16. *Ibid.*, p. 430.
17. G. E. Mingay, 'The Agricultural Depression, 1730–50', *Econ. Hist. Rev.*, 2nd ser., VIII (1955), pp. 323–38.
18. Nottingham University Archives, Manvers Collection, Rentals 4344–8; 4509–48. The bad years in the Hampshire Chalkland may be extended until at least 1747. For a large farmer at Compton 1744 was the worst year in the period 1744–60, and the Rector of Compton abated the tithes, 'in consideration of ye bad Season & cheapness of corn'. See J. S. Drew, *Compton, near Winchester* (1939), p. 120.

19. Papers relating to tenancy of Hants manor of Stoke Charity, HRO: 18M54/Box E, pkt. A.

20. Bolton Collection: Leases for Barton Farm, Weston Patrick, HRO: 11M49/447.

21. Extracts from presentments to Court Baron of King's Somborne concerning stints per yardland, 1724–50, HRO: 2M37/208; Miscellaneous Papers relating to Brook, Eldon, etc., c. 1750–1800, HRO: 2M37/127.

22. Cf. J. K. Galbraith and J. D. Black, 'The Maintenance of Agricultural Production during depression: the explanations reviewed', Journ. Polit. Econ, XLVI (1938), pp. 305–22, and D. E. Hathaway, 'Agriculture in an Unstable Economy Revisited', Journ. Farm Econs., XLI (1959), pp. 487–99.

23. W. E. Tate, 'Field Systems and Enclosures in Hampshire', Papers & Proc. Hants Field Club, XVI (1947), p. 263, agreeing with estimates by Prof. Gonner and Dr. Slater.

24. HRO: 12M37/555.

25. Enclosure at Binley, St. Mary Bourne, 1743, HRO: 3M54/1.

26. Annals of Agriculture, XLIV (1806), pp. 427–8.

27. C. Vancouver, General View of the Agriculture of Hampshire (1810), p. 78.

28. Nether Wallop Estate Papers, HRO: 11M49/466; Register of Copyhold Leases, 11M49/85.

29. e.g. at Chilbolton and Shipton Bellinger, F. R. Goodman, Reverend Landlords and their Tenants (1930), pp. 38–9.

30. Lease of lands at Broughton (1773), HRO: 2M37/358.

31. Noted on a parcel of 165 acres, surrounded by downland, on a map of allotments to heiresses of Roake Manor, Broughton, in the possession of Rev. R. E. Langdon.

32. Note of letting a down (1755), HRO: 2M37/150.

33. K. E. Innes, Hampshire Pilgrimages (1948), p. 42.

34. Downland in the Hampshire Chalkland has been plotted from early nineteenth-century maps by Mr. M. C. Naish at University College, London.

35. HRO: 2M37/Hurstbourne Tarrant, 28, 62; 2M37/53; 2M37/93; Southampton University Library, Abstracts of Torr & Co. leases.

36. Nether Wallop Estate Papers, HRO: 11M49/466.

37. HRO: 18M54/F.1 and Box H, pkt. F, No. 15. See also J. S. Drew, Compton, near Winchester (1939), p. 119.

38. HRO: Chalton Manor Estate, Box 2/3, 4, 5. Dr. Joan Thirsk informs me that she has found instances elsewhere of the temporary cultivation of common pastureland by agreement between manorial lords and their tenants. Dr. Thirsk refers particularly to an agreement in the 1670s between the lord of the manor of Penkridge, Staffs., and his tenants for the tenants to plough a part of the common for five years and then allow it to revert (Staffs. Record Office, D260, 8, 1), and quotes R. Lowe, General View, Notts. (1794), p. 9: 'it has been besides an immemorial custom for the inhabitants of townships to take up breaks, or temporary enclosures of . . . perhaps from 40 to 250 acres, and keep them in tillage for 5–6 years'. Cf. also H. P. R. Finberg, Tavistock Abbey, 1951, pp. 32–5, 105. The Hampshire agreements, Dr. Thirsk suggests, may refer to the continuation of this practice into permanent cultivation. The introduction of turnips, clover, and other green crops made permanent cultivation of the poorer downland possible. See J. Worlidge's letter of 1682 in J. Houghton, Husbandry and Trade Improv'd, 1728 edn., IV, pp. 141–4.

39. See *Annals of Agriculture*, XXXIII (1795), and 'postscript' to A. and W. Driver, *General View of the Agriculture of Hampshire* (1794).

40. A. B. Milner, *History of Micheldever* (1924), p. 245.

41. Valuations, HRO: 33M57/154 and 156/6, 8.

42. Vancouver, *op. cit.*, pp. 55, 58, 78, 80.

43. See e.g. Milner, *op. cit.*, pp. 241–5.

44. *An Account of the Odiham Society for the Encouragement of Agriculture and Industry*, n.d. [1785], p. 49. Simultaneously the Society offered premiums for enclosure, the largest being for the enclosure of 'waste'.

45. Mr. P. G. H. Hopkins, personal communication. It is unsafe, however, to advance as further evidence of concern lease clauses demanding prohibitive rents for pasture converted to tillage. These were the accepted means of maintaining the pasture–arable ratio, and were particularly important in this district, where good pasture was ever scarce.

46. A. and W. Driver, *op. cit.*, p. 22.

47. W. Marshall, *The Rural Economy of the Southern Counties* (1798), II, p. 347.

48. Vancouver, *op. cit.*, pp. 365–74.

49. Vancouver, *op. cit.*, p. 374.

50. *Hampshire Repository*, I, p. 76; II, p. 197.

51. Thomas Edwards's Account Book, 1790–1805, HRO: 2M37/340.

52. A. M. W. Stirling (ed.), *The Diaries of Dummer*, 1934, p. 133.

53. *Hampshire Repository*, II, p. 212.

54. Stirling, *op. cit.*, and HRO: 2M37/340. Thomas Edwards's accounts suggest growing pressure on his fodder supplies as he increased his sheep stock in the first years of the nineteenth century. He began to pay other farmers to winter some stock, bought the feed of Hunton Down, and in 1805 that of 6¼ acres of turnips, and began to purchase rape and swede seed.

55. N. Harvey, 'The Coming of the Swede to Great Britain', *Agric. Hist.*, XXIII (1949), pp. 287–8.

56. For the main features of the system centred on arable sheep see the description of the similar Norfolk four-course in H. G. Sanders, *Rotations*, M.A.F.F. Bulletin 85 (1954), pp. 7–9.

57. Enquiry into the General State of the Poor, 1795, *Hampshire Repository*, I (1799), p. 19.

58. Vancouver, *op. cit.*, pp. 374–88.

59. See Abstracts of Censuses and Returns, 1801 and 1811; and Table of Population, 1801–1901, in *V.C.H. Hampshire*, V, pp. 435–50.

60. Account Book, 1790–1805, HRO: 2M37/340.

61. R. Southey, *Letters from England*, ed. Jack Simmons (1951), p. 42.

62. Farm Account Books, HRO: 2M37/341 (1800–5) and /342 (1805–9).

63. Vancouver, *op. cit.*, p. 106. This was written in 1807–8. Cf. W. H. Chaloner, 'The Agricultural Activities of John Wilkinson, Ironmaster', *Agric. Hist. Rev.*, V, p. 51.

64. A tenant of Sir Henry Tichborne borrowed £2,000 from him and another tenant £2,573 on stock at entry to an additional farm.—General Account of the Hampshire Estates, 1795–1817, HRO: 37M48/10. Thomas Edwards borrowed a total of £700 between April 1799 and July 1800, probably for land purchases at Broughton.—Account Book of Thos. Edwards's expenses, 1789–1800, HRO: 2M37/339.

65 On the contrasting structures of Chalkland farming (in Wiltshire) in recent periods of prosperity and depression, see A. H. Maunder, 'A Study of Farming Change', *The Farm Economist*, VII, August 1953.

66. Cf. A. Simpson, 'The East Anglian Foldcourse: Some Queries', *Agric. Hist. Rev.*, VI (1958), p. 88. A cursory examination of evidence for Berkshire, Wiltshire and Dorset—where the store sheep production also pivoted on Weyhill Fair—suggests that the Hampshire changes were, with local variations, typical of the whole Wessex Chalkland. Cf. G. Slater, *The English Peasantry and the Enclosure of Common Fields* (1907), pp. 234–5.

2. Agricultural Conditions and Changes in Herefordshire, 1660–1815

No comprehensive description of the development of agriculture in Herefordshire during recent centuries is available. An assessment of the changes during the eighteenth century is indeed beset by peculiar difficulty. There are no obvious differences between the cash products at the beginning and end of the century, for the exceptionally varied pattern of the county's farming had been set early in the previous century,[1] and there was no strong movement to enclose or to reclaim land for tillage such as is used to give unity to accounts of the acceleration of agricultural change in some other counties. The best that can be done at present is to compare the exports of produce from the county at the beginning and end of the eighteenth century, in the hope that this will afford some clues as to the growth of production.

The progress of agriculture is commonly assessed by the rate of technological innovation. The criteria, so indiscriminately used by historians, on which judgement is based, are the improvements made in arable farming on free-draining, easily-worked land in the eastern half of England, improvements often grouped loosely as the 'Norfolk system'. Since these criteria are clearly inappropriate to much of the physical environment of the western side of England, they necessarily give an impression of agricultural backwardness there. Professor Ashton is perhaps the most authoritative holder of the view that innovations implying mainly parliamentary enclosure and the four-course rotation, with its 'new' crops, 'spread slowly. It was only in the east and east Midland counties that progress was marked, and in many parts of the country farming was carried on very much as it had been centuries before.'[2] Other criteria than these are needed when dealing with a clayey, early-enclosed, stock-rearing county such as Herefordshire. Some attempt is made here to indicate the degree of receptivity among Herefordshire agriculturists to unfamiliar practices, by considering the chronology of introductions of 'new' field crops and farming methods which can be seen from later experience to have been suited to the county. Finally, the supply and return of landowner-capital, tenant-capital and labour, together with the landowner's role as an innovator, are considered briefly, in the hope of identifying those elements which most influenced the rate and nature of agricultural change.

I

The inadequacy of its road and river communications with the neighbouring English counties was long recognized as stifling to the economic development of Herefordshire. The absence of a sure navigation of the Wye, it was complained, 'choaketh up the Commodities of Corne and fruite in plentifull yeares'.[3] In most seasons a wide range of foodstuffs in excess of local requirements was produced in the county, whereas manufactured goods, coal and almost all the lime had to be imported. The irregularity with which barges could sail the Wye as far up as Hereford, and the consequent necessity of using the very bad roads, raised transport costs enormously[4] but by no means prevented the marketing of produce outside the county. Bristol, where prices for farm products were as high as anywhere outside London, was in 1700 the chief market. London took cattle and the better quality cider, which could bear the high transport charges from Herefordshire.[5]

Bristol received grain, cider and wool which had passed down the Wye. Some produce came down the river to Chepstow, whence it was shipped for Bristol, but much of the grain came as far as Monmouth from Hereford market by pack-horse.[6] Bristol merchants loaded 'great quantities' of grain, notably wheat for Portugal, from Monmouth, which was largely supplied from Herefordshire.[7] The Bristol factors, who travelled widely for their supplies, almost certainly bought Herefordshire grain in Gloucester market, whither it was carried from the Ledbury district and from Wormelow hundred, 'the hither side' of Herefordshire, although land carriage as far as Gloucester was uneconomic from further west in the county.[8] Evidently, in 1700, despite the difficulties of transportation, Herefordshire was important as a source of agricultural produce, especially of wheat, for the Severn vale area in which the focus of trade was Bristol. The schemes in the seventeenth century to improve the intermittent navigation of the Wye were aimed at developing this trade.

By the late eighteenth century the transport situation had hardly improved. The roads, which Celia Fiennes in the 1690s had found 'pretty long miles', were to Marshall nearly a century later, still 'such as one might expect to meet with, in the marshes of Holland, or the mountains of Switzerland'.[9] Hope was no longer pinned on improving the Wye navigation and had been transferred to schemes for constructing canals, principally to connect Leominster and Stourport (put forward in 1777–8, again in 1790, and carried out in 1798) and Hereford and Gloucester, via Ledbury (put forward in 1790 and completed from Newent to Ledbury by 1798).[10] As the Committee for the Hereford and Gloucester canal pointed out about 1790, even if the Wye proved navigable—and the constant frustrations of summer shoals and winter floods were widely felt to be insuperable—it was only the trade with Bristol which would be facilitated.[11] The canals on the other hand offered access to the fast-growing food markets and sources of manufactured goods in the Midlands and north, and these by the end of the century were a greater attraction than Bristol.

A primary aim of the canal promoters was to reduce and stabilize the price of coal, and they succeeded in that the price at both Hereford and Leominster fell by half at the opening of the canals.[12] If coal could be brought cheaply into Herefordshire along a Hereford–Gloucester canal, it was thought that lime could be burnt in the vicinity of Ledbury and conveyed to the lime-deficient clays. Four thousand tons of goods, mainly lime, were indeed landed along the course of the Wye below Hereford in 1809.[13] Bricks could be burnt more cheaply and as a result farm buildings would be kept in better repair. Likewise the canal would mean 'the roads, now bad to a proverb, being less worn by heavy carriages', and that 'the farmers, by diminishing the number of their horses, will have an opportunity of increasing their stock of oxen, which will cause a diminution of the consumption of oats, and a reduction in the excessive price of meat.'[14] Canals seemed to offer to reduce both the prices of 'industrial' goods used in farming and the cost of marketing farm products. With these aims in view work on the Leominster–Stourport and Hereford–Gloucester canals began in the 1790s.

There was no large urban market within the county. The county town itself was thought to have grown by one quarter, to a mere 6,828, during the latter half of the eighteenth century. This was 'not upon that rapid and extensive scale which we see in various other parts of the kingdom',[15] and its effect on absolute levels of demand was minute. The markets for the county's now considerable agricultural surplus were perforce often far afield. A navigation to Gloucester, a nodal point for water-borne traffic, seemed vital for competitive marketing by the farmers of Herefordshire, since the uncertainties of the Wye meant that 'the conveyance of corn, cyder, etc. to the port of Bristol, is sometimes delayed so long as to lower their price; that place being supplied with them in the intermediate time from Somersetshire and other counties; which will always operate to the disappointment of our own farmers, until some other mart is found for the disposal of the produce of the county'.[16]

The promoters of the Hereford and Gloucester canal accordingly made estimates of the actual road and river trade of Hereford and Ledbury, which provide a nucleus of information on the scale and composition of the agricultural export from Herefordshire at the end of the eighteenth century.[17] Nine thousand tons of grain and meal were sent annually from Hereford to Bristol down the Wye, which despite its 'capricious' nature was necessarily prominent among existing trade routes.[18] Grain was also sent overland to towns in Gloucestershire and to Birmingham.[19] In the opinions of Knight in 1804 and Duncumb in 1805, the tillage acreage of the county had fallen owing to rising costs,[20] but, in view of the simultaneous rise in farm receipts and the especially rapid advance in grain prices, it seems unlikely that cereal cultivation was contracting at this time.

Five hundred tons of hops were dispatched annually from Hereford, but the bulk of the crop was sold at Worcester, the main marketing centre for the west Midland hop district. The number of pockets sold at Worcester shows no sustained rise between 1787 and 1798, and hop-growing was somewhat depressed during the Napoleonic wars; nevertheless, the eighteenth century as a whole had seen an expansion of production.[21]

There was a sizeable traffic in cider, perry and fruit. In 1789 the principal cider markets remained Bristol and London, both of which re-exported bottled cider overseas, but the trade was shifting to the Midlands and the north. Home markets were more important than the foreign trade, but both were supplied from the 'Herefordshire district' (Herefordshire, Gloucestershire, Monmouthshire and Worcestershire), 'in which, *only*, *sale* liquor is at present produced in quantity'. The main buying centres were Ledbury and Upton on-Severn, with some purchasing at Hereford, Gloucester and Worcester, while from Bristol and 'of late years' from London travel ling buyers were sent into the district.[22] Two thousand tuns of cider were being exported each year from Hereford alone in the late eighteenth century. Marshall in 1789 estimated the average annual production of the four counties at 30,000 hogsheads, roughly half for sale and half for consumption on the farm. Lodge in 1793 suggested that over 20,000 hogsheads were made in Herefordshire in a good season, and of these about 7,000 were sold to the merchants at Hereford and Ledbury.[23] These statements are not directly comparable, and in any case the measures used were variable, but they serve to indicate the scale of the trade.

'The markets for *sale* liquor has hitherto been confined', wrote Marshall, 'but the late extension of canals ... together with the present facility of land carriage, have already extended, and will in all probability still farther extend the market'.[24] A similar argument for the Hereford and Gloucester canal was that cider, 'now carried to London by a circuitous ... navigation, may be conveyed thither by way of the Stroud canal ...[25] [and] be carried to Stourport, and from thence to Birmingham, Manchester, and all the manufacturing towns of the North'. Lichfield was supplied with cider and perry from Ledbury in 1803 and Birmingham with cider from the Hampton Court estate, Leominster, in 1809.[26] During the French wars the traffic in apples was expanding even faster than that in cider. By 1795 the annual freight charge on cooking apples brought from the cider counties into Manchester alone exceeded £3,000.[27] Apples which were good keepers were sent from Herefordshire and the other cider counties to the west Midland and northern towns for table use at more than twice the price which cider made from them would have fetched.[28] The trade in cider and apples illustrates more clearly than any other how the agricultural export of Herefordshire was increasing and re-orientating at the end of the eighteenth century to cater for the growing markets of the industrial regions.

Livestock production shows signs of a comparable expansion. The traffic in bacon pigs fed on windfall apples or cider refuse for the London market, which had been thriving in the first decade of the century, may have been merged into the growing trade in hogs for fattening at distilleries in London and elsewhere.[29] Sixty tons of wool were sent from Hereford July fair, forty overland to Gloucestershire and Wiltshire, the remainder apparently to Yorkshire. Ross was an even larger wool mart than Hereford, while in 1800 some of the Gloucestershire clothiers had warehouses at Hereford, Ross and Leominster, as they may have had since the seventeenth century.[30] In the 1790s there was much experiment in cross-breeding Ryeland and longwool sheep for heavier carcases. Hereford cattle, which had been driven to the Midland pastures *en route* to the London market for centuries, were spreading geographically 'in every direction' and were now providing beef for a mass urban market.[31]

The traffic in farm products was not all outwards from the county. Herefordshire was poorly supplied with dairies and in consequence Cheshire cheese was brought in by canal, while tubs of Welsh butter came in overland.[32] Nevertheless, the impression remains that the production and export of the farm products of Herefordshire grew substantially during the eighteenth century, especially during the last two decades, although the range of commodities involved hardly changed.

II

The unifying concept of the 'agricultural revolution' is the increase in output following such technological advances (in the broad sense) as parliamentary enclosure, the Norfolk four-course rotation, and systematic stock-breeding. Although the development of a leading breed of beef cattle stands to the county's credit, on the first two counts Herefordshire would appear 'backward'. Neither of these, however, is an appropriate indicator of the progress of agriculture in such an environment.

Only a very tiny fraction of Herefordshire was affected by Parliamentary enclosure, and there were apparently no other formal agreements to enclose open fields.[33] It is doubtful whether more than a handful of townships in the county were ever farmed on a classic open-field system. The most diligent search by historians of field systems, notably H. L. Gray, who based his *English Field Systems* in large measure on Herefordshire material, has failed to produce evidence of more than thirty places where there may have been three-field farming. In 1675 only about 8 per cent of the total county area was open, and only Kent and Essex were more enclosed. At the most, 4 per cent was enclosed by Act, mainly in the nineteenth century, and this included some waste land. The historian of Herefordshire will be better employed in writing a systematic account of the farming of the enclosed land in the county than in seeking further dubious and abnormal instances of open-field survival.

A lengthy process of piecemeal enclosure and disintegration of an open-field pattern, which seems never to have been more than fragmentary, left so little of the county open that by the era of parliamentary enclosure no Herefordshire township was still farmed predominantly on an open-field basis. This process may have been at its most rapid during the second and third quarters of the seventeenth century. There are some signs that adjustment to the downward trend of grain prices in the last quarter of that century took the form of the conversion of arable to grass; the income of the small tenant farmer, especially on clayland, in this part of England seems to have been squeezed hard at this time.[34] There were parliamentary enclosures in 1607–8 (the second in the kingdom), 1779, and a faint burst of activity revealed by seven between 1797 and 1812, paralleled by the breaking-up of some wasteland in the interior of the county. A significant acreage of wood was felled and the land converted to tillage during the latter half of the eighteenth century[35] when grain prices were conducive to this. But, as Tate concluded (p. 190), 'Parliamentary enclosure here was a kind of "mopping up" process applied to the existing scraps of common which . . . had escaped enclosure in earlier years.' Clearly, apart from the slight activity in the final years, the development of agriculture in Herefordshire in the eighteenth century is not at all reflected by its parliamentary enclosure history.

Neither is the rate at which the Norfolk rotation was adopted a useful index of agricultural progress in Herefordshire. The new husbandry of the eighteenth century meant to many contemporaries and to most subsequent writers essentially the Norfolk four-course and, above all, the cultivation of the turnip. Farming everywhere was compared directly with that of west Norfolk, and the comparison was usually as unflattering as it is invidious. Such statements as that of an Essex farmer in 1783, that the growing of turnips in itself constituted 'the basis of all good husbandry',[36] abound unchallenged throughout contemporary literature. Despite its unsuitability for the wet clay or hill lands, the four-course persists as the conventional standard of past agricultural advance.[37] With the rules thus framed with reference to the needs and potentialities of farming on free-draining, easily-worked land, and with propagandists who have never flagged, Norfolk and a handful of similar counties must appear far more 'advanced' than all others.

Since sheep feeding on turnips in winter will poach the ground or pack it hard, it is not surprising that 'this branch of cultivation [was in 1781] not yet generally practised in the Western counties',[38] on clays or in wetter conditions than Norfolk men had to face. Yet turnips were grown much more in the west than the scarcity of fully-developed arable rotations with root-breaks would suggest. They were instead grown as supplementary food for stock-rearing.[39] The classic Norfolk rotation of wheat, turnips, barley and clover, with its counterpart arable flock, was unworkable throughout most of Herefordshire. Husbandry of the Norfolk type came to be tried in the western uplands of the county only during the Napoleonic wars, and from thence it rapidly retreated, as it had from parts of Scotland, although other less drastic changes in rotations became established in the uplands along the Welsh border.[40] The uplands were too wet for wheat,[41] and the sticky clays of the Plain of Hereford were too moist for the barley course and for folding sheep on turnips in winter.

Only on the sandy soils of the Ross district could a version of the Norfolk husbandry thrive. Here it was spreading in 1794 and well established by 1801.[42] This is late for so suitable a district, but the delay is perhaps not hard to explain. Turnip-fed sheep tend to develop a longer and coarser wool staple than those worse fed. The farmers round Ross would be reconciled to this only when convinced that a heavier carcase and coarser fleece would pay better than the light carcase and fine fleece (reputedly the finest among British breeds) of their native Ryeland sheep. This reconciliation seems to have been effected by the rise in meat prices early in the Napoleonic wars. How alien the Ross district under its new regime seemed to farmers elsewhere in Herefordshire may be judged from a note in the account book of Sir George Cornewall's farm at Moccase, ten miles west of Hereford, in 1807: 'on the Ross side, the Norfolk plough is much used—& generally, some plough with two horses, & *one* man—no white crops together—wheat every 4 years —many turnips—& eat off *by sheep*'.[43]

Herefordshire agriculturists were not, however, dilatory in adopting new practices and new crops where these were suitable for the locality. As John Beale wrote in 1657, 'I observe the wisest and best of our Gentry to be very carefull in setting forward such kind of husbandry, as agrees with the nature of the soyl where he inhabiteth'.[44] This principle seems to have been followed, helped by the greater flexibility in management which came with the introduction of new field crops in the late seventeenth and eighteenth centuries.[45] Over much of the county turnips were useful chiefly as a supplementary feed for rearing cattle and sheep. There was not the urgent demand for roots to stall-feed fatstock, nor such a need for dung, as there was in the purely arable areas, with their excess production of straw which needed to be converted into manure. Local demand for meat meant that only a very few cattle had to be 'finished', while the riverside pastures could carry a high stocking density without artificial fodder. Large acreages of turnips, representing a fourth of the cropped area, were not therefore to be expected in the small fields of the Plain of Hereford, although moderate acreages were being grown quite early in the eighteenth century.[46]

Already in 1657 Beale knew that the Ross district was suitable for growing turnips, and it seems likely that he tried them elsewhere (in boggy ground) in 1662. John Noble introduced turnips, at least experimentally, at Much Marcle between 1696 and 1719, instructing his wife to plant them 'in the Nursery' while he was away from home. In 1720–1 a yeoman of Moreton-upon-Lugg referred to 'the country whence the King came, for there nothing did grow but Turnips' with a contempt doubtless born of some familiarity with the root. In May 1726, William Brydges of Tyberton was promised '50[lb.?] of new Turnips Seed'. Edmund Patteshall bought turnip seed for his farm at Allensmore as early as 1743, and limed nine acres of turnips there in 1755 and thirteen acres in 1756, while at Eywood twenty-four acres had been sown in 1755. Turnips were grown at Canon Frome, at Moccas, and at Acton Beauchamp in the 1780s and thereafter; in the first-named locality they were sown with rye, presumably as spring feed for sheep. The crop returns of 1801 show that turnips were grown in many central Herefordshire parishes, and in the north-west in the vicinity of the Knight family homes at Elton and Downton Castle. They were usually grown as extra feed for young stock and feeding-cattle in winter, and some were given to ewes and lambs in spring. Only in the Ross district did they form a full course in an arable rotation. Although the farmers who grew them may have been the wealthier and more alert men, turnips were far from the prerogative of hobby-farming landowners.

The turnip was never rivalled as a symbol of agricultural progress, despite the earlier introduction, wider geographical spread and greater nutritional value of clover and the rotation grasses.[47] Clover leys provided winter feed for sheep on clay or other ill-drained land where turnips could not be fed off, while resting the wheatland and making a direct contribution to soil fertility. Since clover was better adapted than turnips to the conditions of husbandry in much of western England, including Herefordshire, its adoption is a more meaningful index of the assimilation there of novel farm practices. Andrew Yarranton, who had introduced clover into Worcestershire, aimed his book *The Improvement improved ... by Clover* of 1663 at, among others, the farmers of parts of Herefordshire. He had an agent at Ross who sold clover seed and pamphlets on the cultivation of the crop. Yarranton claimed that clover had doubled the value of land in the Ross district. John Beale seems to have informed him in 1662 of the successful growth of some of his clover seed, presumably at Hereford.[48] Further west, a tenancy agreement appertaining to a Hay-on-Wye family refers to a direct reseed with clover in 1686: the tenant 'will not plough or break upp the same [meadow ground] unless it be to the end and intent to sow clover therein'.[49] Clover and the rotation grasses, notably rye-grass, were widely established in Herefordshire throughout the eighteenth century. Early in the 1760s Stillingfleet, the botanist, was carrying out a controlled experiment on grassland on the Price estate at Foxley.[50]

Another aid to stock-farming which was widely adopted in Herefordshire was the water-meadow. Grass could be made to grow faster and earlier in the year if covered for a series of short periods by a warming sheet of water. By this means the problem of the shortage of spring feed, especially acute at lambing, was partly solved. The first English account of floating meadows was written by Rowland Vaughan, who described his works in the flat-floored Golden Valley in Elizabethan times.[51] Similarly, the diversion of streams at Wigmore in 1653 was probably for meadows of this sort, which cannot have been unusual by 1663 when Yarranton claimed that clover effected an improvement of comparable value. Beale remarked in 1657 that 'other helps of pasture we do not omit, every rill of water is carefully conducted to the best use', although this may refer to the more simply designed catchwork meadows. Construction of a large system of floated meadows in the vicinity of Staunton-on-Arrow was begun in 1660 and, after fifty years of spadework, was finally completed in 1710. Other floated meadows, where the water was periodically let on to the land through hatches from a stream and returned via channels and hatches lower down, were those trenched on Lord Scudamore's estate at Holme Lacy in February 1709, and those which William Brydges was having laid out by specialist workmen at Tyberton in April 1712: '30 acres of new Ground laid under ye Improvem^t. They have done for this spring & are to come again next winter.'

The more usual water-meadows in Herefordshire were on the simpler catchwork system, whereby streams were run over hillside

pastures, utilizing some of their natural fall. In the 1770s the benefits of this were said to be immense, but the practice by no means
general. It had apparently spread by the 1790s. Artificial water-
meadows could not be constructed along the deeply-entrenched
Wye, and some other waters were not being exploited because of the
divided ownership of rights over meadows and streams, and the
perennial conflicts caused when mills were robbed of their races.
Despite these difficulties, water-meadows of one sort or another
multiplied during the late eighteenth century, and a few additional
meadows were floated in the first half of the nineteenth century.

The introduction of the swede may be cited as a final illustration
that Herefordshire agriculturists were swift to adopt such new crops
or practices as were relevant to their needs.[52] According to Duncumb, the secretary of the Herefordshire Agricultural Society who
surveyed the county on behalf of the Board of Agriculture, swedes
had been introduced a few years before 1805 by the steward of the
Guy's Hospital estates, although he added that T. A. Knight and
Mr. Davis of Croft had sown them about the same time. Duncumb
did not mention that swedes had been tried by Sir George Cornewall
at Moccas in 1801 and by Edward Wallwyn at Much Marcle as
early as 1795. Wallwyn had written to his agent on 1 May 1795,
sending some turnip seed 'a Single Pound of a New Sort, called *The
Sweedish Turnip*', which, he said, 'is a remarkable hardy Sort—Last
Winter gave it a fair Trial, for the first time, & it was found to stand
the Frost when every other sort was totally destroyed—It is expected to turn out the most useful & profitable Turnip that ever was
grown in this Kingdom ... I must have a fair Trial made of this
single Pound, which I have sent, upon some of our Lands at Marcle
—Desire M^r. Crump to put out a Bit of Ground ... & sow some of
the Seed—He may also have a little of it himself to sow in his own
Ground—M^r. Clinton may also have a little of it—But I expect they
will take Care & give it a fair Trial.' By 1805 swedes had made
'very considerable progress' in the county.

Wallwyn also introduced Dutch clover at Much Marcle in 1795,
when the seed of other clovers and grasses was exceptionally dear.
Duncumb said that Dutch clover had been introduced in the west
of the county about 1791; it was, however, sown at Canon Frome
from 1780.[53] The war period was indeed characterized by the diver-
sification of fodder crops, which doubtless reflects the heavier stocking which followed increasing meat prices. Clark, who first surveyed the county for the Board of Agriculture, had suggested in
1794 that for districts without water-meadow artificial grasses could

E

supply the want of hay, while cabbages planted on the fallows would compensate for the lack of aftermath grass.[54] By this date cabbages, with turnips and potatoes, were commonly sown as a catch crop between the rows in hopyards, where they were fed off by hurdled cattle.[55] Rape was a widespread crop in the lowlands in 1801, and potatoes were becoming important, chiefly as pig food, in the first years of the nineteenth century, although they were also sown as an insurance against grain failures.[56] All these improvements in the supply of fodder in Herefordshire during the eighteenth and early nineteenth centuries were made at dates which compare favourably with similar introductions in more southerly and easterly counties.

It may be objected that the evidence cited refers mainly to innovations made by landowners. There is nothing, however, to suggest that their tenantry was slower to copy new methods than the tenantry elsewhere, and indeed may have been better able to do so than in the open-field counties. Certainly the bounty payments to encourage the spread of flax and hemp cultivation, authorized by an Act of 1796, attracted a growing number of claims from ordinary Herefordshire farmers who introduced these crops on a small scale.[57]

III

Herefordshire was not as isolated from external influence as may at first appear. Welsh cattle drovers, for instance, often passed to and from the London area. Members of the county's landed families were not infrequently in London, even when it was necessary to sail Severn to go there, either on business, or taking a seat in either House, or to settle during term in one of the Inns of Court. When they were in the metropolis, they were able to meet as the Herefordshire Society, established there as a philanthropic institution in 1710.[58] Whilst in London the landowners seized the opportunity to sell the better quality ciders to their acquaintances, and they procured the seed of new crops and gleaned new ideas about improved breeds of sheep or varieties of apples which they put into practice when they returned home. Even their ornamental parks were utilized for grazing cattle 'at tack', that is, at so much per head from those who were short of feed. The landowners were preoccupied with agricultural matters. Where the land was the source of a large part of their incomes and where they had some farming in hand, they had good reason to be attentive to the weather and the harvest prospects, as their surviving letters show them to have been. Thus William Brydges of Tyberton inquired from London of his wife in the country in July 1715 'whether yᵉ Marketts doe not rise upon this wett weather, & how yᵉ corn is like to prove this year'.[59]

By custom the economic role of the landowner was that of provider of farm land and fixed capital. Beyond this, he often disseminated new techniques, and at least one Herefordshire land-owner, T. A. Knight, sometimes called the father of horticultural knowledge, was famed as an initiator of experiments in husbandry. In Herefordshire, according to Beale in 1657, there was 'a great number of admirable contrivers for the publick good', among them Lord Scudamore, the popularizer of redstreak cider; according to Duncumb in 1815 there were still plenty of experimentally inclined agriculturists.[60] Agricultural investment by the county's landowners tended to take the forms of reorganizing the fragmented holdings on their estates,[61] providing the wide range of buildings required by grain, stock, cider and hop production, breeding cattle and sheep, and draining the clays. The priorities were quite different from those of, say, East Anglian landowners.

At the end of the eighteenth century the old, inconvenient timber and thatch farm buildings were fast being replaced by others built of stone and slate. ''Tis a great fault in this County', wrote a con-temporary, 'that of having twice as many Buildings as really ought to be.'[62] On the Herefordshire lands of Lord Malden's large estate, the nucleus of which was Hampton Court, Leominster, when Nathaniel Kent and his colleagues surveyed them in 1786–7 most of the farms had stables, barns with threshing floors, sheds, beast houses, cart houses, a hop kiln, a brew house and a cider mill-house, and some possessed in addition dovecots, pigsties, sheep cotes and dairies.[63] Such a variety meant that the necessary expenditure on upkeep was vastly higher than for farms of equivalent acreages where the products were less diverse.

Similarly, at the end of the century it was noticeable that farms were being enlarged and consolidated. The surveyors of Lord Malden's estate recommended exchanges in order that certain parcels of land might be relet to neighbouring farms where land of that particular type was needed, and suggested that one or two small farms might with advantage be 'melted down into the others'. This was already happening. Harris's and Fay's Farms (78 acres), Upper Moor and Wichurch Farms (77 a.) and Tedstone Court and Woods Mill Farms (153 a.) were pairs which had each been 'now Consolidated in one'. At Newton Farm (177 a.) 'there have been several temporary Exchanges made by the tenant, and if they can be confirmed will tend much to the Improvement of the Estate'. The result of none of these amalgamations was valued at over £106 p.a. and many farms less highly rented remained on the estate, so that ample scope for consolidation remained. One Herefordshire man recommended in 1791 that 'farms from [£]150 to 200 p^r year . . . are the size Estates to do good to Landlord and Tenant'.[64]

Nathaniel Kent and his colleagues would have happily seen consolidation continue. Sometimes they suggested laying two farms together, more often exchanging intermixed and scattered land between tenants or even with other landowners, in order to raise the estate's rentable value. They claimed that 'the improvement most obvious to adopt will be a general Exchange among Lord Malden's Tenants, and if the Lifehold Tenants could be bought in, some material Advantages might be derived from it, as the Land belonging to them lies in small Pieces, and very much intermixed with the estates at Rack Rent'.

Other contemporaries were well aware that holdings were being thrown together. Duncumb feared that this 'left very few opportunities by which an industrious couple can devote their 50l. and 100l. acquired by personal exertions, to stock the number of acres proportioned to their capital'.[65] He suggested that the farmers of relatively large acreages of the Herefordshire clays possessed important advantages over those of the smaller holdings in economies of scale; they had enough teams to haul lime and to plough thoroughly, and they had a large surplus to market and could hold it until prices were favourable. The number of tenants willing to stock the larger acreages rose during the Napoleonic wars, partly because the country banks were induced by agricultural prosperity to lend working capital to farmers.

The advantages to proprietors lay in economy of repairs, ease of collecting rents, and the richer, more reliable tenants. The whole subject of changes in farm size is bedevilled by the failure of contemporaries and of too many historians to distinguish between farm area and size of farm business in terms of total assets. Since, according to Duncumb, even the farms of larger acreage were often under-capitalized, the amalgamation of holdings may exaggerate the rate of increase in the true size of farm businesses, a matter more crucial than mere extensions of area since it relates to the intensity of farming and the production per acre.

The farmers had their own contacts with other districts. They imported seed wheat from the Cotswolds and even from the Berk-shire Downs. Between the early 1790s and 1805 they completely replaced the heavy ploughs native to the county by lighter models, and by 1800 a few of them had tried light wheeled ploughs. In 1799 a tenant farmer of Moreton-upon-Lugg owned a winnowing machine made at Wolverhampton. Yet here again the landowners formed the spearhead of innovators. Sir George Cornewall had bought 'a wheel plough' in 1783, a seed drill in 1785, a threshing machine in 1802 and a plough from Scotland in 1815. Drill ploughs, partly adopted by 1793, were still being tried out in 1805. At Bridge Sollars a landowner had introduced a locally-designed threshing machine.[66]

New ideas spread from the landowners, although a more general diffusion was assured from 1770 when the *Hereford Journal* was founded. One of Sir George Cornewall's farm account books contains a newspaper cutting of 1794 advertising a Radnorshire man's cure for scour in cattle, and another of about 1796 advertising a London sowing-hopper attachment for ploughs. The landowners were instrumental in establishing the Herefordshire Agricultural Society, with Duncumb as first secretary, in 1797. The society immediately set about promoting improved methods. Altogether, in Herefordshire as elsewhere, the landowners must receive much of the credit for initiating the technological changes which overtook farming during the eighteenth century.

IV

At the end of the century and throughout the Napoleonic wars the pace of technical and economic change accelerated. The only long series of farm receipts for an earlier period, those of the Rector of Whitchurch from his sales of cider, wheat, barley, ryegrass and clover seed, hay, straw, cows and calves, show no overall rise from 1730 to 1766. On the other hand, between 1783 and 1815 the profits of farming may have been rising, as they seem to have done on the Canon Frome farm belonging to the Hopton family and on the Cornewall home farm at Moccas.[67]

As the cash return from farming rose, so did the cash return to labour. At Moccas over 100 per cent more was spent on farm labour, excluding the regular farm servants, in 1799 than in 1786.[68] Data collected by the Board of Agriculture[69] show that the cost of labour on arable land in Herefordshire in winter had risen over

28 per cent and in summer over 33 per cent between 1790 and 1804. Reaping wheat cost 50 per cent more and threshing over 33 per cent more. Hands were scarce and the more efficient workers were said to be leaving the land. Duncumb claimed that the male population was 'so much thinned by the levies and operations of war, that the farmer in particular has but little opportunity of selection'.[70] The four harvests of Herefordshire farming, the hay, grain, hops and cider (the last three overlapping) made heavy demands on labour during the third quarter of the year. Local labour was supplemented by contracting bands of men from South Wales for the grain harvest, and in the 1790s half the hop-picking was being done by Welsh women who came into Herefordshire and Worcestershire for that purpose.[71] Nevertheless, labour was so short that in a 'hit' year for apples the overabundant fruit had to be knocked unripe from the trees, thus impairing the quality of the sale cider.

To Clark this scarcity of labour seemed ample justification for enclosing the remaining commons, since 'where there is so much work ... there are few poor that do not deserve to be'. And enclosure, he thought, 'would increase the number of hands for labour, by removing the *means* of subsisting in idleness'.[72] To Duncumb, a decade later, labourers' wages were lagging too far behind the cost of living (which does not mean that the rise in wages was in itself insignificant among farm costs), for wage regulation in Herefordshire had become ineffective in the late eighteenth century.[73] Nominal rates of pay were 'ordered as usual' at each Quarter Sessions and did not reflect the movement of the market rates. The labourer's annual income had not risen fast enough to keep him, if he had a family, off the parish, except perhaps in those few parishes where wage rates were linked by a sliding scale to the price of bread. The labour bill in farming, in the form of cash wages and parish rates, was mounting but not so fast as to provide the labourer with a sufficient real income. Thus, while the cost of labour seemed burdensome to the farmer, the labourer's position continued to deteriorate.

In years of dear bread the labourer suffered direly. In July 1795 the government had to order a ship carrying 500 quarters of wheat into Chepstow, to supply the Forest of Dean.[74] As early as March that year Edward Wallwyn had written to his steward at Much Marcle that 'the prospect of a great Crop of Grain next Harvest is not at present promising—I fear Corn will be dear. I shall plant all the Potatoes I possibly can, and would advise every body else to do the same, & particularly the poorer sort of People.'[75] The same month and thereafter the Hoptons of Canon Frome were selling wheat 'at 8/- to the poor tho' the mark[t] price was then 10/6'.[76] In March 1796, grain barges proceeding from Wilton, near Ross, to Bristol were boarded at Lydbrook by the Dean Foresters who removed much of the wheat and flour.[77] In November 1799, Wallwyn wrote that 'the Crops of grain with us are greatly defective—particularly the lent Corn—Almost all the Barley (which on these Clays is a late Crop) is greatly injured & Much of it absolutely spoiled.'[78] In consequence prices were rising and distress threatened, for heavy rains, 'bad for the Farmer, & still worse for the Poor', continued to impede the sowing of the next season's wheat. In March 1800 a mob seized the cargo of wheat and flour from a grain barge at Redbrook and sold it locally at 10s. 6d. per bushel, which was then a low price; the Hoptons of Canon Frome planted much more potato land that year.[79] In 1801, faced with an unprecedented rise in the price of bread and soaring poor rates, some Hereford shopkeepers were 'compelled to dine frequently on potatoes and water, in order, that eighteen-pence might be saved to meet the demands of the overseer!'[80] That year a subscription flour company was formed in the town ' "for the purpose of reducing the un-exampled prices of bread and flour, and to prevent the adulteration of these articles" ' and in 1802 the company ordered a 20 h.p. Boulton & Watt engine for its mill.[81] The company appears to have gone into liquidation when grain prices fell.

The attempts to cope with the plight of the poor seem to have been serious, and although the poor were hard hit in the worst seasons[82] they apparently escaped the worst sufferings of their counterparts in some southern counties. Nevertheless, high grain prices were not entirely the farmer's gain. As Wallwyn argued, 'tho' to a vulgar Age, it may appear to the Advantage of the Farmer, the fact is otherwise, for having only Half a crop he has only Half his usual Quantity to dispense of, & if he does it at a double price it produces only the same sum. Whereby with other loss of Straw & other Food for Cattle he is ultimately as great a Suferer [sic] as the rest of the Community—for as all must be supplied, Rates, Taxes and Wages increase in prop[t].' He was candid enough to add, 'I will not tell you that I am labouring absolutely in Vain.'[83] Wallwyn ignored the effects of the inelastic demand for grain, whereby a small deficiency of supply would cause a disproportionate rise in price, but his point that high grain and straw prices were disadvantageous to the livestock side of farming is a valid one, although not especially applicable to Herefordshire where few cattle were stall-fed.

There is little direct evidence as to the profits of farming in Herefordshire at this time. The Hopton and Cornewall farm accounts reveal no peaks of profit in the years of dear grain, 1795, '99 and 1801, but rather an uneven rise which became marked after 1805 and especially after 1808. Most farms were probably paying an adequate and increasing return during the wars, some were doubtless paying exceptionally well. The landowner, too, was able to cream off some of the profits by substituting leases determinable every seven years for those binding for a full twenty-one.[84] The boom in mansion building and estate landscaping in Herefordshire during the eighteenth and early nineteenth centuries, 'especially in the richer parts of the county, and in the sections most readily in contact with, and open to influences from other English counties',[85] perhaps reflected rising returns from landed property. Only the labourer's relative position was declining, as the rise in his wages was outstripped by an even more startling rise in the price of provisions.

V

The strain on the agricultural economy at the turn of the century prompted the government to collect information on the grain supply and the general agricultural situation. For Herefordshire only the returns made for the 1801 inquiry seem to survive. These have been analysed and mapped by David Thomas, but unfortunately, besides being incomplete, they are not directly useful for mapping types of farming.[86] Data on the distribution of hop-yards and orchards were interpolated from the 1807 Excise Returns and the original drawings of the Ordnance Survey respectively, but no comparable information was found on clover or the rotation grasses, and none on livestock. There is thus no clue as to how the various enterprises were combined on the farm. The maps which can be drawn are only of the distributions of some crops, not of complete and working farming systems.

The distributions serve to stress how varied were the products of farming in Herefordshire. The Ross district, especially west of the King's Caple meander of the Wye, stands out as an area of wheat and barley growing, where turnips and rape were important but hops were not grown. The main sources of receipts on farms for which accounts survive were barley, wheat, sheep and oxen. Hops and cider were not sold. The proportion of pasture on the farms was small, and clover and ryegrass leys were the main sources of feed.[87] Elsewhere in the lowlands wheat was the dominant cereal. Turnips had not succeeded in the wet and clayey Golden Valley, where they were being tried in the early 1790s, and Thomas concludes that attempts to diffuse the Norfolk husbandry beyond the ecological limits of constituent crops in the western uplands were soon to prove abortive.[88] In the Plain of Hereford proper the importance of cereals, cider-growing and hop-growing gradually lessened from east to west.

'The Herefordshire farmers have so much business between corn, cider, hop, and fattening cattle, on their hands', thought Clark, 'that a part must be, and always is neglected.'[89] The resources devoted to the various enterprises differed from time to time, even from season to season. Hops were blamed for distracting the farmer from more certain lines of production and for absorbing manure needed elsewhere on the farm. During the French wars hop-growing was suffering from the depression of the parent brewing industry and probably from a reaction to earlier over-planting.[90] On the other hand, the production and the profitability of wheat, cattle and sheep, and cider were rising. By and large the county's farming seemed viable and prosperous. The main grievance was the state of communications. It was said of the London auctioneer, Christie, 'that having an estate in Herefordshire to dispose of He had as usual set it off by a flowery oration, but before concluding He said that He felt bound to observe that Herefordshire was a county that had two peculiarities, viz.: "Turnpikes without end",—and "roads without bottom" '[91] The improvement of local agriculture and communications promised dividends to the entrepreneur with capital and energy to spare, while the amenity value of the county was high. The largest purchase of land was that of the 6,000-acre Hampton Court estate, bought by Richard Arkwright, Jr., the cotton manufacturer, for £230,000 in 1809. This was perhaps the best testimony to the potential rewards of owning agricultural land in the county.[92]

NOTES TO CHAPTER 2

1. Notably the establishment of commercial hop-growing and cider making. See e.g. M. W. Barley, *The English Farmhouse and Cottage* (1961), p. 156.
2. T. S. Ashton, *The Industrial Revolution 1760–1830* (1948), p. 63.
3. Quoted by T. S. Willan, 'The River Navigation and Trade of the Severn Valley, 1600–1750', *Econ. Hist. Rev.*, VIII (1938), p. 75.
4. Especially for bulky goods. See e.g. A. S. Wood, 'Sale of Navy Timber on the Whitehouse Estate in the Years 1812–13', *Trans. Woolhope N.F.C.* (1936), pp. 33–4.
5. Daniel Defoe, *A Tour through England and Wales*, 1928 edn., II, p. 52. Lord Scudamore was making cider from the redstreak apples he had popularized in Herefordshire at his seat at Holme Lacy as early as 1667. Apples were also bought from local growers. The product was bottled and sent to London. Weekly Misc. Expenses 1667–8, Scudamore Papers, Hereford City L.C. 631.16. William Brydges of Tyberton was marketing cider to London acquaintances in the early eighteenth century, dispatching it via Bristol and slow coastal shipping. See e.g. Bill of Lading 3/3 and letter to his wife 10 March 1713, Brydges Coll., uncat., Herefs. R.O.
6. G. E. Farr, *Chepstow Ships* (1954), p. 7; 'The Weares . . . Wye and Lugg', 22 April 1696, Papers relating to Wye and Lugg Navigation in the possession of D. L. Arkwright, Kinsham Court.
7. Defoe, *op. cit.*, II, p. 49. There was a similar export to Iberia from Exeter, E. A. G. Clark, *The Ports of the Exe Estuary 1660–1800* (1960), p. 124.
8. Papers *re* Wye and Lugg Navigation, *loc. cit.*, Petition to House of Lords from inhabitants of Eccleswall, etc., *c.* 1696, Hampton Court Collections, Herefs. R.O.: George Bennett, Agricultural Accounts 1705–7, Hopton Coll. pamphlet box, Hereford City 631.16.
9. C. Morris (ed.), *The Journeys of Celia Fiennes* (1949), pp. 233–4; W. Marshall, *The Rural Economy of Glocestershire*, II (1789), p. 223; Edward Wallwyn of Much Marcle was unable to sell hay to owners of colliery horses in Dean Forest in March 1795 because the roads were impassable. Various papers relating to Much Marcle, 1794–1803, Hereford City L.C. Deeds 4253.
10. John Price, *An Historical and Topographical Account of Leominster*, 1795, *passim*; Report and Plan of Intended Hereford to Gloucester Canal, Hereford City, P.C. 626 [1790–1]; John Lodge, *Introductory Sketches towards a Topographical History of the County of Hereford* (1793), pp. 20–1; I. Cohen. 'The non-Tidal Wye and its Navigation', *Trans. Woolhope N.F.C.*, XXXV (1956), pp. 83–101, and 'The Leominster–Stourport canal', *Trans. Woolhope N.F.C.*, XXXV (1957), pp. 267–86; Charles Hadfield, *The Canals of South Wales and the Border* (1960), *passim*. Neither canal was extended further before 1815 and neither was profitable.

11. The Report of the Committee for the Herefordshire and Gloucestershire Canal, n.d. (*c.* 1790), Hereford City, P.C. 626, pp. 2–3. Joseph Farington's journey on the Wye in September 1803 illustrates the difficulties of navigating the river. His boat had several times to be hauled over shoals between Wilton and New Weir, and from Monmouth to Chepstow the journey by boat had to be abandoned because the river was so low. J. Greig (ed.), *The Farington Diary* (1923), II, p. 151.

12. J. Priestley, *Historical Account of the Navigable Rivers [etc.]* (1831), pp. 363, 440.

13. Hadfield, *op. cit.*, p. 188.

14. Report Hereford–Gloucester Canal Committee, *c.* 1790, p. 4; J. Clark, *General View of the Agriculture of the County of Hereford* (1794), *passim,* stresses the great need for lime and for better farm buildings, as do other authorities. For the similar aims of the Leominster–Stourport canal promoters see Price, *op. cit.*, pp. 190–1.

15. John Price, *An Historical Account of the City of Hereford* (1796), p. 59; John Duncumb, *General View of the Agriculture of the County of Hereford* (1805), p. 151, states that the county's population rose 20 per cent over the same period, to 89,191.

16. Report Hereford–Gloucester Canal Committee, p. 1.

17. The two reports relating to the Hereford–Gloucester canal, cited above, are the sources of the following estimates unless otherwise stated.

18. Lodge, *op. cit.*, pp. 7–8.

19. Samuel Rudder, *A New History of Gloucestershire* (1779), p. 64; Simon Moreau, *A Tour to Cheltenham Spa* (1783), pp. 85–6; G. E. Fussell and C. Goodman, 'Traffic in Farm Produce in Eighteenth-century England', *Agric. Hist.*, 12 (1938), p. 364; Duncumb, *op. cit.*, pp. 165–6.

20. T. A. Knight in *Communications to the Board of Agriculture,* V (1806), p. 54; Duncumb, *op. cit.*, pp. 60–3. The increase of cost on 100 acres of arable in Herefordshire, 1790–1803, was reckoned at an average of 13·5 per cent, *Communications . . .* , V, p. 31.

21. John Price, *The Worcester Guide* (1799), p. 51, and D. C. D. Pocock, 'Hop Cultivation and Hop Regions in the West Midlands', *Annual Report,* Dept. of Hop Research, Wye (1958), pp. 75–80.

22. Marshall, *op. cit.*, II, esp. pp. 380–1; Hadfield, *op. cit.*, p. 186.

23. Lodge, *op. cit.*, p. 96.

24. Marshall, *op. cit.*, p. 241; see also Clark, *op. cit.*, p. 43, and Lodge, *op. cit.*, p. 99. However, Michael Biddulph of Ledbury was warned when about to send perry to Stone, Staffs., in 1785, that 'it is not to be ventured on our Canal'. Letters to and from Michael Biddulph, Hereford City, Biddulph Coll., 535.

25. But the Stroudwater Canal carried little cider and that not necessarily from Herefordshire. Tonnage Book, 1798–1813, Glos. R.O.

26. Letters concerning Supply of Cider, 1803, Hereford City, L.C. 663.1; Disbursement Book 'A', 1808–18, Hampton Court Coll., Herefs, R.O.

27. W. H. Chaloner, 'Manchester in the Latter Half of the Eighteenth Century', *Bull. John Rylands Library*, 42 (1959), p. 44.

28. W. T. Pomeroy, *General View: Worcs.* (1794), pp. 29–30; T. Rudge, *General View: Glos.* (1807), p. 238; W. Pitt, *General View: Worcs.* (1813), p. 149. Apples were also sent by 'the fruit boats' to Bristol. Marshall, *op. cit.*, II, (1789), p. 384.

29. G. E. Fussell, 'Crop Husbandry in Eighteenth-Century England—2', *Agric. Hist.*, 16 (1942), p. 43; Defoe, *op. cit.*, II, p. 49; E. W. Brayley and J. Britton, *The Beauties of England and Wales*, VI (1805), p. 420, quoting

Philips's Poem on Cyder (1706): P. Mathias, 'Agriculture and the Brewing and Distilling Industries in the Eighteenth Century', *Econ. Hist. Rev.*, 2nd ser., v (1952), p. 254, n. 5; John Price, *The Worcester Guide* (1799), p. 52.
30. Lodge, *op. cit.*, p. 19; R. Perry, 'The Gloucestershire Woollen Industry, 1100–1690', *Trans. Bristol and Glos. Arch. Soc.*, 66 (1945), p. 104; Arthur Young, *A Six Weeks Tour through the Southern Counties* (1769), p. 151, stated that the best wool used by the Witney, Oxon., blanket makers came from Herefordshire and Worcestershire.
31. T. A. Knight, 'Account of Herefordshire Breeds . . .', *Communications to Board of Agric.*, ii (1800), p. 177; R. Trow-Smith, *A History of British Livestock Husbandry 1700–1900* (1959), pp. 102, 194.
32. J. Duncumb, *Collections towards the History . . . of Hereford*, i (1804), p. 177, and *General View*, p. 68.
33. Enclosure material is drawn from Duncumb, *General View*, pp. 97, 101–2; W. E. Tate, 'A handlist of English enclosure acts and awards Part 15—Herefordshire', *Trans. Woolhope N.F.C.* (1941), pp. 183–90; C. W. Atkin, 'The Evolution of Rural Settlement in Herefordshire', M.A. thesis, Liverpool (1951); W. H. R. Curtler, *The Enclosure and Redistribution of our Land* (1920), pp. 110, 197, citing Professor Gonner and Drs. Gray and Slater; H. L. Gray, *English Field Systems* (1915), *passim*.
34. See Joan Thirsk, *English Peasant Farming* (1957), pp. 195–6, citing Richard Baxter, 1691. Arable land at Tyberton had been grassed down about 1680. 'Wᵐ Watkines affidavit about the Sheep pasture & tithes' [1718]. Brydges Coll., uncat., Herefs. R.O.
35. S. Robinson, 'The Forests and Woodland Areas of Herefordshire', *Trans. Woolhope N.F.C.* (1923), pp. 200, 204.
36. J.L., 'On Sowing Turnips . . .' (1783), in *Bath Soc. Letters and Papers*, ii (1788), p. 236.
36. Even Thomas, who himself demonstrated the unsuitability of the Norfolk rotation for much of the Welsh borderland, continues to use this and more specifically the adoption of the turnip as the index of agricultural change. 'Agricultural Changes in the Welsh Borderland', *Trans. Hon. Soc. of Cymmrodorion* (1961), pp. 102–3, 114.
38. E.N., 'On the Turnip Husbandry' (1781), in *Bath Soc. Letters and Papers*, ii (1788), p. 372.
39. See, e.g. Thomas's map of the distribution of turnips in the Welsh borderland counties in 1801, 'The Acreage Returns of 1801 for the Welsh borderland', *Trans & Papers I.B.G.* (1959), fig. 6, p. 176, and John Rowe, *Cornwall in the Age of the Industrial Revolution* (1953), pp. 223–31. Rowe mentions that potatoes were preferred in Cornwall to turnips, which were more demanding of lime and labour for hoeing. This may also have limited turnips in Herefordshire: of the neighbouring part of Monmouth it was said in 1812 that turnip-growing was concentrated in Abergavenny hundred because lime could be brought there cheaply from the Forest of Dean. C. Hassall, *General View: Monmouth* (1812), p. 48.
40. D. Thomas, 'The Agricultural Geography of the Welsh Border in the late Eighteenth and early Nineteenth Centuries', M.A. thesis, Aberystwyth (1957), pp. 161 ff. and 1961, *loc. cit.*, p. 114; M. Gray, *The Highland Economy 1750–1850* (1957), p. 85.
41. Knight, *loc. cit.*, p. 172.
42. Clark, *General View*, p. 18; Thomas, *loc cit.*, fig. 24.
43. Sir George Cornewall, Farm Account Book 1800–19, Hereford City L.C. Deeds, 5871.

44. John Beale, *Herefordshire Orchards, A Pattern For all England* (1657), p. 2. Barley, *op. cit.,* pp. 98–9, remarks on the speed with which new styles of farmhouse construction were taken up on the Welsh border, especially in Herefordshire, from the end of the sixteenth century.
45. Cf. the changes in the farming pattern of the Ross district described in John Aubrey, *Natural History of Wilts.,* Bodleian Aubrey MSS. II, fol. 152–3, 'Remarques taken from Henry Milbourne, Esq., concerning . . . Herefordshire'.
46. The following instances of turnip cultivation are from: Beale, *op. cit.,* p. 52, and 'I.B.' (probably Beale) in Andrew Yarranton, *The Improvement improved . . .* (1663), pp. 34–43; C. Radcliffe-Cooke, 'John Noble's Household and Farm Accounts', *Trans. Woolhope N.F.C.,* xxxvi (1959), p. 201; Papers relating to Earl Coningesby's Case, 1720–1, Hereford City L.C. 942.44/13, 298; Brydges Coll., uncat., Herefs. R.O.; Patteshall Coll., eighteenth-century farm account books, Herefs. R.O. A95/-; Farm accounts at Eywood, 1756–62, Hereford City Hopton Coll. MS. 3652; Hopton family of Canon Frome farm accounts 1779–87, Hereford City L.C. Deeds 8551; Sir George Cornewall Farm Accounts 1786–99, Hereford City L.C. Deeds 5871; Accounts of farm at Acton Beauchamp, 1785–9, Hereford City L.C. large pamphlet box 631.16; Thomas, *op. cit.,* p. 82, fig. 24; Knight, *loc cit.,* pp. 177, 84.
47. For an authoritative assessment of the relative historical importance of turnips and clovers and rotation grasses see R. Trow-Smith, *A History of British Livestock Husbandry to 1700* (1957), p. 256.
48. Yarranton, *op. cit.,* pp. 31, 34–43; T. W. M. Johnson, 'Captain Andrew Yarranton and Herefordshire', *Trans. Woolhope N.F.C.,* xxxiv (1954), p. 40; G. E. Fussell, 'Agriculture from the Restoration to Anne', *Econ. Hist. Rev.,* ix (1938), p. 71.
49. S. B. Stallard-Penoyre, personal communication.
50. Nathaniel Kent, *Hints to Gentlemen of Landed Property* (1793), p. 36; see also on clover R. G. Stapledon and W. Davies, *Ley Farming* (1948), chap. 1; Aubrey, *loc. cit.*; Farm Accounts of Holme Lacy, Book C, 1708–9, Hereford City L.C. MSS. 361.16; W. H. Howse, 'Farm Operations in 1719', *Trans. Woolhope N.F.C.,* xxxv (1957), p. 301; Radcliffe-Cooke, *loc. cit.,* p. 201; Patteshall Coll. eighteenth-century farm account books, entries for 1729 and 1740s and '50s, Herefs. R.O. A95/-; Daniel Renaud, Rector of Whitchurch, Farm Accounts, 1730–66, Herefs. R.O. A98/-; Farm Accounts at Eywood, 1756–62, Hereford City, Hopton Coll. MS. 3652; Hopton family of Canon Frome Farm Accounts, 1779–87, and 1788–99, Hereford City L.C. Deeds 8550, 8551; Sir George Cornewall, Farm Accounts, Hereford City L.C. Deeds 5871; Duncumb, *General View,* pp. 56, 70.
51. Vaughan claimed to have discovered the principle of floating meadows some years before 1601. *Most Approved and Long experienced Water Works* (1610), no pagination. Catchwork meadows were apparently widely used in the sixteenth century. See also A. S. Wood, 'Comments . . . ', *Trans. Woolhope N.F.C.,* xxxvi (1959), p. 203. The following section on water-meadows draws on D. G. Bayliss, 'The Leintwardine area of Herefordshire', M.A. thesis, Manchester (1957), p. 81; C. R. H. Sturgess, 'Land Drainage and Irrigation', *Trans. Woolhope N.F.C.* (1947), pp. 93–4; Beale, *op. cit.,* p. 52; Farm Accounts of Holme Lacy, Book C, 1708–9, Hereford City L.C. MSS. 631.16; Brydges Coll., uncat., Herefs. R.O.; Diary of John Holder of Taynton, 1691–1730, who was constructing floated meadows on the Herefordshire border 1706–11 (copy in possession of M. A. Havinden); Kent, *op. cit.,* p. 52; Clark, *General View,* pp. 12–13; Price, *Leominster, op. cit.,* p. 208; Duncumb

General View, p. 162; Lodge, *op. cit.*, p. 9; Cornewall Family correspondence, 13 November 1809, *re* Monnington water-course, Hereford City L.C. Deeds 5217; Hampton Court Coll., Herefs. R.O., Memo 1820–2, entries for 9 November 1820, 7 February and 30 March 1821, Thomas Blashill to John Arkwright 12 May and 2 December 1825, John Arkwright to Richard Arkwright, 3 November 1829; *Hereford Journal*, 20 November 1833; John Biddulph's Diary, 9 December 1833, Hereford City Biddulph Coll., 963; Hampton Ct. Coll. John Thomas to Edward Colley, 22 February 1848, James Holland to Colley, 11 September 1861.

52. On the following section see Duncumb, *General View*, p. 67; Cornewall Farm Account 1800–19, Hereford City L.C. Deeds 5871; Various Papers . . . (Wallwyn to Harbut, 1 May and reply 12 May 1795), Hereford City L.C. Deeds 4253; on mangels see Cornewall accounts, 1813, and Letters to Thomas Bibbs . . . (16 May 1816), 1816–34, Hereford City Biddulph Coll., 536.

53. Dutch clover was a white clover suitable for very short leys. See Various Papers . . . (Wallwyn to Harbut, 16 March 1795), Hereford City L.C. Deeds 4253; Duncumb, *General View*, p. 72; Hopton family of Canon Frome, Farm Accounts 1779–87, Hereford City L.C. Deeds 8551.

54. Clark, *General View*, p. 78.

55. Hopton family Farm Account, Hereford City L.C. Deeds 8550; Cornewall Farm Account, Hereford City L.C. Deeds 5871; Lodge, *op. cit.*, p. 39.

56. Duncumb, *General View*, p. 66; Thomas, *op. cit.*, pp. 72, 4.

57. Bounty Payments for Flax and Hemp, 1792–7, Herefs. R.O., uncat.

58. W. H. Howse, 'A Harley Cash Book of 1725–27', *Trans. Woolhope N.F.C.*, xxxvi (1958), p. 54.

59. Brydges Coll., correspondence, uncat., Herefs. R.O.

60. Beale, *op. cit.*, p. 37; Duncumb, *General View*, p. 52; for a less sanguine opinion see 'Extracts from Letters . . .', *Annals of Agriculture*, xxvi (1796), p. 440.

61. See, e.g., L. D. Stamp, *The Land of Britain: Its Use and Misuse* (1948), p. 340, figs. 177–80. The gradual consolidation of holdings in Herefordshire is evident in contemporary documents. Brydges affirmed in 1717–18 that 'it was certainly yᵉ interest of every gentleman to gett his Estate as much together as he could both out of regard of Interest as well as conveniency of managemᵗ'. Brydges Coll., Herefs. R.O.

62. T. Ravenhill to (? Michael) Biddulph, 22 July 1791, in Hereford City, Biddulph Coll., 539; cf. Duncumb, *General View*, p. 29.

63. Survey and Valuation of the Estate . . . Lord Viscount Malden, 1786 and '87, in possession of D. L. Arkwright. In 1793 the larger Kentish hop kiln had 'lately' been introduced, Lodge, *op. cit.*, p. 45.

64. Hereford City, Biddulph Coll., 539.

65. Duncumb, *General View*, pp. 32–5 and 152–3.

66. *Ibid.*, pp. 45–8, 58; Clark, *General View*, pp. 24, 65; E. L. Loveden, 'Notes in Herefordshire', *Annals of Agric.*, xxxv (1800), pp. 103–6; Cornewall Farm Account, Hereford City L.C. Deeds 5871; Lodge, *op. cit.*, p. 26; T. Westphaling, *Communications to Board of Agric.*, ii (1800), p. 422; the first agricultural machine tested by the Royal Society of Arts was a threshing mill by Lloyd of Hereford in 1761, D. Hudson and K. W. Luckhurst, *The Royal Society of Arts 1754–1954* (1954), p. 81.

67. Account Book of Daniel Renaud, Herefs. R.O. A98/-; Hopton family of Canon Frome Farm Accounts, 1779–1815, Hereford City L.C. Deeds 8551, 8550, 8547; Cornewall Farm Accounts, Moccas, 1781–1819, Hereford City L.C. Deeds 5871.

68. Viz.:

1786	..	£96	1793	..	£134
1787	..	99	1794	..	135
1788	..	103	1795	..	121
1789	..	118	1796	..	137
1790	..	126	1797	..	175
1791	..	123	1798	..	178
1792	..	160	1799	..	196

69. *Communications to Board of Agric.*, v (1806), pp. 23–31; see also *Select Comm. on Agric.* (1833), Q.8361.
70. *General View*, pp. 148–9. The scarcity was by no means confined to Herefordshire.
71. See, e.g., Lodge, *op. cit.*, p. 45 note; W. T. Pomeroy, *General View: Worcs.* (1794), p. 49; Goode family Farm Accounts, Amberley, 1805–13, Herefs. R.O. B43/18. The influx of Welshmen at harvest was old-established, see, e.g., Patteshall Coll. Farm Account Books, eighteenth century, entries for 1740s and 1750s, Herefs. R.O. A95/-. In the 1770s most of the hop-pickers had come from Stourbridge and Broseley, Mathias, *The Brewing Industry in England 1700–1800* (1959), p. 492. It is not clear why the Welsh had subsequently tended to replace the west Midlanders.
72. *General View*, pp. 21, 27, 29, 42.
73. *General View*, pp. 40–1, 64, 136–9; Quarter Sessions Minute Book 1792–1797, Herefs. R.O., uncat.; R. K. Kelsall, 'A Century of Wage Assessments in Herefordshire', *Eng. Hist. Rev.*, LVII (1942), p. 119, observes that the Herefordshire evidence does not support the view that wage rates were abnormally stable in the west of England during the eighteenth century. Cf. *Select Comm. on Agric.* (1833), Qs. 8397–8.
74. W. E. Minchinton, 'Agricultural Returns and the Government during the Napoleonic Wars', *Agric. Hist. Rev.*, I (1953), p. 30.
75. Wallwyn to Harbut, 16 March 1795, Hereford City L.C. Deeds 4253. The neighbouring parish of Dymock, Glos., made strenuous efforts to relieve the plight of the poor from 1795, J. E. Gethyn-Jones, *Dymock Down the Ages*, n.d., p. 173.
76. Hopton Farm Account, Hereford City L.C. Deeds 8550.
77. Cohen, 1956, *loc. cit.*, p. 97.
78. Wallwyn to Mrs. Leech, 2 December 1799, Memoranda . . . , Hereford City L.C. Deeds 7833.
79. Cohen, *loc. cit.*, p. 97; Hopton Farm Account, Hereford City L.C. Deeds 8547.
80. Duncumb, *General View*, p. 41.
81. R. A. Pelham, 'Corn Milling and the Industrial Revolution . . . ', *Univ. Birmingham Hist. Jnl.*, VI (1958), p. 173. It may be more than coincidence that potatoes were first planted at Moccas in 1801, Hereford City L.C. Deeds 5871.
82. There had been many complaints in 1795 that Herefordshire millers, mealers and farmers withheld grain and overcharged their poorer customers. A. G. L. Rogers (ed.), *Sir Frederic Morton Eden: The State of the Poor* (1928), p. 204.
83. Hereford City L.C. Deeds 8550.
84. *General View*, p. 41.
85. T. Overbury, 'The Domestic Architecture of Herefordshire', Woolhope N.F.C., *Herefordshire*, n.d., pp. 245–6.
86. Thomas (1959), *loc. cit.*, and thesis *cit.*, both *passim*.
87. Dew family of Brampton Abbots, Hereford City L.C. MSS. 631.16, nos. 20934, 20935; Farm Account for Weir End Farm, Bridstow, 1810–18, Hereford City L.C. MSS. no. 23,747; Lodge, *op. cit.*, p. 11.

88. Clark, *General View*, p. 18; Thomas, *op. cit.*, p. 163.
89. *General View*, p. 42.
90. *Ibid.*, pp. 29–30; Mathias, *op. cit.*, p. 583.
91. J. Greig (ed.), *The Farington Diary* (1923), II, p. 149 (13 September 1803).
92. Papers *re* the acquisition of Hampton Court, Hampton Ct. Coll., Herefs. R.O.; J. R. McCulloch, *A Statistical Account of the British Empire* (1839), p. 534, estimated from the Property Tax Commissioners' figures that the average rent per acre in Herefordshire rose from 15s. 11¾d. in 1810–11 to 19s. in 1814–15.

3. Agriculture and Economic Growth in England, 1660–1750: Agricultural Change

Between the middle of the seventeenth century and the middle of the eighteenth century, English agriculture underwent a transformation in its techniques out of all proportion to the rather limited widening of its market. Innovations in cropping took place on a wide, though not a universal, front and independently of any great expansion of demand, which was to stimulate the extension of improved methods during the classic agricultural revolution of the late eighteenth century. Except in the sphere of stock breeding, the remainder of the century really had little to offer in the way of techniques which were new in principle. Yet the initial introduction of the most important advanced techniques had come during the late seventeenth and early eighteenth centuries, when the slow and ultimately uncertain growth of population and the modest rise in *per capita* national income combined to produce only a gradual growth of demand.

The problems posed are of two kinds: one relating to the economic conditions which induced the developments within agriculture, the other relating to the economic consequences of agricultural change. First, how, in a restricted market, did substantial technical innovation, a rise in output, and an expansion of agriculture's capacity to meet the subsequent burdens of an expanding economy come about? Second, how serious was the fall in agricultural investment and incomes which is thought to have taken place during the second quarter of the eighteenth century, and what were the effects on the course of economic growth? What I shall attempt, therefore, is a thumbnail sketch of the timing and distribution of technical changes before 1750 and of their effect on output. I shall then offer two complementary explanations of these achievements and mention briefly the implications for the aggregate levels of investment and income in agriculture, matters which are germane to any incomes-effect explanation of industrial growth.

It will be plain that my aim is threefold: first, to give a brief overview of present knowledge on the topic,[1] although it must be insisted that limitations of space prevent any but the most cursory discussion of the evidence, and this must therefore be pursued through the footnote references; second, to relate the fragments of evidence so far available in a provisional and speculative explanatory scheme; and third, by the necessary tenuousness of any model constructed at this stage of research, to indicate the programme needed to fill the most critical gaps in our information.[2]

I

What were the early husbandry changes and how were they inserted into the agriculture of pre-industrial England? During the sixteenth and seventeenth centuries, the range of plants at the farmer's disposal had been extended beyond any precedent. The discovery of the Americas, for example, had greatly increased the vegetable species available to England, although most of the introductions to this country were made from or through the more intensive agricultures of the Low Countries, and most of them not until the seventeenth century.[3] By that time, as recent work has shown, farm organization even in the common fields was sufficiently flexible to utilize the new crops. The most influential newcomers were all fodder crops—two legumes (sainfoin and clover) and a root (the turnip).

The most rapid survey of published sources alone shows that the introduction of these plants as field crops came earlier and over a much wider area of England than was once thought. Sainfoin, for instance, was established at Daylesford, Worcestershire, in 1650, and about the same year at North Wraxhall, in north-west Wiltshire, by one Nicholas Hall of Dundry in Somerset.[4] The turnip, after being introduced as a vegetable by Dutch immigrants to Norwich soon after 1565, later spread until by the reign of Anne, according to Defoe, it was to be found 'over most of the east and south parts of England'.[5] Even in western counties, turnips were being grown during the seventeenth and early eighteenth centuries, and by the middle of the eighteenth century they were grown in Cornwall, the westernmost English county (by 1771, farm accounts for Menabilly Barton, Fowey, are referring to 'the Turnip Oxen').[6] In the west, however, turnips were usually sown in small lots as supplementary feed for livestock, not as a full course in the rotation of the whole farm. Considering the high production costs and the unreliability of the turnip crop, and the year-round growth of grass in the south-west, there should be no surprise that it failed to sweep the board. But it was not absent.

Clover leys were sown during the seventeenth century up and down the country from the south coast to Sherwood Forest and across from East Anglia to the Welsh border. Clover was much sown in the west. For example, Andrew Yarranton grew it at Astley, Worcestershire, and in 1662 wrote his *The Improvement improved ... by Clover.* He engaged agents to sell the seed and his explanatory tract in many towns in the west Midlands. Similarly, Dutch woollen merchants living at Topsham on the Exe imported clover seed, which they distributed to markets throughout the south-western peninsula during the second half of the seventeenth century.[7] In addition, the seventeenth century saw an immense spread of floated water-meadows from their points of origin in Herefordshire, Dorset, and probably Shropshire during Elizabeth's reign.[8] By 1700, these irrigated meadows were widespread in the Wessex chalklands and the west Midlands, and were still extending.

From our vantage point these innovations may seem to have come in unhurriedly. As late as 1750, all of them, especially the turnip, still had much ground to conquer. Nevertheless, it is undeniable that they were by then widely established. Grafted on to an agriculture which was already being modified by the creeping consolidation of holdings, they forced open the bottleneck of too little fodder with which to over-winter a large stock of farm animals. The fodder crops and the forced grass of the water-meadows had the same kind of impact: by increasing the supply of feed they enabled more stock to be kept and better fed, giving more dung per acre. This was a crucial advance for a society which lacked efficient artificial fertilizers. Heavier applications of manure would raise the yields of both cereal and fodder crops, more feed would permit still heavier stocking, and the whole slowly expanding circle would unfold once more. Total output would rise unless offset by a net withdrawal of land from cultivation.

The insertion of grass leys into farming routines, which has been acclaimed as a major advance during the sixteenth and early seventeenth centuries, was most unlikely to produce a *comparable* effect on total output. Ley husbandry may improve soil texture but not soil fertility, since on balance the grazing beasts will take out what they put in. While some improvement in yields may have resulted, the biological constraints made any substantial rise in output per acre improbable. The achievement of the 1540–1640 period in this respect must be judged meagre, its increases of output probably more the result of the extension of cultivation. Despite the early examples of floated meadows and a few cropping innovations, and despite many more studies of the farming of individual counties during the 1540–1640 century than have been made of the subsequent hundred years, no major technical transition in agriculture has been identified during the earlier period. That period looks to have been one in which inflationary profits were redistributed from the labourer to the yeoman and to the landowner, to be spent on the 'Great Rebuilding' of farms and on the erection of London houses, rather than one in which productivity far overhauled the growth of population.

The true transformation of crop rotations was accomplished with the adoption on a significant scale in the latter half of the seventeenth century of the innovations in fodder cropping. Nitrogen-fixing by the legumes contributed directly to soil fertility; the improved permanent grass of the water-meadows, washed by lime from the chalk streams, fed animals which were daily moved out to dung and thus to transfer nutrients and minerals to the arable fields. These changes were perhaps revolutionary in their effects although not in their pace.

Direct evidence of a resultant rise in total agricultural output is limited, but M. A. Havinden has provided us with some measures of the impressive increases which were secured in Oxfordshire— on the whole an open-field county which, although it grew the new crops, would not be expected to be in the van of the movement.[9] The figures, derived from large samples of probate inventory data, denote a marked rise in livestock populations, especially of sheep and especially on the light soils. They also show a shift in cereal cultivation in favour of the highest-priced cereal, wheat—a feature which is quite contrary to continental experience during the seventeenth- and early eighteenth-century depression. Unfortunately the evidence on total crop production is extremely slender, although the suggestion is of a rise.

There is evidence from elsewhere. The national sheep population responded to the expansion of feed supplies with a considerable

TABLE 1

		Limestone uplands of Oxfordshire	Thames Valley (clays and loams)
Size of median sheep flock	1580–1640	14 animals	24 animals
	1660–1730	60 animals	51 animals
		%	%
Proportion of cattle herds containing over 5 animals (N.B.: not offset by a fall in the number of herds)	1580–1640	33	39
	1660–1730	46	45
Wheat as a proportion of total crops	1590–1640	14	25
	1660–1730	27	32

expansion during the seventeenth and early eighteenth centuries, and this was of course especially significant for the manuring of the wide expanses of potential new ploughland on the light-soiled uplands. On the other hand, the national cattle population seems hardly to have responded to the stimulus of more and better feed during the first half of the eighteenth century, although it seems to have done so earlier.[10] The output of tallow, hides, and soap remained in the doldrums, while a supply of dairy products was obtained from Ireland. After 1707, the Scots sent more and more store cattle to England, and the Channel Islanders found that they could send growing cargoes of 'green hides' and of re-exported French calfskins to this country, as well as more and more Guernsey and Jersey cattle.[11] Finally, grain prices slowly sank, and a struggle to encourage exports by means of the corn bounty went on (with intermissions like the lean years of the 1690s) from the 1660s to the 1750s.

This may indicate that supply did tend to pull just ahead of demand, despite the withdrawal from arable production of some land in the clay vales. At first sight more striking still, the notching up of agricultural output took place despite difficulties for the producers of grain. There was a high turnover of small farmers on heavy arable lands, especially in central and eastern England, during the extreme scarcity of the 1690s and the low prices of the first years and second quarter of the eighteenth century. Arrears of rent were high on both heavy and light land during some years between 1702 and 1705, 1709 to 1712, and in the 1730s and 1740s.[12] During the last-mentioned decades, a fortuitous run of good harvests raised the supply of grain well above what the home market, the bounty on corn export, the distilling of gin, and the grassing down of the clays could clear. Both grain and livestock prices dropped. Yet the arable acreage continued to be extended and new farms to be created on the light-soiled uplands; fodder crops came more and more into use; and there was a noteworthy re-equipping of farms by landowners.

II

First, we have to account for the improvement in husbandry techniques, chiefly the development of rotations involving fodder crops, during the second half of the seventeenth century and the first half of the eighteenth century. At the general level this may not be so difficult. European work shows the extension of fodder crops to be a regular feature of periods of poor cereal prices, when, *ceteris paribus*, relative prices favour a switch to livestock and therefore necessitate extra animal feedstuffs. The spread of the fodder plants as field crops would have been delayed during the late sixteenth century, when grain prices were relatively high. At that time, although many of the fodder plants were available, there was less incentive to sow them as field crops, so that in England they tended to remain localized and in use only as vegetables, whereas their field cultivation had already become established in the Low Counties during the depression of the late Middle Ages.[13] The mechanics of their subsequent colonization of Enngland need to be more fully worked out, particularly as regards their widespread insertion into common-field regimes which were until recently dismissed as totally inflexible; but it is worth noting that many country gentlemen (including many Royalists from western counties) made acquaintance with the Low Countries during the seventeenth century.

Second, and this is perhaps the surprising and uniquely English feature, we have to consider a rise not only in livestock production but also in cereal production at a time of poor prices for grain. It is certainly unlikely that net cereal output actually fell, while livestock output rose so that aggregate agricultural output would have increased. Two complementary explanations will be suggested for this phenomenon. But even if all the agricultural changes of the period were merely shifts in the locale of production within the framework of a static output of grain, it would still be necessary to postulate how, when cereal prices were falling, production could be so much extended on the light soils of the former sheep downs. The second part of our explanatory scheme could provide such an explanation.

We may first lay stress on English agriculture's built-in mechanism for minimizing differences in the level of investment between spells of rising prices and spells of falling prices. There were two distinct sources of agricultural investment—landowner and tenant. The shifting in their respective shares of estate-maintenance expenditure was (as has been observed of later periods) almost rhythmic. During the 1730s and 1740s, landlords wrote off arrears of rent and reshouldered burdens like the land tax which in somewhat better times they had begun to foist on to the tenantry. Freed from these charges, tenants were able to devote all available resources to productive ends. In addition, in order to compete for and to retain suitable tenants on their farms, landowners even felt obliged to subsidize productive outlays themselves. They provided tenants with grass seeds, rearranged farm layouts, repaired the existing farm buildings and put up new ones, and on the chalk uplands they undertook the heavy capital expenditures needed to float water-meadows and to bring into cultivation commons and sheep downs.[14]

There may have been a shift towards investment in capital items by landowners: in buildings, hedges, and roads, where sheep down was being broken up for arable farms. The agricultural investment of the period, notably of the second quarter of the eighteenth century, was in part therefore the outcome of the estate system. The late seventeenth and early eighteenth centuries had seen the extension of the estates belonging to great landowning families already established in the counties. This was at the expense of the smaller squires, who had been badly hit by war taxation from 1692 to 1715 and (once the hungry nineties had passed) by low grain prices, too. The great estates which had been built up were, in H. J. Habakkuk's phrase, 'units of ownership not of production'.[15] Their owners did not engage directly in anything so demeaning as husbandry; their incomes were lucratively supplemented, and sometimes half supplied, from non-agricultural sources such as army posts and pensions. The physical capital of most estates had been run down during the wars; but when high interest rates dropped after 1720, enclosures and improvements became profitable again.

The larger landowners made it clear that they were in the market for good tenants and that, since they could let at lower rents than the lesser gentry, they would stay in the market even when times became less favourable. During the second quarter of the century, therefore, landowners, notably the great lords, were prepared to subsidize agriculture. For social reasons, and because of their other resources, they were comparatively insensitive to poor financial returns. They accordingly cushioned their tenants against the full force of falling prices and thus raised the level of investment above what it otherwise might have been.

III

A complementary explanation of the considerable innovation in agricultural practice which went on right through the low-price periods of the late seventeenth and early eighteenth centuries is to be derived from the dominant distribution pattern of types of farming. We must first discount the two dichotomies customarily used to organize English agricultural history: the distinctions between open-field and enclosed counties, and between a progressive east and a backward west of England. Research has diminished the sharpness of these divisions and proved them inadequate to explain the course of technical change or the economic experience of agriculturists. Examples have already been cited which make it clear that the east–west division is unhelpful: it is based on inappropriate indices of the rate of technical change—that is, on the adoption of a root break or of the full-blown Norfolk rotation. The link between this dichotomy and the rate of technical change in agriculture was in any case never very explicit. It depended mainly on the fact that East Anglia is nearer than the west country to Holland—the relevance of which seems less striking on a consideration of the actual spread of the new crops within England. Similarly, the divergence between open-field and enclosed areas has been blurred: in Oxfordshire, for example, it has been shown that the introduced fodder crops spread faster on the light soils of the limestone uplands, even in the open fields, than in the more enclosed clay vales like that of Thames.[16] In the case of the open-field-enclosure dichotomy, the link with innovation was supposedly through the 'slowest ship in the convoy' thesis, whereby the most dilatory open-field farmer dictated a snail's pace of adjustment in the system of communal husbandry.[17] Modern work, showing that the new crops were early inserted into many common-field routines, appears to indicate a different power structure, whereby the more pushing and articulate men often secured their neighbours' consent to changes. Both the east–west and open-field–enclosure distinctions do nevertheless refer to important factors influencing the detailed pattern and timing of agricultural innovation, but in no all-embracing or enormously revealing way.

A more fruitful division is offered by the scarp-and-vale topography of lowland Britain. This cuts boldly across county boundaries, dividing agriculture into two main groups of farming systems: on one hand, those on the free-draining, light soils of the chalk and limestone uplands, the lightest loams, and some of the more fertile sand lands; and on the other hand, those on the heavy loams and ill-drained clays. In the former category are the Cotswolds, the Wessex chalklands, the Norfolk 'good sands', and so forth; in the latter, the Midland clay triangle and the clay vales of other parts.[18]

The scope for innovating was not uniform across these two divisions. Although varying from crop to crop, the potential value of the innovations was, in total, greater on the light soils which had previously been too infertile for permanent tillage but which were dry enough for stock (especially sheep) to be kept on the land during winter to feed off the fodder crops, thus returning manure for a following cereal crop. The light land of the Wessex chalk and the Cotswolds benefited, too, from the floating of their valley meadows. Once it became possible to keep their thin soils fertile, cereals could be grown more cheaply on them than on the heavy clays, where, in contrast, traction costs were high, the working season was curtailed, and the land was too wet for stock to be folded on forage crops during the winter months. Because roots grow better in the fine texture of light soils and are difficult to feed off (or even to lift from) heavy, ill-drained land, the turnip was especially slow to penetrate clay districts. On the clays, therefore, less advantage could be taken of the contemporary innovations. The available studies do indeed suggest that such areas were usually very tardy in taking up the new crops.[19]

As a result, during the late seventeenth and early eighteenth centuries, some of the clays went down to grass and specialized more than ever in fattening and dairying, whereas there was a marked extension of cultivation on the former sheep downs of southern England, and as far north as the sand lands of Sherwood Forest. During the third quarter of the eighteenth century this distinction was emphasized, according to contemporaries, when the output per acre on light soils rose, for example on the Cotswolds, to 'equal that of a like quantity of land in the vale, where the rents are double and treble the price and the land will not admit of proportionable improvements'.[20] In other cases, there was a reappraisal of rents in keeping with the altered values of the two kinds of land; for example, it was observed that 'the dry grounds in Hertfordshire, which formerly were lett for a trifling rent, are now lett at twenty shillings per acre, since the introduction of clover & turnips into their poor & barren hills; while the low lying stiff grounds pay only ten shillings, which is the rent they gave near a century ago'.[21]

Thus the centres of arable prosperity were shifting from the heavier lands to the lighter lands. As regards the overall economic condition of the Midlands and the heavy-clay vales, some compensation was probably found in two movements which may have tended to hide the problems of husbandmen on their arable open-field lands. First, cottage framework knitting was spreading into these areas, absorbing under-employed labour or hands ousted from farming as the vale countryside turned more to pastoral husbandry.[22]

Although the relative rates of population growth by land-use divisions have been assessed from nineteenth-century census data, next to nothing is known of their earlier history. Seemingly, there were greater opportunities and pressures towards additional settlement and non-agricultural employment in the vales and on the lowland heaths than on the light-soiled uplands. The conversion of the uplands to tillage and the establishment on them of isolated new farms may have needed some hands beyond those previously present but under-employed; but the new cereal culture could doubtless have been carried on without much of a permanent influx, since the work was seasonal and harvest hands, for instance, were obtainable from the vale and the clothing towns.

Second, the trends of animal production were less unfavourable to the heavier soils. Within the increase in the size of the national flock there was a noteworthy increase in the population of long-wooled sheep in the Midlands. In Defoe's day, Leicestershire was 'a vast magazine of wool'. That county, which in the first half of the seventeenth century had been notable for its tillage, had turned more and more to grass. Wool from Leicestershire, Northampton-shire, and Lincolnshire poured into Cirencester and Tetbury markets for the clothing trade of the west of England; more mutton was in demand as a cheapening loaf released spending power. This was the period which saw the rise of the gentlemen graziers, building William and Mary and Queen Anne houses in the Midland shires; but it was a time which offered unsatisfactory compensation for sinking grain prices to those small farmers in the open fields whose fortunes still depended centrally on the cereal markets.[23]

Although stated very baldly here, this distributional model helps to explain much of the adjustment which was taking place within agriculture. The existence of this broad twofold grouping of farming systems was noted by contemporaries and continues to be recognized by farmers and naturalists. The topographic distinction is often sharp. But a mechanism whereby this could influence the course of innovation and output during spells of low prices and incomes has not hitherto been spelled out. The classification used here does not of course exhaust the ecosystems of lowland Britain, while any simple dichotomy runs the risk of violating some part of the evidence.[24] Nevertheless, the distinction seems to yield a useful categorization of farmers' economic fortunes and of the rates at which they assimilated new techniques. What the present discussion attempts to add is a brief account of the function of the dichotomy in terms of different physical constraints and costs of agricultural production.

Such an account offers a 'pie-slicing' thesis. Producers on light soils were able to take a disproportionately bigger slice of the pie (the market) at the expense of the higher-cost clay-land cereal producers. Their considerable advantage was reinforced by their proximity to the markets: East Anglia to London and the east-coast ports; the Wessex chalk to London, Bristol, and Southampton whence grain was sent to Iberia); the Cotswolds and the Ryelands of Herefordshire to Bristol and Monmouth, whence grain was also exported to Iberia. The Midlands farmers had to dispatch their grain farther and over worse roads to reach any of these outlets. Higher production and transport costs thus placed them in an inferior competitive position even given stable grain prices.

During the gentle subsidence of cereal prices during the late seventeenth and early eighteenth centuries, therefore, light-land farmers found that by innovating they could profitably expand their output. By putting a bigger volume of produce on the market, even at reduced prices, they could at least maintain their incomes. Technically, they had more room to manœuvre than did their clay-land competitors. Except in some years between 1702 and 1712 and during the 1730s and 1740s, there is no reason to think that the

total profits of light-land farmers fell. But the increased output of
grain from the light soils necessarily tightened the screw of low
prices on the higher-cost, technically less flexible, clay-land farms.
The rapid turnover of tenants, the selling out of owner-occupiers,
and the conversions to pasture on the clays suggest that, despite
more modification of their open-field farming than was accepted by
the older writers, the clays were being outcompeted in the grain
markets. There is some evidence that clover was adopted by farmers
on the Chilterns, where the chalk is capped with clay-with-flints,
precisely because they were obliged to improve their yields if
they were to remain competitive with the grain from the freshly
ploughed-up downland of the Salisbury Plain area.[25]

During the sharper price falls of 1702–5, 1709–12, and the
1730s and 1740s, not all light-land farmers escaped. Arrears of
rent mounted up on some estates in those districts. In the last of
these spells there are signs that output went up and the new
husbandry spread faster than ever in Norfolk. It may be suggested
that this was the result of a perverse reaction to lower prices. Faced
with falling prices but with the costs in arable farming incurred
well ahead of selling, farmers would find their incomes squeezed.
The light-land men were the most likely to react to this situation
by increasing output. On the light lands, the fixed, inescapable
costs imposed by high rents on long leases (instead of the annual
agreements and low rents of the clay-land open-field farms) and
by the hiring of a high proportion of the labour input were greater
than on the small wheat-and-bean farms of the clays. Costs were
therefore 'sticky', and although in the long run technical innovation
would reduce them and maintain profit margins, in the short run
there were certain to be adjustment difficulties. Variable cost
could not be cut down fast enough. The burden was to some extent
thrown on to the landlord in the form of high arrears of rents, and
in the long run it was eased by cost-reducing, yield-raising innovation, most of all on the light lands. The possibilities of cutting unit
costs of production by introducing the new fodder crops and associated husbandry regimes were greater on the light soils than on
the clays. Thus the price-cost squeeze on the light soils was most
intense (the clay-land owner-occupier may at times have retreated
into subsistence) and the prospects of eventual repayment for
innovation, in the form of higher rents or at least by abolished rent
arrears, were brightest. Certainly higher rents were sometimes a
condition of the landowner's outlay on capital items on light-land
farms—as an illustration, forty pounds was 'allowed towards build-

ing a New Rickhouse 1738 as per Agreement on Farmer Morgans taking an advanced Rent' on a farm at Broughton, Hampshire.[26] And light-land farmers were willing to turn to the new crops specifically as a way out of their dilemma: for instance, in 1745 a farmer at Stoke Charity on the Hampshire chalk attempted to extricate himself from financial entanglements with his landlord by proposing to sow large acreages of 'Cinque Foyle' in future years.[27]

Combining our explanations, some of the agricultural development of the period may be attributed to the rhythms of the landlord–tenant system and to the growing social motives for the ownership of agricultural estates, and some of it to the disparate technical and cost situations of light-land and heavy-land farmers. Light-land farmers, during the prolonged, gentle deflation of cereal prices, were persuaded or obliged to exploit their opportunities of taking a larger share of the market. During the sharper falls in agricultural prices, they inclined more energetically to expand their output to protect their incomes. This response was what the nineteenth century was to call high farming. In the first half of the eighteenth century, agriculture was even less free to contract if faced with a fall in prices than during the nineteenth century, since in a pre-industrial society there were comparatively few attractive alternative occupations, although there was a gradual drift of labourers into framework knitting and into certain towns. A land-use inversion between the uplands and the vales lasting fifty or one hundred years was not, in the circumstances, a particularly sluggish adjustment. It is possible that the rise in national cereal output to be expected from the breaking up of new land could be held in check by a much more limited grassing down of the clays; for, after an initial spurt of fertility, yields per acre on the light lands were usually lower than in the vales. But there does seem to have been some pressure of excessive production because of the inability of resources to flow freely out of clay-land agriculture.

IV

What might the implications of this analysis be for the totals of agricultural investment and income? As regards investment, the scraps of evidence at hand do not point to striking changes in aggregate levels. Instead of producing more when his income was squeezed, the small clay-land owner-occupier may merely have worked harder himself to avoid buying inputs or hiring labour (he was, after all, likely to be under-employed much of the year), and to that extent cash spending on inputs may have fallen. But on larger holdings where labour-intensive fodder crops replaced a grain course or permanent pasture there was presumably a net increase in employment. On the light lands, farmers seem to have invested more vigorously in improved techniques in attempts to extricate themselves from the price-cost squeeze. And landowners certainly in many cases stepped up their agricultural investment during the 1730s and 1740s. The tentative conclusion (which is all that can be drawn) is that total investment, on balance, probably went up by some modest proportion.

When it comes to assessing changes in total agricultural income, we are making bricks quite without straw. I suggest as a working hypothesis that during the late seventeenth and early eighteenth centuries as a whole, when the small farmers of arable clay land were often embarrassed, any fall in their incomes may have been offset by the gains of the more successful innovators, predominantly light-land men. This perhaps implies the concentration of income in fewer hands, with implications for the ratio of basic to luxury goods purchased. During the 1730s and 1740s, total agricultural income may have dropped, for there were spells when on both heavy and light lands rents fell and farmers were in distress. Yet, as far as spending by agriculturists on the products of an incipient industrial economy is concerned, it has yet to be shown that this in itself had enormously depressing consequences. The period saw a sharper phase of the secular shift in resources and distributions in agriculture, whereby the clays tended to go down to grass and the light lands to be converted to tillage, with concomitant expenditures on new building, floating meadows, paring and burning the grass downs prior to their cultivation, and so forth. These undertakings were primarily located on the light lands, whereas during the third quarter of the eighteenth century when grain prices were rising, landowner investment may have been lower on the light lands,[28] concentrating instead on Parliamentary enclosure (perhaps an attempt to create in the jumbled open fields of central England the physical setting of an improved agriculture which had earlier and more readily been provided on the empty sheep downs of the light soils) and on transplanting Norfolk-type rotations *en bloc* to less developed regions like Scotland. But the income generated by the undertakings of the second quarter of the century may have balanced any fall at that time in the purchase of consumer goods by the farm sector. In addition, most big landowners could bear their part in such enterprises from non-agricultural funds and without foregoing conspicuous forms of consumption. The checks and balances of landlord and tenant and of the two dominant groups of farming system, therefore, tended to circumscribe a fall in total investment or income.[29]

Any net decline in consumption in the farm sector might be expected to have been offset by the surplus real income created among the buyers of food, although the gain in income for the consumers of a cheaper loaf was spent partly on white bread as a replacement for rye bread, partly on more meat, partly on tea and sugar, partly on gin, and some of it surely was taken out in increased leisure. The second quarter century was not unreasonably described as a 'golden age' for the labouring man.

Within agricultural production, systems were being regrouped, however much subsequent periods of high grain prices might rejuvenate clay-land arable farming and thus, temporarily, put the clock back. But by comparison with later periods (though not with earlier ones) resources were still choked up in agriculture as a whole. This, together with the near stagnation of population growth, meant that the rise in purchasing power brought by cheaper food was not yet strong enough to throw down the final barriers against large-scale industrial expansion. This was to come in the third and fourth quarters of the century, when prices rose because a long run of inclement weather depressed yields and (rather later) when the growth of population extended the market. At that time the upsurges of investment and income in agriculture seem to have swamped any damage done to expansion elsewhere in the economy by higher food prices.

NOTES TO CHAPTER 3

1. Especially as revealed in the following key sources: H. J. Habakkuk, 'English Landownership, 1680–1740', *Economic History Review*, x (February 1940), 2–17; A. H. John, 'The Course of Agricultural Change, 1680–1760', in L. S. Pressnell (ed.), *Studies in the Industrial Revolution* (London: Athlone Press,1960), pp. 122–55; G. E. Mingay, 'The Agricultural Depression, 1730–1750', *Economic History Review*, 2nd ser., VIII, no. 3 (April 1955), 323–38. The present article is a slightly revised version of a paper given to the joint conference of the Economic History Society and British Agricultural History Society, at the University of Reading, 10 April 1964. Comments by Gordon Mingay and Donald Whitehead, and by B. H. Slicher van Bath and his staff at a seminar in the Department of Rural History, University of Wageningen, Netherlands, have been most helpful.

2. In order to extend our knowledge of agricultural output, an analysis of eighteenth-century farm accounts has since been made at Nuffield College, Oxford, under the direction of R. M. Hartwell and the writer.

3. The account of crop innovations which follows is drawn from references listed below; a good contemporary summary is to be found in O. Lawson Dick (ed.), *Aubrey's Brief Lives* (Harmondsworth: Peregrine Books, 1962), especially pp. 28–9.

4. R. C. Gaut, *A History of Worcestershire Agriculture and Rural Evolution* (Worcester: The Worcester Press, 1939), p. 97; F. Harrison, *North Wraxhall, Co. Wilts* (London: Macmillan, 1913), p. 155.

5. K. J. Allison, 'The Sheep-Corn Husbandry of Norfolk in the Sixteenth and Seventeenth Centuries', *Agricultural History Review*, v, no. 1 (1957), 27; Daniel Defoe, *A Tour Through England and Wales* (London: Dent & Sons, 1928), p. 58.

6. Rashleigh Farm Accounts, uncatalogued, Cornwall Record Office; J. Rowe, *Cornwall in the Age of the Industrial Revolution* (Liverpool: University Press, 1953), p. 221; on another western county, see E. L. Jones, 'Agricultural Conditions and Changes in Herefordshire, 1660–1815', *Transactions of the Woolhope Club*, XXXVII (1961). [See Chapter 2 above.]

7. Charles Wilson, *Holland and Britain* (London: Collins, n.d.), p. 108.

8. Rowland Vaughan, *Most Approved and Long Experienced Water Works* (London, 1610), no pagination; letter to Humphrey Weld from his tenants of Winfrith manor, 1598, Dorset Record Office, Weld Collection D10/E(103). A floated water-meadow is one in which river water is conveyed for a series of short periods over adjacent, gently sloping meadow land by means of a complicated system of hatches and ditches. This is in contrast with the older and simpler system of catchwork meadows, watered by washing stream water over hillside grassland. The effects are irrigation, raising the temperature and thus facilitating grass growth, and fertilizing.

9. 'Agricultural Progress in Open-Field Oxfordshire', *Agricultural History Review*, IX, no. 2 (1961), 73–83.

10. There is much scattered evidence on the size of the sheep and cattle populations and the output of their products, the most convenient summary being Phyllis Deane and W. A. Cole, *British Economic Growth* (Cambridge: University Press, 1962), pp. 68–74.

11. Southampton Civic Record Office, Petty Custom and Wharfage Books from 1723.

12. See especially G. E. Mingay, *English Landed Society in the Eighteenth Century* (London: Routledge, 1963), pp. 54–5.

13. B. H. Slicher van Bath, 'The Rise of Intensive Husbandry in the Low Countries', *Britain and the Netherlands*, I (London: Chatto & Windus, 1960), pp. 130–53.

14. E. L. Jones, 'Eighteenth-Century Changes in Hampshire Chalkland Farming', *Agricultural History Review*, VIII, no. 1 (1960) [see Chapter 1 above]; M. C. Naish, 'The Agricultural Landscape of the Hampshire Chalklands, 1700–1840' (unpublished M.A. thesis, London University, 1960), *passim*.

15. Habakkuk, *Economic History Review*, X, p. 5.

16. Havinden (cited in n. 9), *passim*.

17. Compare the categorical dismissal of the ability of open-field farmers to utilize the new crops and the statements (culled from the biased 'improving' literature) about the slowness of innovation, in Lord Ernle, *English Farming Past and Present*, (6th edn.; London: Heinemann, 1961), pp. 122, 134.

18. Many studies by historical geographers have attempted to measure agricultural differences between light-soiled uplands and heavy-soiled vales, and sometimes between finer units. Such work includes S. E. J. Best, *East Yorkshire: A Study in Agricultural Geography* (London: Longmans, 1930); D. R. Mills, 'Enclosure in Kesteven', *Agricultural History Review*, VII, no. 2 (1959), pp. 82–97; J. A. Sheppard, 'East Yorkshire's Agricultural Labour Force in the Mid-Nineteenth Century', *ibid.*, IX, no. 1 (1961), pp. 43–54; D. B. Grigg, 'Changing Regional Values during the Agricultural Revolution in South Lincolnshire', *Transactions of the Institute of British Geographers* (1962), pp. 91–103. But these writers have hardly generalized their findings or pursued the economic implications, while historians are usually content to work with administrative units which often blur agricultural distinctions.

19. See, for example, G. H. Kenyon, 'Kirdford Inventories, 1611 to 1776, with Particular Reference to the Weald Clay Farming', *Sussex Archaeological Collections*, XCIII (1955), pp. 78–156; and C. W. Chalklin, 'The Rural Economy of a Kentish Wealden Parish, 1650–1750', *Agricultural History Review*, X, no. 1 (1962), pp. 29–45. The problems of the rates of assimilation of the new crops by different farming systems are discussed in E. L. Jones, *Transactions of Woolhope Club*, XXXVII [see Chapter 2 above], and in his 'English Farming before and during the Nineteenth Century', *Economic History Review*, 2nd ser., XV, no. 1 (1962), pp. 145–7.

20. Simon Moreau, *A Tour to Cheltenham Spa* (Bath, 1783), p. 62.

21. J. H. Smith, *The Gordon's Mill Farming Club, 1758–1764* (Edinburgh: Oliver and Boyd, 1962), p. 149.

22. J. D. Chambers, 'The Vale of Trent', *Economic History Review*, Supplement 3 (1957), p. 13, n. 8; W. G. Hoskins, *The Midland Peasant* (London: Macmillan, 1957), p. 227; Joan Thirsk, 'Industries in the Countryside', in F. J. Fisher (ed.), *Essays in the Economic and Social History of Tudor and Stuart England* (London: Cambridge University Press, 1961), pp. 70, 88.

G

23. Defoe, II, p. 89; W. G. Hoskins, *The Making of the English Landscape* (London: Hodder & Stoughton, 1955), p. 124.

24. The third main division in terms of area, the lowland heath, may however be ignored here as consisting of sandy soils also termed 'light', but too infertile for cultivation except for a little temporary enclosure during periods of exceptionally high prices, such as the Napoleonic wars. See E. L. Jones and C. R. Tubbs, 'Vegetation of Sites of Previous Cultivation in the New Forest', *Nature*, CXCVIII, no. 4,884 (June 1963), pp. 977–8.

25. John (cited in n. 1), p. 147.

26. Jones, *Agricultural History Review*, VIII [see Chapter 1 above], quoting Nottingham University Archives, Manvers Collection, Rentals.

27. *Ibid.*, citing Stoke Charity Papers, Hampshire Record Office: 18M54/Box E, pkt. A.

28. See Naish, *passim.*

29. English experience contrasts sharply with that of Europe, where the fall in population and depression in agriculture were very severe. This is of particular consequence with respect to the Low Countries, which had formerly been ahead of England in agricultural techniques but which failed to respond so energetically (or perversely) to the fall in prices. In the reclaimed areas of Holland, the drainage network remained a fixed charge on agriculture when farm-product prices were falling. The status of landowning was lower than in England (seignorial rights could be acquired without buying land) and did not attract investment in the same way. And when returns from agriculture fell after 1650, the one hundred or so Amsterdam merchants who owned land in the Beemster, north Holland—the reclamation of which they had financed—quit their estates and retreated to the city. On the European experience, see B. H. Slicher van Bath, *The Agrarian History of Western Europe, A.D. 500–1850* (London: Arnold, 1963), pp. 206–20. I am also indebted to that author for a typescript of his lecture, 'Die Europaischen Agrarverhältnisse im 17. und der ersten Hälfte des 18. Jahrhunderts', and to Drs. A. M. van der Woude for showing me the Beemster.

4. Agriculture and Economic Growth in England, 1650–1815: Economic Change

By any measure of resources used or value of output, agriculture was still much the largest sector of the economy at the end of the period which this essay surveys. Figures for 1811 and 1812 indicate that one-third of the total occupied population of Britain was engaged in farming, forestry, and fishing; that the value of land plus farm capital comprised almost two-thirds of the national capital stock; and that over one-third of the total national income was produced by agriculture.[1] Since the middle of the seventeenth century the country had made remarkable headway as measured by real income per head of the population, had seen forceful developments in several manufacturing industries and considerable expansion and sophistication in many other branches of technology and economic life. No matter if the changes to come in the nineteenth and twentieth centuries were to dwarf those of the preceding period: England had already achieved a higher level of economic development than the more backward countries in the world today. Our problem is to isolate the contribution which her agricultural sector made to this advance.

The web of rural activities was so vast and formed the setting for so many of the other productive enterprises of the time that it naturally clamours for attention from students of the entire process of economic growth. Accordingly, while studies of changes within agriculture continue to appear, any discussion of the development of the national economy is virtually certain to touch on agriculture's role. For a time this wider sphere was greatly taken up by analysis of the possible short-run influences of the size of harvest. Then, following the publication in 1962 of Deane and Cole's *British Economic*

Growth 1688–1959, with its aftermath of erudite review articles, attention switched to the longer-run involvement of agriculture and the remainder of the economy. This is strictly in accord with the current preoccupation with the less-developed countries of the modern world, where almost by definition agriculture bulks large. Britain, it is often said, is the worst exemplar for the population-swamped, backward lands. Professor Kuznets has calculated that already in the seventeenth century as little as 60 per cent of its labour force was in farming, whereas even in the other advanced countries of western Europe (with the probable exception of Holland) the agricultural proportion did not fall to this level before the first quarter of the nineteenth century.[2] Special circumstances operated in Britain's favour, as also in the other early developed countries of western Europe and North America, with Japan and European Russia. All these were quite industrialized before the First World War and they have held their lead ever since. The identification of the advantages in any one of them may thus be of value to those other countries which still seem bereft of a good hand of cards. No one should expect the historical record, with all its gaps and uncertainties, to offer a precise programme for economic development, yet it may surely indicate priorities.

In the case of eighteenth-century England, however, such a range of suggestions about the relation of agriculture to economic advance is current that confusion reigns. At one extreme it has been claimed that agriculture's greatest contribution was to contract smoothly, shedding factors of production to industry *en route*, and at the other that agricultural development was an indispensable prerequisite of industrial progress.[3] Surprisingly few writers have set out to list the ways in which agriculture may have contributed to economic growth and gone on to provide any really informed historical appraisal of each transaction.[4] Much of the literature therefore contains *ad hoc* suggestions running well ahead of real empirical knowledge and scattered among broad surveys of eighteenth-century economic history. The whole debate is further confused by diverse opinion about the respective chronologies of industrial and agricultural advance. The recent tendency has been to push the origins of industrial change well back into the eighteenth century while simultaneously bringing its main weight forward to the railway era in the nineteenth century.[5] Modern research has also spread developments within agriculture over a longer time-span, although it is still not generally conceded that techniques began to improve strikingly in the seventeenth century, far earlier than was once thought.[6]

It is therefore difficult to bring the developments in agriculture into relation with those elsewhere in the economy. Farming in particular is so diverse regionally and in the mix of its products (each evolving continuously but unevenly) that its advance almost defies summing up. In a short space there is nothing for it but to resort to somewhat heroic simplification. I shall of necessity take a rather simple-minded view of the contributions of agriculture to the growing English economy, dealing one by one with a number of exchanges which in the real world were inextricably entangled and sometimes pulled in opposite directions. The whole field of study is experiencing the familiar paradox of the early stages of any academic inquiry, that is a 'query explosion'. The modern literature has multiplied the number of problems of which we are aware without keeping pace either in solving them or accumulating relevant data. What is needed now is a more intensive drive to assemble evidence: there are plenty of minds ready to build or demolish economic models based on any historial material which is to hand, but so far there is barely enough in this sphere for their activities to be rewarding. The words of the nineteenth-century polymath, Charles Babbage, seem to apply: 'Political economists have been reproached with too small a use of facts, and too large an employment of theory ... the errors which arise from the absence of facts are far more numerous *and durable* than those which result from unsound reasoning respecting true data.'[7]

On these counts, I shall try to describe what we now know of the springs, form, and timing of productivity changes in agriculture, and then to treat sequentially the main flows of resources between agriculture and industry in the eighteenth century. There is a grave danger of making probabilities and possibilities much too categorical when coping with them in a brief space, and it is certainly possible to give only illustrative examples of tendencies and trends, but given the space constraint little more can be done than to note the danger. Professor Habakkuk pointed out in 1958 that the problem is twofold—to explain 'why the output of English agriculture was so much more "responsive" in the eighteenth century than in the sixteenth' and to decide in what manner a rise in agricultural investment and incomes stimulated industrial investment.[8]

THE SPRINGS OF AGRICULTURAL PRODUCTIVITY

Do you or I or anyone know
How oats and beans and barley grow?

First the farmer sows his seed,
Then he stands and takes his ease,
Stamps his feet and claps his hands,
And turns around to view the land.
Waiting for a partner,
Waiting for a partner.
Open the ring and take one in.

This traditional children's singing game might almost be an allegory of the primitive state of farming until the middle of the seventeenth century. It is thoroughly fatalistic. Despite the beginnings of a literature exhorting farmers to improve their techniques, there might as well have been no body of scientific knowledge about husbandry matters. Farmers are presumed to have exerted little or no control (through their cultivations or fertilizer inputs) over the growth or yield of their crops—' 'Tis not the husbandman, but the good weather, that makes the corn grow', wrote Thomas Fuller, whose *Worthies of England* was first published in 1662. As the song suggests, farmers were at the mercy of the elements. Agriculture might in effect have been waiting, as it had waited throughout history, for some agency to burst the age-old ring of inflexible organization, rudimentary methods, and insufficient capital.

A partner was indeed about to unite with the farmer, when in the late seventeenth century England was the special beneficiary of a 'commercial revolution'. Much wealth was generated by the rapid expansion of the export and re-export trades and much of it was invested in land by the successful merchant class, so great has the social magnetism of a country estate always been to Englishmen. As Josiah Child remarked as early as 1668, 'if a merchant in England arrives at any considerable estate, he commonly withdraws his estate from trade before he comes near the confines of old age'.[9] The rich merchant bought a country seat. Agriculture could not but be the gainer from this transfusion of trading capital, allied as it was to new farming practices spreading among a more progress-minded rural community. Several strands thus wove into one in raising the productivity of agriculture. They may for convenience be divided into advances in husbandry technique and improvements in agrarian organization.

Advances in Husbandry Technique

The old view of an 'agricultural revolution' firmly placed in the second half of the eighteenth century still persists despite mounting evidence that it was merely a phase, although an agitated one, of changes which stretched well before and far beyond that time. Its organizing conception was of the Norfolk four-course shift (wheat/ turnips/barley/clover) spreading on land enclosed by Acts of parliament, and accompanied by brand-new advances in stock-breeding. Between the 1760s and 1815 Arthur Young was propagandizing for the Norfolk rotation; the parliamentary enclosure movement was at its height (supposedly sweeping away the static, forage-scarce farming of the open fields); and the renowned breeders like Robert Bakewell were selling their over-fat animals to hobby-farming aristocrats amidst a blaze of publicity. But the choice of these indicators makes the notion of 'agricultural revolution' in that period a self-fulfilling prophecy.

A more up-to-date interpretation would expand the base of the relevant changes and extend their time-span appreciably. The middle of the seventeenth century seems the most appropriate starting-point for the infinitely expansible improvement of farming practice. Observers like Charles Davenant, John Aubrey, and John Houghton were certain it was then that new husbandry systems flowered. Houghton pointed out 'the great improvements made of lands since our inhuman civil wars, when our gentry, who before hardly knew what it was to think, then fell to such an industry and caused such an improvement, as England never knew before'.[10] Documentary sources bear this out. The crucial innovations pertained to the supply of fodder, partly the diffusion of the turnip as a field crop but much more important at that early date the first widespread cultivation of clover, sainfoin, and ryegrass, with the vigorous 'floating' of water-meadows (i.e. the irrigation of stream-side pasture).[11] These crops and practices, with later additions like the swede (a much hardier root), went on spreading into new counties, new estates, new farms, and new fields throughout the period which this essay covers. What is especially important to note is that well before the middle of the eighteenth century they had already colonized sizeable chunks of the country: this is of the utmost significance to understanding the chronology of agricultural change and its consequences.

What may have inspired this long movement was a probable swing in the ratio of cereal to livestock prices from approximately 1650 to 1750 in favour of expanding livestock production. Fodder crops which had lain almost dormant in England during Tudor and early Stuart times, when grain prices were high relative to those for stock, were therefore extended. They were rotated with cereals in new systems of mixed farming. They fed fattening stock, the dung from which raised the yields of the cereal courses. By the second half of the eighteenth century, when there was renewed pressure on cereal production, there was no danger of a recession of forage crops. Mixed farming had come to stay, since either its fatstock or its cereal enterprises offered reasonable returns under most market conditions. Often both paid well.

The mechanism by which new crops and methods were diffused was evidently less through the early didactic literature reviewed by Lord Ernle in his various historical works than by a combination of landlord endeavour and the entrepreneurship of the larger farmers.[12] Landowners themselves were not enormously active in promoting the new techniques in detail, except perhaps in 'underdeveloped' districts like the Yorkshire Wolds,[13] but they and their agents were by no means inert.[14] Their direct participation was probably most important in the seventeenth century, when many of them returned from an exile which had afforded ample leisure for inspecting the advanced practices of Flanders.

In considering the spread of cropping innovations it is simplest to envisage English agriculture as made up of three parts. Firstly, there is the rearing country of the Highland Zone, which may be left aside as it seems hardly to have been penetrated by the 'new' crops. Then alternating across the Lowland Zone are the light soils of the chalk, limestones, light loams and more fertile sands, and the heavy soils of the clay vales.[15] Left for centuries under sheep pasture, the light soils were now found to hold the advantages for mixed farming. They were free-draining, their working season was long, their traction costs were low. Unaided, they had been too infertile to sustain permanent cropping, but with the introduction of fodder crops—notably legumes which fix their own nitrogen—rotations of these and cereal courses could be maintained. The Norfolk four-course was only one rather limited variant of these light-land rotations. Novel farming systems appeared early in many light-soiled localities besides the famous 'good sands' of west Norfolk. Everywhere these systems disturbed the existing dependence of the light lands on access to the better 'natural' (that is, unsown) pasture of the low vale country. For example, the steward of an estate at Croft wrote of the Lincolnshire Wolds about 1725 that 'of late, since the practice of improveing Lands with Turnops is set up, they take y^t [that] way of so improveing their own lands, & feeding ye sheep themselves . . . a great detriment of letting ye Marsh Lands so well as heretofore'.[16]

The ill-drained vales and heavy soils, for long one of the country's main 'granaries', could not take up the 'new' crops so readily. Such soils were especially unsuited for growing roots. Further, although there was no exact correspondence, many of the heavier soils in central England were farmed on the old common-field plan and within their communal system were sociological rigidities and a lack of capital to buy lean stock to fatten which impeded the adoption of fodder crops. Available case studies show only a sluggish uptake of the 'new' crops in heavy-land localities. The rigidities were not as severe a constraint as was once believed, but they were present.[17] Had they not been, common fields might have survived to this day as more than rare museum pieces like Laxton and Yarnton.[18]

The large, privately occupied farms freshly taken into cultivation on the light-soiled uplands suffered no comparable disabilities. Their forage and grain courses were pinned together by the device of the sheepfold, which had made much of the southern chalkland fertile by Defoe's day. ''Tis more remarkable still', he observed, 'how a great part of these downs comes by a new method of husbandry, to be not only made arable, which they never were in former days, but to bear excellent wheat, and great crops too ... for by only folding the sheep upon the plow'd lands, those lands, which otherwise are barren, and where the plow goes within three or four inches of the solid rock of chalk, are made fruitful.'[19] The sheep were fed during daylight on the 'artificial' forage crops and folded at night to dung and tread the land sown to cereals. Higher crop yields were one result, though as has been mentioned the system was perhaps first brought into being by a desire to increase the output of livestock products. On the light lands the rise in total output beyond the previous return of scanty mutton and a wool clip was clear. On the heavy lands the small farmers were financially distressed because of the new competition from the light soils or because they could not adapt to market changes, but although they do not seem to have been able to amend their ways, neither—in a pre-industrial society—did they have much option but to keep on farming. The net effect was surely an expansion of output in agriculture as a whole. To take a single illustration, the situation in Gloucestershire was summed up by Thomas Rudge in 1803 as follows: 'The HILL district includes the Cotswolds ... Within the last hundred years a total change has taken place on these hills. Furze and some dry and scanty blades of grass were all their produce, but now with few exceptions the downs are converted into arable inclosed fields ... The VALE includes the whole tract of land, bounded by the Severn on the west and the Cotswolds on the east . . . The produce . . . has continued nearly the same for many centuries.'[20]

In addition to the better nutrition which new forage crops ensured,[21] livestock were being more systematically bred. This was not restricted to the heyday of the market in pedigree fatstock in the late eighteenth century but was under way long before, although the earlier exchanges between breeders have left few traces.[22] Few as they are, signs of an early and quite widespread concern with the systematic breeding of both cattle and sheep are to be found. Peter Mathias has suggested to me that this interest may have been an outgrowth of the attention which Restoration gentlemen lavished on breeding swifter fox hounds and Arab horses. This is very plausible.

About 1670 John Franklin was already upgrading the cattle and sheep of his enclosed farm at Cosgrove in Northamptonshire with an eye to the London market and the dealer who came down by coach every autumn to purchase his fatstock.[23] Franklin catches our gaze through the exceptional chance of having a descendant who has written about his farming. There must have been innumerable unsung agriculturists who about the same time were mating picked sires and dams. Their choice of pairs was guided still by intuition rather than performance records, but at least they were making cattle and sheep more docile and easier to fatten, by selection 'for frank mental deficiency'.[24]

Some other early selective breeders come more fully into view. Sir Thomas Gresley of Drakelow, Derbyshire, was recorded as owning a dairy of Longhorn cows all chosen for similarity in colour and conformity by 1720. He was followed by Webster of Canley, Warwickshire, who began with Drakelow stock. And to show that the eminent breeders of the late eighteenth century were not blazing an untrodden trail, Robert Bakewell himself then started with some Canley heifers, lineal descendants of one of which were still in his herd at his death.[25] Even more indicative of a sturdy trade in carefully bred animals, though it barely breaks the surface of the historical record, is an observation of the 1730s that 'of late years there have been improvements made in the breed of sheep by changing of rams and sowing of turnips and grass seeds, and now there is some large fine combing wool to be found in most counties in England'.[26]

Improvements in Agrarian Organization

These developments in the methods of farm production were a yeast trying to ferment a rather cold agrarian structure. They come first because they represent the most sharply changing element within agriculture and the one which contributed most obviously to rising production during our period. The matrix of tenurial arrangements, farm-size distribution and field layout within which they acted did alter consistently in favour of large-scale production for the market, but comparatively slowly. The organizational evolution formed a centuries-old continuum in England; so did technical advances, but as decisive an upturn as can ever be detected in the rate of agricultural change occurred in their case in the mid-seventeenth century. Novel systems of husbandry thus account much more for the new 'responsiveness' of agricultural supply than do improvements in agrarian organization. Only during the French wars at the end of the eighteenth century was structural change greatly accelerated. Further, while in the long run organizational improvements did make agriculture flexible—particularly compared with the Continent—they did not inevitably lead to increasing productivity. Often their impact was on the shares of the proceeds of agriculture which different social classes received. Better farming practices on the other hand led straightaway to rising productivity.

The most dramatic aspect of change in the agrarian framework was parliamentary enclosure, the chronology of which may be indicated as follows:

TABLE 1

Numbers of Enclosure Bills, 1730–1819		Acres of common pasture and waste enclosed by Acts of parliament	
1730–1759	212	1727–1760	74,518
1760–1789	1,291	1761–1792	478,259
1790–1819	2,169	1793–1815	1,013,634

Source: Deane and Cole, *op. cit.*, pp. 94 n. 3, 161 n. 1, 272 n. 1, drawing on State Papers, 1836, vii; Slater; and Gonner.

This conveys the impression that the reallocation of common fields and the reclamation of 'waste' (lightly grazed land) welled up late in the period. It throws the weight of change very heavily on the later years. This is partly an artefact of excluding enclosure by agreement and all reclamation on privately held land. Since these procedures were simpler and cheaper than those of parliament they were usually carried out early and legislation was resorted to only in more stubborn instances. The non-parliamentary evidence has never been codified—to attempt it for more than local areas would be a prodigious task, rendered incomplete in any case by gaps in the manuscript sources[27]—but if it could be included a different chronology would emerge. Parliamentary enclosure would appear as the culmination of a process of land reallotment, reclamation, and fencing into separate parcels stretching far back in time. Similarly, since parliamentary enclosure was strongly concentrated in central England, the inclusion of adequate data from the eastern and western flanks where piecemeal enclosure and reclamation had long preceded it would reinforce the account of a steadier rate of structural change. The apparently rapid upswing represented by the parliamentary enclosures of the second half of the eighteenth century[28] would not be steam-rollered out of existence by the inclusion of other evidence, but it would be somewhat flattened.

Tenurial and managerial organization also gradually improved. The latest summary of work on the distinctively English landlord–tenant symbiosis refers to the pattern of land distribution as 'of great continuity and stability coupled with a definite but gradual growth of great estates'.[29] The great estates did expand between the end of the seventeenth century and 1790, but the mid-eighteenth century marks no upturn, while 'relative growth, it must be emphasized, was always very gradual'. The estates of the lesser gentry were also expanding and a class of absentees among the smaller landowners was emerging, but again only steadily. These developments were largely the outcome of social factors—'prestige-maximization' on the part of England's well-to-do, to whom the social values of an estate made up for the lower monetary return than trade or industry.

Farming proper was something done by tenants. Landowners provided the capital-in-land. They threw farm units together in order to create more efficient holdings and they paid for the fixed capital on the farm. The growth of an estate system where the owners often possessed large extra-agricultural resources which they were willing to invest in the land was crucial in raising English agriculture from the rut of capital-starvation in which the continental peasantry remained stuck. Investment by landowners was helped by the appearance of the long-term mortgage about the middle of the seventeenth century, together with a fall in the rate of interest. This had usually been 10 per cent to landowners before 1625 but was seldom above 5 per cent after 1680.[30] At first landowners met barriers of inadequate working capital, ignorance, and lack of initiative among the farm community, so that in the early eighteenth century 'there was in fact a market in good tenants, and the inducements which competing landowners offered were improvements'.[31] Management and enterprise among farmers did, however, become more satisfactory.

Part of the increased managerial efficiency stemmed from the intervention of the landowners' stewards or agents: thus in 1749 a tenant at Tong in Shropshire agreed that 'with respect to my Tillage, I am to be governed by his Grace's Steward, and to lay down each year so much in clover and Grass Seed as I shall be allowed to take up of Ley Ground'.[32] But much of it evidently came from the emergence of a more informed class of farmers, tenants many of them, especially on the new farms carved from the sheep downs of the light lands. One substantial Hampshire chalkland farmer repeatedly interspersed his accounts with the eager phrase 'Land for money and money for Land'.[33] Up on the Cotswolds the occupier of Bowldown Farm near Tetbury, a John Smith who arrived there in 1744, wrote down what he termed his 'system of farm management' (it was a six-course rotation which extended the four-course by keeping the seeds down for a second year and taking oats after wheat) and sent rules for the economical running of a farm business to a Major Ogilvie at Montrose. The occupier of a nearby farm at Didmarton recorded the annual produce from 1774, switched from a five-course rotation to John Smith's six-course about 1781, and left among his papers observations on the merits of threshing by hand or by machine, with calculations of the cost of almost every task on the farm.[34] And down on Romney Marsh it was reported in 1786 that the graziers

> keep a register of all their stock, noting down the number of the whole, and in what fields . . . how many of each have died—what their skins sell for—when any are sold, the price they are sold for and to whom. The number of Bullocks they take in from the Farmers and at what charge per head per week—the price they sell their wool at and the number of Packs—their rent—their assessments and their other expenses, with every other particular relative to their businesses during the course of the whole year; and by casting up the Debtor and Creditor's side they know to a farthing the profit or loss of every year.[35]

On all sides there was evidence of a constant advance in farm business methods.[36]

The units on which farmers operated were changing for the better, at least on the reasonable assumption that larger and better-equipped holdings were a benefit to agriculture. This was the result of the amalgamation of farms and their consolidation from inter-mixed open-field strips and scattered fields. Landowners were seeking more professional advice about these matters. They received recommendations like that offered by Nathaniel Kent when he was brought in to survey Lord Malden's extensive Herefordshire lands in 1786–7. He proposed exchanges so that certain parcels of land might be relet to neighbouring farms where land of that particular type was more needed, and pressed that some small farms might with advantage be 'melted down into the others'.[37] This was indeed already happening on Lord Malden's estate, and in fact widely. 'In general,' it has been concluded, 'eighteenth-century conditions en-couraged a persistent bias towards larger farms occupied by tenants rather than freeholders', while 'there was a long-term ten-dency towards larger and more efficient units even in open-field villages, and enclosure merely tended to hasten this process'.[38]

Nevertheless, the small farmer was neither swept away by enclo-sure nor entirely bought out of existence by the bigger landowners. The growth of population from the mid-eighteenth century actually increased the demand for small farms, which (since quite high rents were offered) it often paid to satisfy. Very large and very small tenanted holdings may have been increasing at the expense of the intermediate range. At the upper end of the scale the amalgamation of farms into larger units operated by a smaller number of more capable tenants was not, however, always accompanied by the thorough consolidation of their newly enclosed fields. The process of building larger farm units and bringing them within ring fences was being accomplished by the buying-out of small freeholders, by private exchanges and by enclosure. Since larger enclosed farms were more progressive technically the drift was advantageous. Yet it was slow. It has not always reached its goals today.

The pattern of the countryside and the agrarian organization which evolved in England made production more flexible and far more responsive to the market than a peasant system could have been. However, structural improvement was a sedate procession winding its way down the years, while better husbandry practices made the real running. Technical advance made a more conclusive contribution to rising agricultural productivity.

CONTRIBUTIONS TO ECONOMIC DEVELOPMENT

The Supply of Food and Raw Materials

The self-evident functions of an agriculture are, firstly, to supply food and certain desirable beverages. Secondly, it should afford industrial raw materials, notably for clothing and footwear but also in our period for other goods like soap for washing and tallow for candles so that the well-scrubbed results may be seen and admired. To these might be added, thirdly, the provision of fodder for the large number of horses which was vital to keep traffic moving by pulling wagons on the roads and barges along the waterways.

Napoleon's dictum that an army marches on its stomach applies *a fortiori* to a nation. Had agriculture failed in its primary task (given no overseas sources of supply), so that the population was regularly thinned by famine or alternatively growing equally fast as the supply of food, we need proceed no farther. The interest of agriculture would be restricted, as with any stagnant system, to understanding its built-in constraints. Society would have been so occupied in struggling to maintain output from the land that at best there would have been a minute surplus of income for spending on industrial goods: economic growth would have been checked by the inflexibility of agricultural supply. This was the fate of France through much of our period, just as it is the misery of mankind in many less-developed countries today. English agriculture was more vigorous. It shook off the dead hand of the 'crises of subsistence' which periodically afflicted wide areas of France.

English agriculture started well. Until the 1760s the country exported more and more grain. This was reversed during the third quarter of the eighteenth century. Plenty was again attained at the end of the seventies and in the eighties (when temporarily the tide of parliamentary enclosures and transport improvements ebbed), but shortages returned in the French wars with which one century ended and the next began. There were cases of starvation among the very poor in 1795–6 and 1800–1,[39] and presumably other deaths from hypothermia due to insufficient food and fuel. Even the rich suffered the shocking embarrassment of requiring a certificate to show that they were burdened with more than a brace of unmarried daughters before the girls could titivate themselves with hair-powder made from flour which their less fortunate neighbours might have been glad to eat.

Taking the long view to which twentieth-century comfort conduces we can, however, see that these shortages did not last, but served to spur the heavy agricultural investment of the Napoleonic wars. After a bumper harvest in 1813, our period ended with ample food supplies. In any case, neither the export of cereals before 1750 nor much less the import subsequently was equivalent to more than a small fraction of home consumption. It is reasonable to conclude that agriculture more than adequately supplied the country's wants until the mid-eighteenth century (without fatally depressing farmgate prices) and failed to do so afterwards only by the slenderest margin.

The expansion of output was helped by definite economies in the use of the materials produced. Striking illustrations of this increased efficiency are displayed by Professor Mathias.[40] He shows how the waste grains from important agricultural processing plants—distilleries, breweries, and starch yards—were all absorbed in fattening large numbers of hogs for the metropolitan market. Later, many lean cattle were fattened too. This novel and sophisticated 'industrial agriculture' was based on several thrifty linkages. For instance, the waste grains became available in the cooler months, when the processes of brewing and distilling were carried out, precisely when feed for livestock was otherwise scarcest. Ordinary farmers might, of course, winter-feed barley to animals, but if the harvest were poor and barley dear they would buy fewer beasts to fatten and the price of store stock would fall. The distillers would then be well-placed since they had to buy barley come what may and were, of course, left with waste grains to dispose of—while animals to fatten were cheap. They could thus offset the costs of their main business by comparatively high returns from the sideline of stock fattening. The only weakness of the system was that manure from the city-fed animals was flushed away instead of being returned, as it would have been on the farm, to the soil. The dung was too bulky to collect from the London distilleries.

Otherwise, the eighteenth century saw a more economical interlocking of the harvest and the leavings of the drink trade with the production of fat hogs and cattle for the butcher, the tallow chandler, the soap boiler, and the leather currier. Like mixed farming, 'industrial agriculture' neatly reused most of its byproducts. At this most advanced end, the business of agriculture had become enormously complicated, with subtle changes in productive methods taking over from one another as the costs of different feedstuffs altered from season to season.[41]

English agriculture, then, was approximately successful, even when most strained by the inflation, population pressure, and glowering blockades of the Napoleonic wars. Valuable results flowed from this, beyond the fundamental go-ahead which it gave to the growth of population. Sufficient food supplies and raw materials helped to minimize the upward movement of industrial wages and input costs. Consumers found elbow room for the purchase of industrial goods. In addition, there was a small but useful contribution to the balance of payments. As Professor John has repeatedly urged, grain exports ensured command over foreign currency in the first half of the eighteenth century when European markets for British manufactures were dull. France paid 10·5 million *livres* for British cereals in 1748–50. A similar exchange was noted in 1739: 'there being at present a great scarcity of corn in many of the provinces of *France*, the duke of *Orleans* caused 2,000,000 of livres (near 100,000 *l.* sterling) to be expended in the purchase of corn from this country, to be distributed at a moderate price among the poor in those provinces where he had any interest'.[42] Even when the export of grain was converted into a net import at the end of the century, resulting in an outflow of bullion, there were occasional panics in the money market but the effects do not seem to have been serious.[43]

All in all, the 'responsiveness' of English agriculture was a victory, an excellent underpinning for an economy which was growing in all directions—in population, average income per head, and capital stock. The advantages are perhaps seen most clearly when contrasted with the sour experience of that other early commercial and industrial nation, the Dutch, which in the freer years before the mid-eighteenth century had set its economy squarely on imported cereals. When the cost of these mounted and sources of supply were sometimes cut off by wars in the second half of the century, the Dutch burnt their fingers badly, suffering high costs for labour which damaged the competitiveness of their industry.[44] England escaped only a little singed and for all the frictions of growth retained an agriculture of great potential.

The Release of Factors of Production

1. LABOUR. For long the chief contribution of agricultural change to the development of industry was depicted as the 'institutional' creation of an urban proletariat. Enclosure was the supposed means. It was treated as if consciously contrived to dislodge countrymen

H

from the land and herd them into the new factories. In this form of a concerted, disappropriating recruitment drive the view was never very coherent and it was thoroughly exploded by Professor Chambers.[45] The conspiracy theory of parliamentary enclosure may linger in the doctrinaire wings of economic history but it is no longer a serious proposition that the enclosure commissioners were a kind of capitalist press-gang.

Professor Chambers more plausibly points out that the newer systems of husbandry (especially the labour-intensive root breaks), the reclamation of barren land, and the physical processes of enclosure and improvement (hedging, in-fencing, building, farms, and laying out accommodation roads) all demanded more labour, not less. Where forests, fens, and moors were enclosed and reclaimed totally new settlements were sometimes established. Apart from threshing machines, labour-saving machinery on the farm was unimportant before the middle of the nineteenth century. Far from the land giving forth its sons, between the first census in 1801 and that of 1851 the absolute numbers engaged in agriculture, forestry, and fishing never ceased to climb. They were 1·7 million in 1801 and 2·1 million in 1851.[46] This of course does not mean that productivity per man was not rising alongside productivity per acre.

Neither does it mean that enclosure did not influence the character of the rural workforce. Professor Chambers emphasizes the protection which the small owners of rights on the land usually received,[47] but he observes that the frequent appropriation of almost all the common grazing by the *legal* owners tore down the curtain, 'thin and squalid' though it may have been, which shielded men with only customary rights from utter proletarianization. And as Dr. Martin shows,[48] whatever the correctness with which the small owner was treated, the cost of enclosure lay disproportionately heavily on him. Many small owners sold out. They did not do so simply to grasping landowners but often to other relatively small operators, including numerous professional gentlemen who crowded to get farms at the height of the war boom.[49] Of those who sold, many doubtless quickly ran through the cash they had realized and sank into the ranks of common labourers. For example, at Broughton, Hampshire, the expenditure on poor rates was slashed by half for the one year 1791, following the enclosure award of 1790, but thereafter soared away up far into the years after the Napoleonic wars.[50] In the affected parishes, parliamentary enclosure brought fast changes in agrarian structure at the turn of the eighteenth and nineteenth centuries.

Whatever the fate of the small owner, the labourer who merely rented property to which common rights once attached, and the small tenant farmer whose holding might be amalgamated with others to form bigger units, were often converted into workers to be hired and fired at will. More impersonal labour relations in farming were here to stay. While common-field husbandry had seldom been as inflexible as Lord Ernle insisted, the new, brisk, businesslike agriculture was clearly more efficient in production.

Enclosure hurried the process whereby rural labour became wage-dependent, though Prof. Mingay has made the telling point that the very old enclosed areas of Kent and Sussex suffered exceptionally grim rustic poverty.[51] There is a conflict of emphasis between Professors Chambers and Mingay on one side and some other writers on the creation of a proletariat by enclosure.[52] Chambers and Mingay stress the alternative force of a blindly swelling rural population. Others wish still to stress the role of enclosure in destroying village culture and the quasi-independence afforded by common grazing,[53] but it is not clear how long they think that this 'thin and squalid' curtain could have stood between the burgeoning population and dire want. Social issues are, however, aside from our purpose. It is apparent that enclosure was not the creator of a labour force for industry.

Enclosure itself tended to mop up labour from the countryside. Rural labour resisted being sucked into the industrial sector. Much of it remained immobilized and poor in southern and eastern England long after our period. Switching freely from skilled land work to skilled work in industry was hardly possible. A nineteenth-century Wiltshire incumbent who saw both sides of the fence commented that, 'in-door and out-door habits, the loom and the plough, the shuttle and the sickle, the soft hand and the hard hand, cannot be interchanged at pleasure'. He noted that the Spitalfields silk weaver did not dare do her own housework since if she chapped her palms they would catch and spoil the threads, and that this applied, though less, even to woollens.[54] Dairying could be combined with industry but hard field work could not.

Industrialists could not therefore draw quickly on reserves of rural labour. The English were long accustomed to a working holiday at harvest time, combining high earnings with a social occasion and permitting the women and children to glean the fallen ears for their winter flour. Joseph Veale reported from Exeter in August 1717 that 'our markett have advanced ocationed chifly by

busy harvest times. when few goods are made', and William Will-
mott wrote from Sherborne in the 1770s of his workpeople that
'they rather chose to do very little of the short silk and get into
the Fields a leasing as it is harvest time'. The Yorkshire woollen
industry was interrupted by the dispersal of men, women, and
children to haymaking and harvesting in the Vale of York, the
East Riding, Lincolnshire, and Nottinghamshire. Equally, throughout the eighteenth century iron furnaces and forges were brought
to a seasonal halt by the preference of their operatives to go harvesting.[55] These habits were frustrating to manufacturers striving to
stockpile goods for sale immediately after harvest when the whole
agricultural population was most flush with money.

In the Midlands and north during the late eighteenth century
the demand for hands in the cotton industry became acute and
the old system of part-time work on a putting-out basis could
not stretch to meet it. The supply of such labour among the wives
and daughters of small farmers and rural labourers was drained
and this, it seems, provided a stimulus for mechanization in the
industry during the 1770s.[56] It would be tendentious to praise
agriculture because its inability to release enough labour prompted
inventiveness, but it must be concluded that it was not usually an
immediate source of labour for industry. Arthur Young's farming
correspondents in Cheshire, Lancashire, and the West Riding in
1792 would not have agreed, but they were witnessing localized
competition for workers between agriculture and industry.[57] In
general, agriculture itself secured bigger absolute numbers of
hands, and its ancient seasonal rhythms long continued to disturb
the work flow in industry. Industry, in fact, had creamed off part of
the surplus growth of the rural population for its own workforce.
We must look to the deeper currents of demographic change
for the source of the labour which fed all-round economic expansion.

2. CAPITAL AND ENTREPRENEURSHIP. The industrialization
of a predominantly rural society will understandably draw
where possible on agrarian resources of capital, entrepreneurial
talent, and technical skill. If these do not originate in agriculture proper, they may well come from its penumbra of servicing
and processing trades. Conceivably industry might be wholly
financed and staffed from the mercantile enclave which even
weakly developed economies usually possess, but this was
the English experience only in so far as capital originally gener-

ated by foreign trade was often filtered into agriculture through the buying of country estates, and out again through the early industrial activities of landowners.

Landowners did play a noteworthy role in fostering industry.[58] Where their estates overlay deposits of coal or iron and carried standing crops of timber for pit-props or charcoal-burning they were well placed to do so. They were also active in the fields of transport and urban housing: the aristocratic nameplates of west London squares are a tribute to enterprise, not gentility. Landowners were able to command finance for such developments and could call readily on professional or technical advice. Often their enterprises were no more than an extension of the exploitation of the natural resources of their land, but their willingness to engage in them at all gave the English an edge over the more aloof European aristocracies. Nevertheless, as the eighteenth century progressed and industry became firmer on its feet, English landowners withdrew more and more from active participation in non-agricultural ventures, leasing off their mines and ironworks.[59] Admittedly, there were always individual landowners who opposed industrialization. In Nottinghamshire and Derbyshire some of the magnates tried to exclude textile mills from access to water power, though all they succeeded in doing was to drive mill-owners to set up steam engines as a substitute. But landed society by and large was tender to the manufacturer, presumably because the sources of wealth in the English economy had so long been very varied. The ironmasters, the Foleys and the Knights, and the cotton spinners, the Arkwrights, were freely admitted to county society in that most rural of shires, Hereford, while the Peels were greeted respectfully in Staffordshire, even though they set up cotton mills on their land.

Like the landowners, practising farmers also made early moves into industry. This was even more true of their sons, who shifted into the towns to become apprentices. On average during the eighteenth century about 50 per cent of the immigrant apprentices to the cutlery trades of Hallamshire were the sons of men engaged in farming, but the proportion was falling over time; in 1720, 60 per cent of youths apprenticed in Leicester hosiery trades came from villages outside, though by 1780 the proportion had fallen to 45 per cent.[60] Those of their families who attained the status of minor gentry or clerics thus had an open line through which they could place their investments with relatives in manufacturing. Benjamin Franklin's English forebears were in this category. His family had lived for at least 300 years on a freehold at Ecton in Northamptonshire, but of his father's generation in the late seventeenth century all except the eldest brother, who inherited the land, moved away to become dyers in the textile trades.[61] The Crowley family rose from small farmers to the heights of the iron industry in three generations. Small farmers in northern England and the north Midlands had, of course, long engaged in part-time manufacturing, but the emphasis shifted until their agricultural connections wore thin. More advanced processes of manufacture and more insistent demands for industrial goods became too absorbing for half a man's attention to remain occupied with crops and animals.[62] In remote parts of the Peak district, away from the purview of urban putting-out merchants, a handful of workshops on isolated farms evolved into full-blown cotton factories, but agriculture otherwise figured rarely among the original occupations of the principals of cotton firms established in the Midlands after 1769. There was already a big enough base in older textile industries to supply most of the founding personnel for cotton. The same was the case in the iron industry which drew most of its eighteenth-century entrepreneurs not from the yeomen, as Toynbee and Mantoux thought, but from a wide spectrum of secondary metal workers. Agriculture was a source of industrial entrepreneurs but it tended to be at a generation or so's remove.

From the case studies of the careers of industrialists, it is not immediately apparent whether agriculture gave more than it took away. The English pattern was for a small farmer, dealer, or craftsman to become a rich manufacturer and for him or his son to become a country gentleman. A nice example is Joseph Wilkes (1735–1805), Peel's partner, who came of a farm family, prospered by promoting transport improvements, became a cotton manufacturer and then a landowner in Staffordshire. Capital equipment in industry was naturally created in the course of such a progression, and something possibly added to technology, but a man's descendants commonly bled his factories to subsidize their life as country gentlemen and the improvement of their estates.[63]

There are innumerable instances of this outflow of capital from industrial undertakings into the financially less profitable business of landowning. The pattern is much complicated by regional questions—by the possibility that industrialists more readily quit the older industries of southern England and thus speeded their contraction. It was, for example, customary for west country clothiers to buy estates and become 'Gentlemen Clothiers'.[64] In Gloucestershire the practice was said to have caused the failure of clothiers whose assets thus became too illiquid to tide over trade depressions. A Stroud banker stated that many had borrowed half the capital to buy estates at 5 per cent interest when the land yielded at most 3 per cent. Others were alleged to have become so enamoured of landed pleasures that they dissipated their fortunes in gambling, entertaining, and other forms of social display. In Berkshire the preference for buying land instead of reinvesting in the woollen industry has been put forward as the reason for the industry's decline, though this presupposes that returns from the trade were inadequate or that abnormal local rigidities prevented replacement investment by fresh personnel. The latter might just have been true of Gloucestershire if outgoing clothiers hung on too long to the strictly limited number of watermill sites. Although as in Nottinghamshire steam engines could have been substituted, and were slowly, it is a possibility that a prolonged and unfortunately timed withdrawal from industry into land may have persuaded 'free' capital that it was better meanwhile to set up new firms on the northern coalfields. Even this is not altogether likely, for Gloucestershire had access to Somerset coal. It is rather more probable that the movement of capital from the declining southern and eastern sections of the cloth trade into agriculture was not simply the universal prestige buying of landed estates but a recognition that local industrial investments were no longer very rewarding. There is some support for this in the case of Thomas Griggs (1701–60) in Essex, who transferred his surplus funds from textile manufacturing into speculations in real estate, fattening livestock, and malting barley. Agriculture and agricultural processing had become the more productive outlet for funds in the south and east.

An assessment of agriculture's contribution of entrepreneurial and managerial skills, and capital, to industry must thus take special account of locality and date. Landowners and farmers promoted valuable industrial undertakings in the earlier part of the period. They were instrumental in getting many manufactures started, though later the industrial sector was able to produce the men it needed to continue expanding. While fortunes made in industry did leak into landownership, from the common-sense point of view it appears that since manufacturing did expand, the counter-attractions of rural life may have retarded but could not block industrialization. Indeed, the drying-up of the land market in the late eighteenth century may have been important in holding much industrial and mercantile money in the capital market. As Professor

G. E. Mingay has concluded, 'the limited amount of land available for purchase meant that such newcomers [to estates] were less numerous than at any time in the two previous centuries'.[65]

There was no overall shortage of capital in the economy. A pool of funds existed in rural and market town society. Many small towns and villages were devastated by fire, with very high computed losses, but money was usually forthcoming to rebuild them promptly—for example, after the 110 fires which destroyed ten or more houses each (over 100 houses in five cases) in Berkshire, Dorset, Hampshire, and Wiltshire alone between 1650–1815.[66] Sir F. M. Eden, who was not accustomed to withhold information on poverty, maintained that some working-men, by dint of extreme parsimony, had hoarded considerable sums. He thought they should be persuaded to put these out at interest. In Gloucestershire he knew a village shoemaker with £300 and a barber with £800.[67] In addition, there are instances like that of the labourer at Eynsham, Oxfordshire, who in 1773 lent £160 to a shoemaker in the village.[68] In the Midlands and north, as Professor John has shown, these local pools of capital were already being drawn on by industrialists in the early eighteenth century. What was needed was a means of mobilizing rural savings in the south and east for the use of manufacturers elsewhere.

Much has indeed been made of a chain of banking arrangements which siphoned the surplus profits of farmers in the arable areas of southern and eastern England to the expanding industries of the more northerly areas. With the stimulus which the 'new' forage crops had given to mixed farming on the light lands in the south and east—but not to the poorer environment of the north and west —there had occurred a separation between the zones of highest agricultural profits and highest demand for industrial investments. Country banks in the arable districts received deposits when the crops were threshed and sold in the months after harvest, remitted the cash to London clearing banks, which in turn lent to the manufacturers. Banks like Barnard's in Bedford sent an increasing flow of country money along this channel, to finance the cotton spinners of Lancashire and the metal workers of Birmingham.[69]

The proportionate significance of this flow until the very end of the period is, however, doubtful. The credit needs of arable farmers in the southern parts of England were high between the spring sowing and harvest, higher and longer-lasting than in the livestock districts of the north,[70] and at that time surely required a reverse flow of lending. This must have been inconvenient for manufacturers who also spent the summer trying to accumulate stocks of goods for post-harvest sale. Before harvest, supplies of working credit in the country as a whole must have been stretched to their limit. And since country banks were few before the late eighteenth century and only began to lend to farmers on any scale rather late in the Napoleonic wars, it may be wondered whether farmers had hitherto been willing to dispatch substantial sums even after harvest through the banking system to industry. May they not have preferred to hold their receipts against summer needs which the country banks did not yet meet? They may have had a high liquidity preference, simply hoarding cash as it came in, as for example in 1774 when one agriculturist near Canterbury noted his 'current silver in the iron chest' as '50 crown pieces, 80 half crown pieces, 520 shillings, 180 sixpences'.[71] I have examined a number of account books which seem to indicate that farmers became serious lenders, and then locally, only on the strength of their windfalls during the profit inflation of the French Revolutionary and Napoleonic wars.[72]

The direction in which agriculturists channelled their non-farming outlays may have been of more consequence than the volume. Landowners and farmers invested heavily in the infrastructure of the economy, that is in its communications network. With other rural residents like attorneys, merchants and parsons many of them were prominent shareholders and promoters of regional transport improvements. Only in the canal mania of the 1790s were non-local investors much drawn to these schemes. Admittedly, Professor Mingay has emphasized the suspicion with which landowners sometimes regarded improved communications. Although better routes would cheapen industrial inputs to agriculture (much of the interest was in securing coal to burn in making lime for the claylands and bricks for farm buildings), certain landowners opposed the schemes for fear that an easier flow of grain would glut the markets, depressing prices and rents. The sideline of carting in which their tenants engaged during slack seasons might also be damaged.[73] Yet such opposition was greatly outweighed by the involvement of the rural community as a whole in promoting better communications.[74]

Agriculturists were concerned for their own reasons. The majority did want to obtain cheaper industrial inputs and to dispatch their farm products more easily. For instance, the landed promoters of the canal from Andover, Hampshire, to Redbridge at the head of Southampton Water offered their hefty subscriptions in 1788 not to turn Andover into a second Birmingham but specifically to send out grain and bring in building materials, grass seeds, and woollen rags for manure.[75] Aims were closely similar and pressures even greater in the more isolated county of Hereford. There, in the late seventeenth century, schemes to improve the navigation of the River Wye were put forward. By the late eighteenth century local attention had shifted to canals on the grounds that further work along the Wye would merely speed up connections with Bristol, whereas canals could link the county to the faster-growing food markets and sources of manufactured goods in the Midlands and north.[76]

These schemes did not always bring the anticipated profits. One half of agriculture was perhaps uninterested—the livestock producers still moved their animals about on the hoof, using the green lanes to avoid turnpike tolls and finding the canals both too slow and too little focused on the London market. Only the railways could work a great change in their mode of transport. But grain growers became better served. The opening, for example, of a turnpike to Wantage market and its hinterland of barley fields on the Berkshire Downs greatly increased the production of malt at Wallingford for shipment down the Thames to London. The average annual make of five years ending 1754 was 49,172 bushels, of five years ending 1774, 113,135 bushels.[77]

Even if efforts at improving transportation were directed at strengthening the rural economy, they had an obvious effect in permitting the wider diffusion of industrial goods. The narrow island of Britain was well placed for linking coastwise and inland water traffic, which was so much cheaper than overland carriage. A striking example of the results was to be seen at Reading during the Napoleonic wars. Once the Kennet and Avon canal connected with the Thames, with the Oxford canal a few miles up-river tapping the Midlands, Reading was able to import cheap coal, cheap hardware, and iron from Birmingham, pottery from Staffordshire, stone from Bath, and groceries from London or—when they came from the West Indies or Ireland—across from the west coast.[78]

Two major interactions of agricultural capital and the remainder of the economy remain to be considered. Firstly, it has been argued that high spending on enclosure and follow-up improvements caused a transfer of funds into agriculture during 1760–1815. 'It may very well be', writes Professor Landes, 'that in the early decades of heavy enclosure, that is, the very years that also saw the birth of modern industry, British husbandry was taking as much capital as it was giving; while in the period from 1790–1814, when food prices rose to record levels, the net flow of resources was probably towards the land.'[79] His cited cost of £5–£25 per acre for enclosure plus subsequent improvements seems high for England compared with, say, the figures provided by Dr. Martin for Warwickshire. It is a fair point that much enclosure did not pay at once, that there was no necessary improvement of agriculture immediately, and that the full force of the increased capacity was only felt at the end of the Napoleonic wars. Yet it is undesirable to isolate enclosure as if it were the sole occasion for moving capital between agriculture and industry. If agriculture was so long neutral and for the last twenty-five years of our period an actual drain on resources it is surprising that industry managed to grow. In fact, although the contribution of farming to the British national income increased in the war years, faster than that of industry, the agricultural share in the national capital did not increase.[80]

Against the enclosure-based view that farming was a drain on the country's capital during the wars can be set the contrary argument that it was agriculture which carried much of the burden of the state at war, through the yield of the land tax plus the relative ease with which Pitt's income tax could be collected from the agricultural community. From 1803–4 to 1814–15, whereas incomes assessed for tax in the trade and industry sector rose by less than 10 per cent, those of the land sector rose by almost 60 per cent. Miss Deane concludes that 'had the commerce and industry sectors paid their "fair share" of the mounting cost of the French wars it is likely that the industrial revolution . . . would have suffered a severe setback'.[81]

Aggregating the fragments of evidence on the exchanges of capital and entrepreneurship between agriculture and industry is hazardous. It does seem that agriculturists contributed handsomely to the earlier industrial enterprises. Later their entrepreneurial involvement with industry lessened, but they were contributing much by helping to construct the communications system. For all the serious rigidities of the capital market in the countryside, all the feedback of investment by industrialists keen to acquire the social colouring of landed society, and all the expense of enclosure, the balance of probabilities is that agriculture did make a net contribution to the formation of industrial capital and did release entrepreneurs who played a significant role in industrialization. Agriculture paved the earliest paths to growth.

INCOME EFFECTS OF AGRICULTURAL CHANGE AND
THE DEVELOPMENT OF A MARKET FOR INDUSTRIAL GOODS

Thus far we have been in territory where economic historians have erected a few signposts. The signs do not mark every route or always agree about directions, but at least someone has been there before. With the subject of demand for industrial goods we enter virtual *terra incognita*. This is a land full of uncharted levels of income for different regions and social and occupational classes. Many scholars have preferred to stress the role of export markets for British industrial production in the eighteenth century, for on this more figures survive—dangerous to play with, no doubt, but definite series bearing some relation to the output of major branches of industry.

More recently writers have begun to study the home market, which was clearly so very much larger than the export market.[82] In the present state of knowledge we can discuss this only generally; budgetary studies are urgently needed for further progress. However, the agricultural sector was certainly of great significance for incomes right through the period, accounting for one-third of the occupied population at its close quite apart from affecting the level of demand among all consumers of foodstuffs.

Firstly, there is an effect of agriculture on the development of the economy which has been largely overlooked.[83] The low cereal prices from the Restoration to about 1750 (low compared with long periods before and after) were damaging to the incomes of small farmers in northern districts and in the common-field parishes on the Midland clays, where advantage was not readily taken of the innovations of the time. These farmers were squeezed by the flow of grain from the newly cultivated light lands or could not expand production to offset poor prices. Regional differences in agricultural prosperity intensified as the south and east became increasingly superior at producing grain and fatstock. Agriculturally inferior districts in northern and western England and the Midlands (despite improvements to Midland river navigation) were edged into stock-rearing and fattening, dairying, and taking up domestic industries. A strong growth of domestic manufacturing in several industries can definitely be assigned to the late seventeenth and early eighteenth centuries. It was important as a supplement to inadequate farm incomes, or in cases like Midland hosiery a remedy for the loss of agricultural work among those dispossessed by the enclosure of parishes which were laid down to pasture. Northern graziers and men on the Midland clays attempted in the late seventeenth century to have the new fodder crops, which were shifting the agricultural advantage southwards, suppressed by legislation. These stultifying efforts failed and regional differentiation continued. Domestic industries like cloth-making, hosiery, lace and leather work and nail-making thickened in the areas less favoured for farming long before the fortuitous presence of coal beneath many of them brought heavier manufactures based on the steam engine or coke-smelted iron.

In this early and gradual fission southern England became increasingly agricultural and its old industries withered.[84] Northern and some Midland districts became more industrial precisely because the readier uptake of the 'new' crops on light land in the south had made them relatively poorer agriculturally. 'North' and 'South' thus evolved as complementary markets which it became worth linking by better communications. When food prices rose later in the eighteenth century part-time farmers in the 'North' might have been expected to revert to full-time agriculture, but by then the growth of industrial demand (including for export) was sufficient to sustain the manufacturing sector. And these areas were now able to realize a superior industrial technology based on advances in the use of coal.

Professor John's work[85] brings us more directly into contact with the agriculturally-induced demand for industrial goods. His case is that the cheap grain of the first half of the eighteenth century, especially 1730–50, raised the incomes of consumers of bread. This was particularly beneficial to the poorer groups in society, among whom an appreciable margin for spending on industrial wares may have been released for the first time. The high proportion of wage-earners in England, compared with Europe, would benefit both from cheap food and more work during the run of good harvests. This was exactly what Malthus thought about these years. Professor John cites evidence for a greater consumption of the products of the woollen, metal goods, and pottery industries at this time, although some of the income freed by cheaper bread was doubtless spent on other food (meat), imported produce (tea and sugar), and on grain in a potent guise (gin).

It may be thought that gains for food consumers would be cancelled by falling farm incomes and rents, but apart from some short spells this was apparently not so. There was no general depression. Losses in the heavy-land districts were probably offset by the gains of innovators on the light lands, a situation neatly summed up by John Aubrey in the 1680s:

> Great increase of sainfoine now, in most places fitt for itt; improvements of meadowes by watering; ploughing up of the King's forests and parkes &c. But as to all of these, as ten thousand pounds is gained in the hill barren countrey, so the vale does lose as much, which brings it to an equation.[86]

Total agricultural purchases from the industrial sector therefore held up. They may not have risen, but since purchases by the buyers of cheaper food did there was a net expansion of demand before 1750.[87]

Professor John's thesis has been criticized by Professor M. W. Flinn on the grounds that the statistical evidence on wheat prices is too narrow and can be rearranged to suggest that there was not a great fall.[88] In that case the price data might not be able to bear the weight of the argument for an income-induced expansion of home demand for industrial goods which Professor John has built on them. Admittedly, the decennial figures of retained imports of industrial raw materials and production in the few industries for which series have survived show little rise before 1750, with another spurt after 1770 or more especially 1780,[89] and Professor John has had to piece together other items which suggest a more favourable view of production and consumption in the first half of the century.

Professor Flinn may be moving towards an alternative explanation of similar phenomena. He refers to two recent articles (by Tucker and Youngson) which indicate that the population may have grown more steadily throughout the eighteenth century than is usually thought.[90] If this is so, the demand for industrial goods might have risen simply because there were more people to buy them and the fall in grain exports from the 1750s might be explicable in terms of greater numbers of consumers—though the rise in population would surely have had to be sharp to account for all the observed fall. Such an interpretation would need two further props. Firstly, the economy would have had to possess some different thrust to maintain the purchasing power of a growing population. This might have come partly from the 'commercial revolution' of the late seventeenth century and partly from early industrial and transport improvements which, instead of being the *result* of income released by greater agricultural productivity, contributed to it and raised the real incomes of some farmers even during the first half of the eighteenth century.[91] But this leaves the earlier industrial and transport developments inadequately explained. Secondly, it would still need to be shown why mixed farming should have developed through the vigorous extension of forage crops right from the mid-seventeenth century.[92] This is easiest to explain by accepting the customary view of slight population growth, with needs for bread more readily satisfied and the price of grain thus low relative to the prices of livestock products. A mild incentive to expand the animal enterprises would be favourable to the spread of the 'new' fodder crops. More and better-fed livestock would then have given more dung and thus boosted the rise in grain production.

More recently still, Professor D. E. C. Eversley has written an important paper which extends Professor John's thesis.[93] Professor Eversley considers that demand did not fall between 1750 and 1780 but went on deepening very largely because of the expansion of a middle-class market which was immune to erosion from such rise as occurred in food prices. Starting from Gregory King's social accounts he demonstrates the early existence of a sizeable middle class of consumers, and he attributes much of the increased demand for industrial goods between 1750 and 1780 to its further growth.[94]

A systematic connection between food prices or agricultural incomes and the movements of industrial output is unclear. What may conceivably have happened is that transport improvements from the fifties were sufficient to narrow the gap between farm-gate prices and the price to the urban consumer, so that returns to agriculturists were reasonable while consumers were less pinched than they would have been by any previously comparable rise in the price of grain. The effect on the market for industrial wares of changes in the incomes of agricultural producers *vis-à-vis* changes in the incomes of food consumers are almost impossible to separate on present evidence. Since farmers were such important employers, the two were closely linked. At the end of the eighteenth century wages were high during boom years but poor rates were high during slumps.[95] Up to a point the social security of the poor law constantly shifted income between employers (including farmers) and labourers, so that total demand approximated more closely than it might have done to the curve of population growth.

Professor Eversley urges that expanding middle-class demand between 1750 and 1780 was backed by continued working-class demand on the grounds that the size of the labouring population did not much increase before the final quarter of the century, and meanwhile growing employment for industrial workers in many cities bolstered real wages. Labourers could therefore continue to buy 'decencies' (goods half-way between necessities and luxuries) in all but occasional years of high food prices. The rise in food prices was not drastic, he claims, until after 1780 and the bad weather which is often supposed to account for difficulties in agriculture from the 1750s has been exaggerated. Working-class income on this view was only reduced at brief intervals. This does not wholly agree with the Phelps Brown index of real wages and the Gilboy wage material, which show slight losses for labourers in the south of England in the 1750s and 1760s, while the gains in real wages in the north during the early part of the century were reduced (though not eliminated) during the middle decades.[96] Perhaps the economic development of the third quarter of the eighteenth century, which after all was not impressive compared with the final quarter, should be attributed more simply to a rise in middle-class income. An important component of this would have been the income of agricultural producers.

Compared with the second quarter of the century, the third quarter was not a time of favourable weather. According to one of the most reliable contemporaries, the years from 1764 to 1774 were wet ones and there never was known 'a greater scarcity of all sorts of grain, considering the great improvements of modern husbandry. Such a run of wet seasons a century or two ago would, I am persuaded, have occasioned a famine.'[97] The 'corn vales' were drowned. But the centre of gravity of grain production was shifting to the drier, light-soiled uplands, and Professor Eversley is clearly right to point out that food supplies were successfully maintained in most seasons. By the late 1770s and again in the mid-1780s agriculture was more than adequately filling the markets, farm incomes fell and landlords found it difficult to collect their rents.[98]

Although, as John Aubrey put it, the losses among heavy-land farmers in the 1650–1750 period may have been so offset by gains for the innovators on the light lands as to come to 'an equation', this need not mean that the rise in the incomes of agriculturists in the third quarter of the eighteenth century was unimportant. Some tentative suggestions may be made about the impact of regional swings in agricultural improvement on the incomes of producers. During the third quarter of the century the previous energetic reclamation of downs and floating of water-meadows on the southern chalklands seems to have slackened. This is not too far out of line with Arthur Young's version of the periodicity of development on the 'good sands' of Norfolk: 'for 30 years from 1730–1760, the great improvements of the north western part of the county took place ... For the next 30 years to about 1790 they nearly stood still; they *reposed upon their laurels*.'[99] Possibly the explanation is that having already created a viable mixed husbandry where once only sheep had grazed, light-land agriculturists found that they could make satisfactory profits without additional expensive reclamation. Prices were moderately high; rotations could be improved without the heavy outlays necessary to bring new land into cultivation. Only the steep price rise at the end of the century was to spur renewed activity in every sector of agriculture. From 1750 it was the turn of the heavy-land sector to try to catch up.

Here, notably in the clay triangle of central England, the heavy, ill-drained soils were overlapped by the zone of densest common-field husbandry. This sector was resistant to change. Professor John has argued that the failure of agriculture to respond swiftly to the demands of the 1750s and 1760s was important because it prompted legislation to admit Irish tallow, meat, and dairy produce, and because it diverted resources to industrial expansion.[100] The pertinent area of resistance would surely have been the heavy lands, especially where common-field farmers were numerous. It was overcome but only at high cost. In parts of the Midlands where the land had belonged to a few proprietors enclosure had come early, the 'new' crops had been sown and farmers specialized in fatstock breeding.[101] More usually the 'peasant' farming of the Midland clays defied any change except the pungent expedient of parliamentary enclosure. Professor Chambers pointed out that of twenty-one Leicestershire villages enclosed by Act after 1790, ten were on clays too stiff for mixed husbandry based on the turnip. In others the communal system had maintained itself by partly adopting the new methods, but most small farmers in the Midlands lacked the capital to carry out thorough reform. Dr Martin has demonstrated that in Warwickshire, too, only the inflationary prices at the turn of the eighteenth and nineteenth centuries made it worth while to enclose and bring the advanced methods to parishes on cold, unproductive clay or where large numbers of small proprietors meant that reallotment costs must be high. In a more recent paper Dr Martin gives further details of the successive waves of enclosure in Warwickshire, costing least before 1750, more between 1750 and 1779, and more than ever after 1780.[102]

I

During the second half of the eighteenth century agriculture thus ran into high cost barriers to the further expansion of output. It had jumped one fence by the eighties, when parliamentary enclosure slackened and the proceeds of farming seem to have been low. The inflation of prices after 1790 then overrode the highest obstacles of soil and sociology. Both waves of enclosure were doubtless profitable, though not necessarily very quickly. It seems therefore that in one region or another gains were being made by agricultural producers throughout the eighteenth century. Before 1750 the gains in one area counterbalanced the losses in another (not counting the gains of food consumers). After 1750 the gains tended more than to balance any losses. The periods 1730–50, 1750–80, and 1790–1815 may approximately mark phases in the development of tastes for industrial consumer goods among the farm community.[103]

The purchase of industry-made producer goods by farmers lagged well behind. Chambers and Mingay comment that 'a remarkable feature of the agricultural revolution was the slow pace at which improved tools and machinery were brought into use'. This is certainly true compared with some other institutional or technical changes in agriculture. Winnowing, chaff-cutting, and threshing machines were introduced mainly during the Napoleonic wars. It was only at the close of the eighteenth century that iron ploughs widely replaced wooden ones. However, little is known in detail about the purchase of producer goods by farmers and an analysis of the ledgers relating to the Hedges family's four forges at Bucklebury, Berkshire, from 1736 to 1763, is accordingly of interest.[104] Ploughshares were pointed by this firm twenty or thirty times for every new one supplied. The plough beams, mouldboards and handles, and the frames of harrows, were all made of wood. While quantities of nails were sold, the preciousness of iron is illustrated by the constant return of nails and small bolts for repair, while it is clear that the forges relied heavily on scrap returned by customers.[105] 'Turnup pickers' were made, but only a single drill plough and a solitary winnowing fan were repaired. Only about 10 per cent of the ledger entries refer to household goods, but by 1750 there are signs that some agriculturists were buying such factory-made items as cast-iron bedsteads, mended but not made locally. Wealthier members of the rural community were already using consumer goods from distant factories, while relying much longer on local forges and blacksmiths for producer goods on the farm.

It is unlikely that higher food prices ever seriously eroded the expansion of the home market for consumer goods by eliminating the margin for such spending among the working population. Agriculture constantly demanded more labour. The 'golden age' of the labourer in the second quarter of the eighteenth century apparently engrained in him tastes for manufactured goods which he was willing to work harder thereafter to gratify. Old haphazard working habits and slackness when food and drink were plentiful may thus have gradually disappeared without much goading from real physical want. The marginal propensity to consume was seemingly high among the rural poor, whose purchases, though individually small, were large in aggregate. Gilbert White remarked in 1775 that 'little farmers use rushes much . . . but the very poor, who are always the worst economists, and therefore must continue very poor, buy an halfpenny candle every evening, which, in their blowing open rooms, does not burn much more than two hours. Thus have they only two hours' light for their money instead of eleven.'[106]

Even the final years of war probably failed to wipe out the demand for industrial goods among the poorest employed group, the farm hands, except in spells of extraordinarily high prices for food like 1795–6 and 1799–1801. During the wars the conjunction of a removal of workers into the armed forces and war trades with the need to produce more food in Britain put pressure on the agricultural labour market. This helped to sustain real incomes just as it induced farmers to introduce threshing machines to save labour.[107] In any case, so far as the total consumption of industrial goods by the labouring population is concerned it must be recalled that whatever happened to their average income, their numbers grew fast in the last quarter of the eighteenth century. This was the period when the output of the mass-production industries really rose. In so far as any conclusion is as yet possible on agriculture's contribution to the demand for industrial goods it is that living costs were held down remarkably well, freeing money to buy manufactures while the total income received by agricultural producers bore up before 1750 and rose afterwards. Agriculture played no small part in the expansion of the home market.

CONCLUSIONS

In terms of the balance sheet which has been presented the agricultural sector made a valuable net contribution to economic growth in the 1650–1815 period. The exact nature of the exchanges was not always that of the textbooks—in particular labour was not ejected into factory industry by the force of the parliamentary enclosure movement—nor was every contribution a positive one. It must be obvious how very much more sheer historical research remains to be done on items in the accounts. But of the overall picture there seems no reasonable doubt.

England was early in the field with a productive, expansible agriculture, which as the eighteenth century went by increasingly spread its influence by means of books, correspondence, and personal inspection to willing pupils in other countries. The tough resistance of mainland Europe's peasant agriculture, a much less flexible system than the landlord–tenant nexus in England, delayed the acceptance of new methods there. In our nearest and greatest rival, France, Arthur Young saw the rigidities of a society where 'you pass at once from beggary to profusion' and where men with money refrained from investing as freely as they would in England.[108] Our earlier commercial and industrial rival, the Netherlands, was not well suited to cereal growing and was in any event much embarrassed in the later eighteenth century by an excessive reliance on dearer and dearer imported grain. Landed society was much more cut off from economic enterprise in Europe than in England so that the diffusion of new techniques was slow. Nevertheless it continued. Even in southern Europe, where climatic considerations limited the effectiveness of the 'new' roots and grasses, and where an already dense population lacked reserves of land comparable with the open-field fallows and 'wastes' of northern Europe, efforts were made to copy England. For example, in backward Corsica General Pasquale di Paoli, who from 1755 to 1769 tried to free the island from Genoese rule and actually brought it briefly under George III's protection, was an agricultural propagandist of some success. Perceiving Corsica's shortage of farinaceous foods he was proud to become known as the 'Generale delle patates', the Potato General.[109]

English influence on American agriculture was greater than is usually thought and would have been greater still had America needed to intensify her farming instead of being able to spread to untold fresh territory in the west. Links between well-to-do and highly similar 'improving' circles spread English methods to Virginia, Pennsylvania, New Jersey, and Massachusetts in the second half of the eighteenth century. Some Americans imported English seeds and above all improved strains of livestock. Coke of Holkham remained pro-American throughout the Revolution; his estate was visited by several Americans. Others were made honorary members of the British Board of Agriculture, while Arthur Young and Sir John Sinclair corresponded with Washington at Mount Vernon and Sinclair with Jefferson at Monticello.[110]

Agriculture had thus contributed in real, if complicated, ways to the emergence of industrialism in England. In turn in the nineteenth century English industry communicated its technology to the more receptive countries in Europe and to the United States. Besides this, English agricultural methods were taught directly to these other advanced lands. The development of progressive farming in England was thus vital to growth over much wider areas than simply its home ground. It was one of the leading forces of economic advance.

NOTES TO CHAPTER 4

1. Phyllis Deane and W. A. Cole, *British Economic Growth 1688–1959* (Cambridge, 1962), pp. 142, 161, 271.
2. Simon Kuznets, 'Underdeveloped Countries and the Pre-industrial Phase in the Advanced Countries: an Attempt at Comparison', in A. N. Agarwala and S. P. Singh (eds.), *The Economics of Underdevelopment* (New York, 1963), p. 143. This measure may mislead unless the extent to which farm workers engaged in rural domestic manufacturing is also stated, but for present purposes it is a sufficient index.
3. The latest fashions are to play down the possibility that agriculture was an 'engine of growth' or to persist in asserting that agricultural and industrial developments were contemporaneous. See e.g., Phyllis Deane and H. J. Habakkuk, 'The Take-off in Britain', in W. W. Rostow (ed.), *The Economics of Take-off into Sustained Growth* (London, 1963), p. 69; Phyllis Deane, *The First Industrial Revolution* (Cambridge, 1965), p. 50; and M. W. Flinn, *The Origins of the Industrial Revolution* (London, 1966), p. 96.
4. Exceptions are M. M. Postan, 'Agricultural Problems of Underdeveloped Countries in the Light of European Agrarian History', *Communications*, Second International Conference of Economic History, Aix-en-Provence (1962); Deane, *op. cit.*; and H. J. Habakkuk, 'Historical Experience of Economic Development' in E. A. G. Robinson (ed.), *Problems in Economic Development* (London, 1965), esp. pp. 123–5.
5. See the succinct survey by Deane and Habakkuk, in Rostow, *op. cit.*
6. J. H. Plumb, 'Sir Robert Walpole and Norfolk Husbandry', *The Economic History Review*, 2nd ser., v (1952), should have long since prompted sharper questioning of the conventional notion of an 'agricultural revolution' limited to the later eighteenth century. Since 1952 there has, of course, been further work pushing widespread innovation back to the mid-seventeenth century, but resistance to this conception remains strong. It is still asserted that early instances of the growing of 'new' crops like clover or turnips were highly localized and that agricultural investment and innovation were crippled by low farm product prices until the mid-eighteenth century.
7. Quoted by Jeremy Bernstein, *The Analytical Engine* (London, 1965), p. 42. Italics supplied. Of facts on some themes we do have a superabundance —it is sobering to realize how little specialists in this field have failed to respond to Professor Fisher's tilt, a generation ago, at their peculiar obsession with the 'recondite niceties' of land tenure. ('The Development of the London Food Market, 1540–1640', *Econ. Hist. Rev.*, v [1935]).
8. H. J. Habakkuk, 'The Economic History of Modern Britain', *Journal of Economic History*, xviii (1958), esp. p. 500. Professor Habakkuk and Miss Deane have since urged that 'earlier bursts of economic growth had been checked by the production barriers in agriculture'. (In Rostow, *op. cit.*, pp. 68–9.)

9. Quoted by H. J. Habakkuk, 'English Landownership, 1680–1740', *Econ. Hist. Rev.*, x (1939–40), p. 11.

10. R. Bradley (ed.), *Husbandry and Trade Improv'd: [by] John Houghton* (1727), p. 56. The authoritative new *Agrarian History of England and Wales*, vol. IV, 1500–1640 (Cambridge, 1967), edited by Joan Thirsk, contains few references to the forage crops though it notes that they became prominent after the mid-seventeenth century. The stock of ideas about new farming systems, and the range of plant species available, grew during Tudor and early Stuart times and seems first to have been drawn on heavily under the Cromwellians, when Samuel Hartlib was granted a pension for publicizing various utilitarian plants, and garrisons as far afield as Kirkwall taught the locals how to grow cabbages. See Mea Allan, *The Tradescants* (London, 1964), p. 184, and Eric Linklater, *Orkney and Shetland* (London, 1965), p. 81.

11. These innovations and their consequences are further discussed in my article, 'Agriculture and Economic Growth in England, 1660–1750: Agricultural Change', reprinted above as Chapter 3.

12. As one example, by the second half of the eighteenth century Thomas Johnson of Wild Court Farm, Hampstead Norris, Berkshire, was selling turnip and clover seed to other farmers from a wide area of Berkshire, Hampshire, and Oxfordshire. Journal, Berkshire Record Office, D/Ex 62/2, 1764–94.

13. See G. E. Mingay, 'The Large Estate in Eighteenth-century England', *Contributions*, First International Conference of Economic History (Stockholm, 1960), p. 378.

14. See for example Edward Wallwyn's instructions to his agent on introducing the swede to his Herefordshire tenantry in 1795. E. L. Jones, 'Agricultural Conditions and Changes in Herefordshire, 1660–1815', *Woolhope Transactions*, xxxvii (1961). [See above, Chapter 2.]

15. The management advantages of light land and disadvantages of heavy land are described in E. John Russell, *The World of the Soil* (London, 1961), pp. 244–55. My discussion also leaves aside the infertile lowland heaths.

16. G. Eland, *Shardeloes Papers of the 17th and 18th centuries* (O.U.P., 1947), p. 61.

17. A new study of a common-field village in Buckinghamshire emphasizes how belatedly the fodder crops often came in. (A. C. Chibnall, *Sherington* [Cambridge, 1965].)

18. Laxton in Nottinghamshire is properly preserved by the Ministry of Agriculture. Yarnton Lot Mead in Oxfordshire ought to be.

19. Daniel Defoe, *A Tour through England and Wales*, Everyman edn., 1928, I, p. 187.

20. *The History of the County of Gloucester* (Gloucester, 1803), I, pp. xviii–xix.

21. By 1674 Anthony Wood reported that meat was now rarely spiced, probably because meat from animals fed on the new forage crops was of better quality (and being in greater supply was not stored so long) than formerly. David Ogg, *England in the Reign of Charles II* (Oxford, 1934), I, pp. 68–9.

22. I was wrong to exclude systematic stock-breeding from the pre-1750 innovations discussed in my essay above [Chapter 3]. Relative price movements probably favoured attention to better breeding, while the growing number of enclosed pastures assisted farmers to determine which animals mated.

23. T. B. Franklin, *British Grasslands* (London, 1953), p. 90.

24. P. B. Medawar, *The Future of Man* (London, 1960), p. 120.
25. C. S. Orwin, 'Agriculture and Rural Life' in *Johnson's England* (Oxford, 1932), p. 277.
26. Arnold Toynbee, *Lectures on the Industrial Revolution of the 18th Century in England* (New York, n.d.), pp. 41–5, quoting a *Pamphlet by a Woollen Manufacturer of Northampton* (1739).
27. The most instructive effort is W. G. Hoskins, 'The Reclamation of the Waste in Devon, 1550–1800', *Econ. Hist. Rev.*, xiii (1943), esp. pp. 90–1.
28. Especially in the final war years. Since the procedures were increasingly costly this means that there was a rise then in this component of agricultural investment.
29. F. M. L. Thompson, 'The Social Distribution of Landed Property in England since the Sixteenth Century', *Econ. Hist Rev.*, 2nd ser., xix (1966), pp. 505–17.
30. H. J. Habakkuk, 'The English Land Market in the Eighteenth Century' in J. S. Bromley and E. H. Kossman (eds.), *Britain and the Netherlands* (London, 1960), p. 160.
31. Habakkuk, 1939–40, *loc. cit.*, p. 14.
32. G. E. Mingay, *English Landed Society in the Eighteenth Century* (London, 1963), p. 173. Cf. note 14 above.
33. Farm Book of James Edwards, 1744–53, Hampshire Record Office, 2M37/338.
34. J. C. Morton, 'A Lifetime on the Cotswolds', offprint from *Gardeners' Chronicle and Agricultural Gazette, c.* 1863, pp. 4–6. Subsequent occupiers at Didmarton were still continuing the annual production records when Morton wrote.
35. [Daniel Jones], 'Sheep Farming in Romney Marsh in the XVIII Century', *Wye College Occasional Publications*, 7 (1956), pp. 14–15.
36. The keeping of farm records was not confined to an exceptional few. See E. L. Jones and E. J. T. Collins, 'The Collection and Analysis of Farm Record Books', *Journal of the Society of Archivists*, iii (1965), pp. 86–9, and E. J. T. Collins, 'Historical Farm Records', *Archives*, vii (1966), pp. 143–9. The collection which Mr. Collins assembled from private hands for the University of Reading in 1965–6 bears this out.
37. See Jones, 1961, *loc cit.* [See Chapter 2 above.]
38. Mingay, *op. cit.*, pp. 89, 183.
39. T. S. Ashton, *An Economic History of England: The 18th Century* (London, 1955), p. 235.
40. 'Agriculture and the Brewing and Distilling Industries in the Eighteenth Century', *Econ. Hist. Rev.*, 2nd ser., v (1952).
41. The complex business history involved does not come out well in most agricultural histories, which tend to emphasize the supply side. They emerge best when the viewpoint is inverted and farming is looked at from the market side. Almost the only substantial attempts at this for our period are the sections on barley and hops in Peter Mathias, *The Brewing Industry in England 1700–1830* (Cambridge, 1959).
42. *The British Chronologist*, ii (London, 1789), p. 228.
43. T. S. Ashton, *Economic Fluctuations in England 1700–1800* (O.U.P., 1959), pp. 47–8.
44. Charles Wilson, 'Taxation and the Decline of Empire', *Bijdragen en Mededelingen van het Historisch Genootschap, Utrecht*, lxxvii (1963), pp. 10–26; E. L. Jones, 'English and European Agricultural Development, 1650–1750' in R. M. Hartwell (ed.), *The Industrial Revolution* (Oxford: Basil Blackwell, 1970), esp. pp. 75–6.

45. J. D. Chambers, 'Enclosure and Labour Supply in the Industrial Revolution', *Econ. Hist. Rev.*, 2nd ser., v (1953).
46. Deane and Cole, *op. cit.*, table 31, p. 143.
47. Until at least 1851 the Crown itself possessed no machinery to throw open an *encroachment* on its land in the New Forest—'an interesting reflection on an age which is usually blamed for "stealing the common from the goose" by means of enclosure Acts'. C. R. Tubbs and E. L. Jones, 'The Distribution of Gorse (*Ulex europaeus* L.) in the New Forest in relation to former Land Use', *Proc. Hants Arch. Soc.*, xxiii (1964), p. 5.
48. J. M. Martin, 'The Cost of Parliamentary Enclosure in Warwickshire', *University of Birmingham Historical Journal*, ix (1964).
49. According to Henry Hunt, *Memoirs* (London, n.d.), ii, p. 39, in 1801–2 'there was scarcely an attorney in the whole country that did not carry on the double trade of quill-driving and clod-hopping'. But much seems to have depended on the exact locality and period. See J. M. Martin, 'The Parliamentary Enclosure Movement and Rural Society in Warwickshire', *Agricultural History Review*, xv (1967), pp. 19–39.
50. Broughton Poor Book 1791–1802, and annual series of sums spent since 1692, seen by courtesy of Rev. N. G. Powell.
51. *Op. cit.*, p. 185.
52. See the long review of J. D. Chambers and G. E. Mingay, *The Agricultural Revolution 1750–1880* (London, 1966), in *The Times Literary Supplement* for 16 February 1967, and W. G. Hoskins, *The Midland Peasant* (London, 1957), pp. 267–72.
53. From acquaintance with commoners in the New Forest and the Forest of Dean I entirely accept that common rights conduce to an independence of mind not found among hired farm hands. But it is a luxury made possible precisely by economic growth stemming from the replacement of communal farming by commercial agriculture over most of the country.
54. J. Wilkinson, 'History of Broughton Gifford', *Wilts. Arch. Mag.*, vi (1860), p. 37.
55. Delmé Radcliffe correspondence, 13A, 1706–85, Hertford C.R.O.; Maureen Weinstock, *Studies in Dorset History* (Dorchester, 1953), p. 91; H. Heaton, *The Yorkshire Woollen and Worsted Industries* (Oxford, 1920), p. 342; T. S. Ashton, *Iron and Steel in the Industrial Revolution* (Manchester, 1963 edn.), p. 197.
56. J. D. Chambers, 'The Rural Domestic Industries during the period of transition to the factory system, with special reference to the Midland Counties of England', *Communications*, Second International Conference of Economic History, Aix-en-Provence (1962), p. 442.
57. Arthur Young, 'Of Manufactures mixed with Agriculture', *Annals*, xxxii (1799), p. 221.
58. See Mingay, *op. cit.*, Chapter viii, 'The Landlords and Industrial Development'.
59. See, e.g., R. L. Downes, 'The Stour Partnership, 1726–36: a note on Landed Capital in the Iron Industry', *Econ. Hist. Rev.*, 2nd ser., iii (1950), pp. 90–6. Occasional landowners whose family fortunes had originated outside agriculture sometimes sold off their other assets to finance farm improvements. For example, Sir Christopher Sykes sold his interests in stock and shipping in order to develop the Yorkshire Wolds at the end of the eighteenth century. Mingay, *op. cit.*, p. 165.
60. D. L. Linton, *Sheffield and its Region* (Sheffield, 1956), p. 173; Hoskins, *op. cit.*, pp. 257–9.
61. Lewis Leary, *The Autobiography of Benjamin Franklin* (New York,

1962), p. 17. Similarly the major London brewer, Samuel Whitbread, was the son of a prosperous Bedford yeoman and set up in business with his £2,000 patrimony. Peter Mathias, 'The Entrepreneur in Brewing, 1700–1830', published in a separate issue of *Explorations in Entrepreneurial History* (1957), p. 35.

62. See Chambers, 'The Rural Domestic Industries', *loc. cit.*, pp. 433, 436–7; S. D. Chapman, 'The Transition to the Factory System in the Midlands Cotton-Spinning Industry', *Econ. Hist. Rev.*, 2nd ser., xviii (1965), pp. 526–43; Ashton, 1963, *op. cit.*, pp. 209–10.

63. See the summary in my 'Industrial Capital and Landed Investment: the Arkwrights in Herefordshire, 1809–43', in E. L. Jones and G. E. Mingay (eds.), *Land, Labour and Population in the Industrial Revolution* (reprinted below [Chapter 7]). In 1809 a single cotton spinner, Richard Arkwright Jr., may have spent on buying one of his estates a sum equivalent to 30 per cent of the total annual investment in the cotton industry. His father, Sir Richard, had, however, once probably pulled out of land for a few years to release capital for mill-building. The first generation of successful industrialists typically held off from land purchases until they were satisfied with the size of their fortunes, and only then plunged into estates in a big way. Cf. also Mathias, *loc. cit.*, p. 37.

64. Lists of clothiers who bought estates are given by G. D. Ramsey, *The Wiltshire Woollen Industry in the Sixteenth and Seventeenth Centuries* (O.U.P., 1943), p. 127; R. Perry, 'The Gloucestershire Woollen Industry 1100–1690', *Trans. Bristol & Glos. Arch. Soc.*, 68 (1945), pp. 112–14; and J. de L. Mann, *Documents illustrating the Wiltshire Textile Trades in the Eighteenth Century*, Wilts. Arch. Soc. Records Branch, xix (1964). See also R. F. Dell, 'The Decline of the Clothing Industry in Berkshire', *Trans. Newbury District Field Club*, x (1954), pp. 60–1; W. Hicks Beach, *A Cotswold Family* (London, 1909), pp. 38–9; E. A. L. Moir, 'The Gentlemen Clothiers' in H. P. R. Finberg (ed.), *Gloucestershire Studies* (Leicester, 1957), pp. 242–4; and K. H. Burley, 'An Essex Clothier of the Eighteenth Century', *Econ. Hist. Rev.*, 2nd ser., xi (1958), p. 291.

65. Mingay, *op. cit.*, p. 47.

66. E. L. Jones, 'The Reduction of Fire Damage in Southern England, 1650–1850', *Post-Medieval Archaeology*, ii (1968), pp. 140–9.

67. *The State of the Poor* (London, 1797), i, p. 496.

68. Bond of Hercules Humphreys, one of a collection of documents seen by courtesy of Mrs. C. Bolton of Eynsham.

69. T. S. Ashton, *The Industrial Revolution 1760–1830* (O.U.P., 1948), p. 106; L. S. Pressnell, 'Joseph Barnard: Westminster's Predecessor in Bedford', *Westminster Bank Review* (February 1960), p. 10.

70. M. Marks, 'The Measurement of Agriculture's Seasonal Credit Requirement', *The Farm Economist*, ix (1960), pp. 449–56.

71. Lee Warley Disbursements Book, 1766–1825, Rothamsted Collection, now in the University of Reading archive of historical farm records.

72. Tax on farm incomes rose from £18·87 million in 1803 to £26·7 million in 1814. P. K. O'Brien, 'British Incomes and Property in the Early Nineteenth Century', *Econ. Hist. Rev.*, 2nd ser., xii (1959), p. 262; Hunt, *op. cit.*, i, pp. 398, 477, 534–5; ii, pp. 38–9, provides a contemporary description of high profits in Wiltshire but stresses how much farmers spent on conspicuous consumption; see also L. S. Pressnell, *Country Banking in the Industrial Revolution* (Oxford, 1956), pp. 346–7.

73. Mingay, *op. cit.*, pp. 196–9, 201.

74. Consideration of this should not be limited to canals and turnpikes,

figures for which exaggerate late eighteenth-century developments. River improvements were well under way in the second half of the seventeenth century.

75. E. L. Jones, 'An Agricultural Canal', *The Hampshire Farmer*, 14 (1959), p. 2.

76. Jones (1961), *loc. cit.* [See Chapter 2 above].

77. Eden, *op. cit.*, II, p. 18.

78. Charles Hadfield, *The Canals of Southern England* (London, 1955), pp. 164–5.

79. David Landes, 'Technological Change and Industrial Development in Western Europe, 1750–1914', in H. J. Habakkuk and M. Postan (eds.), *The Cambridge Economic History of Europe* (Cambridge, 1965), VI, p. 307, and his 'Japan and Europe: Contrasts in Industrialization', in William W. Lockwood (ed.), *The State and Economic Enterprise in Japan* (Princeton, N.J., 1965), pp. 166–7. Professor Landes's figures of the costs of post-enclosure improvement come from A. Pell, 'The Making of the Land in England: a Retrospect', *Journal of the Royal Agricultural Society of England*, 2nd ser., XXIII (1887), pp. 355–74, which is overweighted by the costs of reclaiming Wychwood Forest in the 1850s and by other high costs (especially for drainage) during the third quarter of the nineteenth century.

80. Deane and Cole, *op. cit.*, pp. 160–1, 271.

81. Deane, *op. cit.*, p. 50.

82. Deane and Cole, *op. cit.*, p. 42 and n. 1.

83. I have advanced a similar case for several early developed countries in 'Agricultural Origins of Industry', *Past and Present*, 40 (1968), pp. 58–71 [reprinted as Chapter 5 below].

84. See E. L. Jones, 'The Constraints on Economic Growth in Southern England, 1650–1850' in *Contributions*, Third International Congress of Economic History (Munich, 1965) (forthcoming).

85. A. H. John, 'Agricultural Productivity and Economic Growth in England, 1700–1760', *Journal of Economic History*, XXV (1965).

86. J. Britton (ed.), *John Aubrey: The Natural History of Wiltshire* (Oxford, 1847), p. 111.

87. Professor A. W. Coats seems to accept this two-pronged argument in his inaugural lecture, 'Economic Growth: The Economic and Social Historian's Dilemma', University of Nottingham (1966), pp. 12–13.

88. 'Agricultural Productivity and Economic Growth in England, 1700–1760: A Comment', *Journ. Econ. Hist.*, XXVI (1966), pp. 93–8. See also his *The Origins of the Industrial Revolution* (London, 1966), p. 66. Dr Flinn does not provide any new series and rests part of his case on the irrelevant failure of wheat prices to fall in Scotland, while the strongest construction he can put on the available English price series still leaves them weak compared with, say, the first half of the seventeenth century or the second half of the eighteenth century.

89. Deane and Cole, *op. cit.*, table 15, p. 51; table 18, p. 72. Habits of consuming boughten goods were first engrained in the mass of the populace by the collapsing prices and soaring (retained) imports of tobacco, sugar, calicoes, tea, coffee and porcelain in the late seventeenth century. See Ralph Davis, 'English Foreign Trade, 1660–1700', in E. M. Carus Wilson (ed.), *Essays in Economic History* (London, 1962), II.

90. Flinn, *op. cit.*, pp. 24–5.

91. Something along these lines was suggested by A. J. Youngson, *Possibilities of Economic Progress* (Cambridge, 1959), p. 123, n. I.

92. I am indebted to a 40,000-word digest of manuscript and published

material on improvements in fodder supplies between 1600 and 1800 prepared for me at Nuffield College by Mr. E. J. T. Collins in 1965.

93. D. E. C. Eversley, 'The Home Market and Economic Growth in England, 1750-1780', in E. L. Jones and G. E. Mingay (eds.), *Land, Labour, and Population in the Industrial Revolution* (London: Edward Arnold, 1967), pp. 206-59.

94. Flinn, *op. cit.*,pp. 65, 67, illustrates the difficulties of the literature by revealing the different definitions and emphases attached by authors to labouring, middle, and upper income groups.

95. Arthur Young, *loc. cit.*, pp. 220-1.

96. See the summary in Flinn, *op. cit.*, p. 63.

97. Gilbert White, *The Natural History of Selborne* (Everyman edn., 1949), p. 169.

98. See, e.g., Lincs. R.O. TYR IV/I/87 and IV/I/100, referring to 1778-9; Hertford C.R.O. DE 5003 referring to 1779; Clementina Black, *The Cumberland Letters 1771-1784* (London, 1912), p. 229, referring to 1779; and Oxford C.R.O. DIL I/C referring to 1786.

99. *General View ... Norfolk* (London, 1804), p. 31.

100. A. H. John, 'The Course of Agricultural Change, 1660-1760', in L. S. Pressnell (ed.), *Studies in the Industrial Revolution* (London, 1960), pp. 152–155. But as has been mentioned, the restricted land market of the second half of the eighteenth century may also have dissuaded as much capital from entering agriculture as would otherwise have been the case.

101. See. e.g., Franklin, *op. cit.*, p. 90.

102. Martin, 1967, *loc. cit.*, pp. 27-30. The development of the clays, where liming was essential, may have given a special impetus to transport improvements from 1760 to 1800. Cf. Mingay, *op. cit.*, p. 201.

103. Types of goods bought, indicative of solid comfort for many farmers by the late seventeenth century, may be seen from Mingay, *op. cit.*, pp. 235–239. See also Chambers and Mingay, *op. cit.*, p. 69 and the detailed studies by G. H. Kenyon, 'Kirdford Inventories, 1611 to 1776', and 'Petworth Town and Trades', *Sussex Arch. Colls.*, XCIII–XCIX (1954–61).

104. Felicity A. Palmer, *The Blacksmith's Ledgers of the Hedges Family of Bucklebury, Berkshire, 1736-1773*, Research Paper no. 2, Institute of Agricultural History, University of Reading, 1970. Christopher Hill, *Reformation to Industrial Revolution* (London, 1967), p. 196, asserts that the high cost of iron tools was 'a bottleneck in agriculture', but unfortunately offers no authorities or evidence.

105. According to *The Field Book* (London, 1833), p. 38, gun barrels were still extensively made from the iron of 'old horse-shoe nails, procured from country farriers, and from poor people who gain a subsistence by picking them up on the great roads leading to the metropolis'. The Woodstock steel jewellery industry relied exclusively on spent horse-shoe nails. Metallurgists are not unanimous whether or not these were merely convenient scrap or possessed special properties.

106. White, *op. cit.*, p. 191.

107. E. L. Jones, 'The Agricultural Labour Market in England, 1793-1872', *Econ. Hist. Rev.*, 2nd ser., XVII (1964), pp. 323-5 [reprinted as Chapter 10 below].

108. *Travels in France 1787-9*, quoted by Chambers and Mingay, *op. cit.*, p. 204.

109. Moray McLaren, *Corsica Boswell* (London, 1966), p. 148.

110. See, e.g., R. C. Loehr, 'The Influence of English Agriculture on American Agriculture, 1775-1825', *Agric. Hist.*, XI (1937), pp. 3-15; E. E. Edwards

(ed.), *Washington, Jefferson, Lincoln and Agriculture* (Washington, D.C., 1937), *passim*; C. R. Woodward, *Ploughs and Politicks* (New Brunswick: Rutgers University Press, 1941), *passim*; and C. and J. Bridenbaugh, *Rebels and Gentlemen* (New York, 1942), pp. 184, 191, 220.

5. Agricultural Origins of Industry

Economic historians tend to look on agriculture's role in industrialization as complementary but unenergetic.[1] After noting that all successful nineteenth-century industrializations were accompanied in their early stages by an increase in agricultural output, Professor Habakkuk nevertheless remarks that 'this increase in agricultural output is not to be regarded as a pre-condition of growth, if only because it usually accompanied rather than preceded the acceleration of growth'.[2] Professor Flinn has recently written of Britain that 'it must remain extremely doubtful whether the agricultural developments themselves would be sufficient to have played more than a modest part in stimulating an industrial revolution'.[3] Much the same view is often expressed by development economists, of whom Professor Nicholls observes, 'in theory and policy, economists have largely neglected the *initial* importance of the production side of agriculture'.[4] The present chapter amounts to a tentative suggestion that developments on the production side of agriculture were indeed instrumental in bringing the earliest advanced countries to the brink of industrialization. It seeks an insight into the evolution of the early industrializers only up to the point at which heavy and continuous industrialization began.

The evidence available for this temerarious exercise is thin and very scattered, but an attempt will be made to review the cases of England, some parts of western Europe, and North America. By the late eighteenth century these areas were economically ahead of the rest of the world except for Japan (also discussed below), where surprisingly similar trends were evident. How had these lands succeeded in advancing so far? Some of the reasons lie far back in history, even prehistory,[5] but it will be proposed here that others lie in the agricultural progress of the seventeenth and eighteenth centuries. Better farming techniques were then adopted in the doubly favoured context of countries with cheap waterborne transport and relaxed, or sometimes even falling, population pressure. The significance of river or tidewater access was remarked by Adam Smith.[6] As to demography, the 1650–1750 period in England saw a relatively weak growth of population; much of western Europe saw a net fall; Colonial America hardly suffered from the pressure of numbers on food supplies; while the latest view on the Japanese situation is that after quite strong growth in the first half of the Tokugawa period there was a marked slackening, but not stagnation, between 1720 and 1840.[7] In most of these societies, therefore, *per capita* incomes may have been rising because there were few more—and sometimes fewer—mouths to consume the output of the existing or gradually expanding productive apparatus. The income elasticity of demand for grain was probably low, so that consumers had a margin to spend on other commodities, including livestock products, which compensated farm incomes while contributing to a slow growth of manufacturing. In these circumstances an actual increase in agricultural productivity could have important consequences, which may be considered for each of the countries in turn.

I

Agricultural output increased in England.[8] There is now ample evidence that a number of forage crops (clovers, sainfoin, ryegrass and to a lesser extent turnips) and floated water-meadows (that is irrigated pasture) spread very widely, though far from uniformly, from the middle years of the seventeenth century. The effect was to afford a much greater supply of fodder, enabling more animals to be kept. There is plenty of evidence pointing to an expanding 'national flock'. This represented the lifting of a constraint on productivity in an agriculture dependent on organic fertilizer. More livestock made more manure; this meant heavier yields of grain, or, more to the point, enabled cultivation to be extended on to relatively infertile soils on the chalk, limestone and sandlands which had previously been sheepdown. More manure also secured heavier yields of the forage crops which meant in turn that still more fatting beasts could be kept.

The outcome was an increase in the physical output of both crops and livestock. London provided a large and growing market. Its population rose 70 per cent from 1650 to 1750, from 400,000 to

675,000, or from 7 per cent to 11 per cent of the national population
—a proportion in the capital matched only by Amsterdam in the
United Provinces.[9] Dr Wrigley has calculated that feeding this increase in London, together with an increasing number of non-farm
workers outside, plus securing improvements in diet through greater
livestock production and also exporting (by 1750) 6 per cent of total
grain output, called for a rise of at least 13 per cent in agricultural
output between 1650 and 1750. This was a formidable rise for an
agriculture lacking significant industrial inputs and it released much
income and labour for secondary and tertiary industries. It need not
be assumed that it was the growth of urban demand which drew out
agricultural supply: there was a surplus over any English needs
which was exported. Even so, grain prices still sagged. But the
social mechanisms which permitted London to grow and rural industrial concentrations to emerge did ensure that the surplus could
be traded. In return the farm population received cash to spend on
colonial wares and industrial consumer goods. They did not need to
eat up the food surplus in home population growth.

Within England there developed pressure from excess grain and
fatstock production on farmers in less-favoured situations, such as
the wetter, more elevated parts of the north and west and on the
heavy Midland clays. Faced with competition these men sought in
the 1680s, according to John Worlidge, legislation 'to suppress the
Improvements in the Southern Parts', while William Ellis heard too
how the men of the Vale of Aylesbury, on the Buckinghamshire
clays, had at that time striven 'with great might to suppress the
sowing of the [clover] grass in the Chilterns or hilly Country'—an
improvement made necessary if the Chilterns themselves were to
remain competitive with the freshly-cultivated downland farther
west.[10] These attempts to fossilize the distributions of English agricultural production did not succeed. Grain and fatstock markets
must have become tighter for the higher-cost producers of the less
favoured districts, some of which, in the Midlands, were being
brought more and more into the London market area by improvements in the navigability of rivers in the late seventeenth and early
eighteenth centuries. Farmers in these districts reacted by concentrating on dairying, rearing store beasts (leaving fattening to the
men with the new forage crops in the south and east), and above
all by seeking supplementary income from by-employment in
industry.

Industry had penetrated the countryside in the late Middle Ages.
Rural dwellers had then been glad to offset the slump in cereal

prices by taking up manufacturing for the market in their own homes. Town merchants had been glad to put out work to them because their labour was cheaper than the towns could supply—because countrymen still had *some* agricultural earnings and could offer themselves to industry for a small supplement. Concentrations of rural domestic industry appeared in areas of densely-populated pastoralism which were not well placed for cereal growing. They were strengthened in late Tudor times by the pressure of population, magnified, in such areas, by the existence of systems of partible inheritance which finally sliced the size of holding too small to support a family purely by farming.[11] The division of the country into cereal surplus areas and areas of pastoralism with rural domestic industry was in accordance with the principle of comparative advantage. Of the West Riding, for instance, Mantoux could argue that producing cloth was an essential side occupation for small farmers struggling with poor soils under wet skies.[12] 'Every clothier', according to Defoe, 'must keep a horse, perhaps two . . . a cow or two, or more, for his family, and this employs the two, or three, or four pieces of enclosed land about his house, for they scarce sow corn enough for their cocks and hens', and instead drew their grain from Lincolnshire, Nottinghamshire and the East Riding, and their fatstock from counties all round.[13]

What we have to show, however, is that there was a further shift in comparative advantage as a result of the improvement of agricultural techniques between 1650 and 1750, when population pressure had eased. Evidence is available that southern England was quicker than the north to take up the new fodder crops.[14] The expansion or intensification of rural domestic industry in the north and west and Midlands is less easy to demonstrate, for this is a topic always impoverished of facts and figures. Yet some examples stand out. In east Devon the so-called Honiton lace industry spread into the countryside during the seventeenth century, to all the settlements from Axminster to Torquay. In the south Midland counties of Bedfordshire, Buckinghamshire and Northamptonshire the spread of the lace industry during thirty years at the end of the seventeenth and beginning of the eighteenth centuries was phenomenal. In addition, says Defoe, straw-plaiting, especially for hats, was spreading rapidly from Hertfordshire into Bedfordshire. The lace manufacture was a supplement to low family incomes in agriculture, since an estimate of 1699 was that total labour earnings in the trade were £300,000 per annum, indicating an average weekly return for a workforce of 100,000 of slightly under two shillings per head. This was a bonus

K

seized eagerly in agriculturally-poor Devon hill parishes like Luppit and Upottery and in densely-populated, agriculturally-distressed Midlands villages.[15]

The nailing industry saw a comparable growth in a not dissimilar situation. Professor Court cites as a fair illustration the parish of Rowley Regis, seven miles west of Birmingham, where in the seventeenth century nailers and locksmiths found it convenient to settle and graze their livestock on the extensive common lands.[16] The needle-making village of Long Crendon, Buckinghamshire, underwent a considerable growth of population and needle production from 1700. This was associated with the relaxing of manorial restrictions on the use of common pasture and on taking-in the manorial waste. Numbers of hovels sprang up in corners of the village; the age of marriage fell; work was available in the needle trade, no longer simply on the land.[17] Another case is paper-making. Before 1650 paper milling was negligible, with only thirty-eight mills in England. By 1712 there were approximately two hundred, many of them significantly conversions of corn mills on streams in poor hill country like the Mendips.[18]

A final example is framework-knitting. From the middle of the seventeenth century the hosiery industry began to raise shoots and then to spring up like wildfire in the villages of Nottinghamshire, Derbyshire and Leicestershire. Villages round the edges of Sherwood Forest and on the north Derbyshire border, with ample 'waste' where squatters might locate, and the populous villages south of Leicester became the main centres. London capital only came into the area to unite with cheap rural labour from the final decade of the seventeenth century, a generation after the colonization of the countryside by framework-knitting began.[19] This indicates that the original impetus came from a search for ancillary work by the local population. The switch to pasture in the Midlands was ousting labour from farming in many parishes, driving them into the 'open' parishes where it was possible to work at framework-knitting or, in the south Midlands, where outwork could be done for the lace merchants.[20] The hosiery industry itself hardly brought about the switch to pasture, since wool production in the Midlands was far greater than local industry required; Leicestershire by Defoe's day was a 'vast magazine of wool', which was poured out of the region to the cloth towns of the west of England.[21]

There was no sign of comparable concentrations of rural domestic manufacturing for the market in arable districts such as the Wiltshire downs, the sandlands of Suffolk or the Lincolnshire wolds, however close these were to zones of rural industry, although in many areas some goods were made for family use. Industry in the arable areas tended to be of the kind which processed farm products. It was punctiform and its plant, such as watermills or windmills, required larger doses of capital than the simple equipment of home industry. Although agricultural processing was capital-intensive rather than labour-intensive, the nature of its products offered little scope for transformation into manufacturing industry. The accumulation of capital in the arable areas in the hands of millers, merchants and lawyers, was used either for the expansion of their own businesses, for the purchase of land, or was possibly siphoned off to the agriculturally-poor areas,[22] for it was there that industry was growing.

II

The internal production of a surplus is less easy to show for the agricultures of continental western Europe. Something may perhaps be made of the rise in seed-yield ratios evident in the data collected by Professor Slicher van Bath,[23] but since he states that cereal acreages were retreating between 1650 and 1750 it is difficult to come to a conclusion about aggregate production. A relative surplus was however available on many western European markets as a result of two changes. On the demand side the demographic recession was severe. On the supply side there was a stream of imported grain brought by the Dutch shippers from the Junkers of the sandy Baltic plain and the landed magnates of eastern Europe.[24] These imports fell during the period because there *was* seemingly an increase in the production of some cereals in parts of southern and western Europe, as well as a rise in the import of American rice.

With grain quite plentiful in north-western and west-central continental Europe,[25] similar regional patterns of economic activity to those in England emerged. Relatively infertile areas, uncompetitive in cereals, took up rural domestic industry. In the Netherlands areas like Twente developed a textile industry and the Veluwe developed textile and paper manufacturing.[26] In Belgium, whereas better soils remained mainly agricultural, the sandy *chatelleine du Vieuxbourg* saw agriculture give way throughout the period to linen production, accompanied by a falling standard of living.[27]

The Alps formed another zone where industrial by-employments sprang up in the familiar setting of pastoralism. Textile manufacturing was to be found in most cantons. In the French Alps, Cluses became the pre-eminent centre for clockmaking because its soil and hence its alternative agricultural prospects were decidedly inferior, and because about 1720 a local man returned from learning the trade in Nuremburg to set up a training school for clockmakers. Nail-making began in the Bauges towards the end of the seventeenth century and had developed its main outlines by 1730. Grenobloise gloving was also growing in the early eighteenth century. Young men from the Swiss Alps often became mercenary troops for princes throughout Europe, but in eastern Switzerland numbers took to staying at home, making cuckoo clocks for sale and wooden toys for children. A census of cotton spinners and weavers round Zürich in 1787 did not reveal a circular net round the city but found the industrialized areas to be far out, in the mountains of the pre-Alpine zone. These districts had come late under the putting-out system, but they offered a labour supply so cheap as to offset their poor communications and worse climate. The putting-out industry offered alternatives to emigration for younger sons who would not inherit land holdings. Here industry ceased to be a by-employment and became a full-time occupation for young people who had no chance of entering local agriculture.[28]

By-industries also became important to German peasants on the more thankless soils now that grain was available from the serf-farmed plains east of the Elbe. In Silesia there was a growth of the linen industry in the foothills of the Riesengebirge after the Thirty Years War, the number of rural workers rising while the number of town workers fell.[29] In the Black Forest the construction of wooden clocks began between 1670 and 1730, and the men also made light iron work in the home, with dolls, tubs and musical instruments, while their womenfolk sewed gloves and made coarse lace.[30] If some of these home-made wares sound trivial, it should be recalled that they were responsible for the diffusion of manufacturing skills beyond those which an agricultural peasantry would have possessed; they reflected, or occasioned, the expansion of a mass market for goods sold for cash by pedlars; while time-pieces, as we have lately been reminded, were crucial to the emergence of an industrial society.[31]

The densest German industry arose in the Rhineland, where the Aachen woollen merchants in the seventeenth and eighteenth centuries put out wool to be spun and woven by the peasants of the near-by Eifel mountain villages and later among the dairy farmers of the Limburg, and in Silesia and Bohemia, where the great feudal landowners set up putting-out industries among the serfs and peasants on their estates. In Bohemia Count Kinsky noted in a government survey in the 1720s that populations in mountainous areas were especially suitable for industrialization because their farming opportunities were poorer than on the plains, and it was in the mountains that industry did grow up.[32]

Finally, a regional divergence of the same type appeared in Sweden and Denmark in the late seventeenth and early eighteenth centuries, although crown policy severely restricted the chances of further rural industrialization in the latter country. Agriculturally poor areas in both countries did develop dense part-time rural industries while areas better suited to crop-growing concentrated on producing a surplus of food for sale.[33] Parts of Denmark exported grain to Norway. This was the pattern which was very much intensified and added to in much of northern and western Europe in the 1650–1750 period.

III

In North America there was agricultural abundance soon after the first settlement. Despite near-starvation in their first winters, by 1650 the New England Puritans were provisioning the sugar islands of the British and French West Indies (and the older Virginia colony), and by 1675 the boats and settlements of the Newfoundland fishery.[34] However, apart from a few spots like the Connecticut river valley, the granite land of New England possessed little soil to match for fertility the Hudson and Mohawk valleys in New York state or the valley of the Susquehanna in Pennsylvania. These middle or 'bread' colonies therefore succeeded New England as sources of the crops exported (albeit largely by New England merchants) to the West Indies, Newfoundland and the Iberian peninsula. They made 'flower and Beer a drug in all the Markets'.[35] New England turned to sending livestock products from her coastlands to the Atlantic markets. Massachusetts, with the highest proportion of non-farming artisans, started to import wheat for her own consumption from Virginia and Maryland (as well as Pennsylvania) when these former tobacco colonies switched to cereals after 1740. In the mid-eighteenth century, when the shallow soils of eastern Connecticut were nearing exhaustion, increasing numbers of farmers were obliged to seek alternatives. Some found the answer in craft manufactures. It was thus in Massachusetts, Connecticut and Rhode Island that part-time manufacturing was taken up by farmers. In winter and eveningtime the children, too, made nails at forges set up in the chimney corners of eastern Massachusetts farmsteads. These were the parts of southern New England which became heavily industrialized early in the nineteenth century. The seed had been sown.[36]

This was in sharp contrast with the South, where an export crop economy produced no food which artisans could have bought and which still at the end of the eighteenth century preferred to import even slaves' clothing from England, though New England finally penetrated its market.[37] The Middle Colonies occupied economically as well as geographically an intermediate position. They exported grain and established large flour mills, but regions like the back country of Pennsylvania still lacked adequate market access. Hence farmers here, as well as in New England, were driven into part-time manufacturing.[38]

IV

Finally, there is evidence of a substantial rise in agricultural productivity in seventeenth- and eighteenth-century Japan.[39] Row cultivation was introduced; commercial fertilizers were more heavily applied; the number of plant varieties and their exchange between districts increased, as did deliberate seed selection; while irrigation by treadmills and Dutch pumps was improved and extended. Some new implements were introduced. New crops like sugar cane, sweet potatoes, peanuts, maize and some European vegetables were added. There was a change from large holdings with numbers of subordinate labourers to independent, small-scale farming by nuclear families in early Tokugawa times, and this seems to have been beneficial.

The innovations in Japanese agriculture were regionally skewed. Peripheral districts to the north-east and south-west of the central plains were the ones with fresh land on to which cultivation could still be extended and where the supply of food was most increased. In the older settled regions of central Japan there was no such outlet and grain crops were not produced in sufficient quantity for local consumption—here food was purchased, industrial crops were grown, and household manufacturing sprang up. The success of Japanese agriculture may be gauged from the degree of urbanization, estimated at 22 per cent by 1750. In addition the agricultural sector paid taxes equivalent to 15 per cent of national income, which went to support the samurai class.

In the case of Japan it is more difficult to correlate these shifts with the distribution of rural industry, partly because few of the available English-language studies disaggregate by region[40] and partly because the pattern was not quite the European one. But it is clear that the hinterlands of Edo (later Tokyo), Osaka, Nagoya and to a lesser extent Kyoto were thick with rural industry. Often this was processing, such as oil-pressing and brewing, but there was also much cottage manufacturing staffed by farmers who had not prospered,[41] that is, who had been competed out of agriculture by the superior producing districts. Outwork for urban merchants appeared on a large scale. Other centres of cottage industry were in remote and agriculturally-insignificant provinces like Echigo. Significantly they do not seem to have been in the north-east and south-west flanks of the central plains where the big expansion of food crop production for the market had come.

V

These brief surveys may now be brought together. In the countries discussed the agricultural advances were regionally uneven. In areas not very favourable for the production of cereals, concentrations of household manufacturing thickened and new ones arose. The argument which links the agricultural and industrial changes is one about the intensification of interregional economic competition. Parts of each of these countries were better endowed for crop-growing than were other parts. What happened in the seventeenth and eighteenth centuries was that the divergence was accentuated by improvements on the side of agricultural supply. This took the form of new agricultural 'technologies' in England, Japan and to a lesser extent Colonial America, and to differing degrees it also took the form of extensions to the cultivated area. Mainland western Europe, or rather parts of it, probably increased its own food output but was also the beneficiary of cheap grain exported from the great estates east of the Elbe, where serfdom was being imposed at this time.[42] The crop-surplus areas scooped the urban markets (not necessarily in their own national market area), supplying them most cheaply. Less-favoured areas tended to concentrate on livestock production and to switch into rural industry, which, when operated part-time, fits so much more readily with raising or milking stock than with crop-growing.

The slackening rate of population growth worked in the same direction. The pressure of demand, and hence the price, for staple foodstuffs was reduced. At the same time rising agricultural productivity was increasing the supply of food and tending to reduce its price, though the preponderant effect was to release young people from agriculture. Their mouths, whether they moved to the towns or became workers in rural industry, did succeed in keeping the demand for foodstuffs at quite a high level and staved off what might otherwise have been a serious depression for farmers. The technically-progressive, crop-surplus regions could therefore sell their surpluses and use the proceeds to buy manufactures and colonial goods. Regional specialization on either crop-raising or livestock production plus rural domestic industry depended on this reciprocal trade.

Before the seventeenth century the two sets of regions had been much more nearly equal at producing their own modest agricultural and industrial requirements. From that time one set became substantially better at crop-growing. Given the slow maturing of agricultural innovation or rural social change in the past it is not surprising that a demographic lull was needed for this to show itself to effect. In such areas resources switched into farming, and manufacturing industry, such as it was, tended to wither away. A case in point was southern England and East Anglia, where there are strong signs of a movement from cloth manufacture and other industries into corn milling and malting.[43] The other set of regions (in this case much of the Midlands and north of England) became inherently no better at either pursuit, but agricultural innovation in the former set had made them *relatively* poorer at producing food crops. They could compete less and less well in that direction; and if they were to buy the tropical and industrial *desiderata* of the age they had to find something else to sell. Rural industry was their recourse and retreat. The argument, therefore, is that in a back-handed way agricultural surpluses, arising at a fortunate demographic juncture, played a large part in generating rural industrialization in England, several western European countries, America and Japan.

VI

What advantages accrued? On the agricultural side, where surpluses had been achieved by improvements in the methods of husbandry these could usually be extended to give indefinite increases of food supply. And because, although agricultural prices were low, the extension of both urban and rural-industrial markets for food had prevented them from being fatally depressed, the farming community was able to acquire tastes for purchased goods. Further, plentiful food had permitted the growth by migration of towns, those efficient solvents of rural customs inconvenient to industrialization.

On the industrial side, institutional arrangements had evolved in the commercial, financial and distributive fields and a wide spectrum of rural manufacturers had acquired capital and entrepreneurial experience. The main contribution was certainly to the quality of the human agent, particularly the conditioning of a semi-proletariat appropriate to the future needs of large-scale industry.[44] Unlike the residents of pastoral districts, the field labour of arable areas (especially under export crop monoculture) did not work rhythms conducive to domestic manufacturing. Called on for intermittent spells of monotonous effort, it did not practise skills useful in industry. By contrast the workforce which engaged in by-employments acquired the technical expertise of industry. It was slowly being severed from agricultural concerns and sometimes (as a function of certain inheritance patterns) separated altogether from the ownership of land. It was poor, sometimes possessing only a few tools, perhaps none but what could be rented. It worked for cash payment. It increasingly bought food instead of growing its own. It was loosed from customary restraints on marriage and household formation. In the more advanced of such communities the population increased fast during the second half of the eighteenth century; for example, the industrialized rural communes in the Swiss Alps experienced a greater rate of population growth even than Zürich, through the numerous progeny of the 'beggar weddings' contracted by youngsters confident of finding employment in the textile industry.[45] A malleable and trained workforce was central to an industrializing country. Without this conditioning process, the outcome in large measure of powerful but regionally uneven increases in agricultural supply, industrialization would surely not have occurred where and when it did.

NOTES TO CHAPTER 5

1. A much longer treatment in Italian, including some discussion of countries which did not conform to the suggested pattern, appeared as 'Le Origini Agricola Dell'Industria', in nos. 3–4, 'Agricoltura e sviluppo del capitalismo', of *Studi Storici*, IX (1968). I am indebted for comments to J. K. Bowers, A. W. Coats, E. J. T. Collins, R. M. Hartwell, W. N. Parker, and R. Zangheri.
2. H. J. Habakkuk, 'Historical Experience of Economic Development', in E. A. G. Robinson (ed.), *Problems in Economic Development* (London, 1965), p. 123.
3. M. W. Flinn, *The Origins of the Industrial Revolution* (London, 1966), p. 96.
4. W. H. Nicholls, 'An "Agricultural Surplus" as a Factor in Economic Development', *Jl. of Political Economy*, LXXI (1963), p. 2.
5. Cf. V. Gordon Childe, *The Prehistory of European Society* (Harmondsworth, Penguin Books, 1958); C. S. Coon, *The History of Man* (Harmondsworth, Penguin Books, 1967); W. M. S. Russell, *Man, Nature, and History* (London, 1967).
6. Adam Smith, *The Wealth of Nations* (London, Everyman edn., 1910), I, pp. 16–19.
7. For Europe, see tables in B. H. Slicher van Bath, *The Agrarian History of Western Europe A.D. 500–1800* (London, 1963), p. 80; for Japan, see Akira Hayami, 'The Population at the Beginning of the Tokugawa Period', *Keio Econ. Studies*, IV (1966–7), pp. 1–28; for colonial America as a whole the statement above seems fair, though Kenneth Lockridge has now shown 'overcrowding' in New England: 'The Evolution of New England Society', *Past and Present*, no. 39 (April 1968), pp. 62–80.
8. E. L. Jones, *Agriculture and Economic Growth in England, 1650–1815* (London, 1967), *passim* [and see Chapters 3 and 4 above].
9. E. A. Wrigley, 'A Simple Model of London's Importance in Changing English Society and Economy, 1650–1750', *Past and Present*, no. 37 (July 1967), pp. 44–5.
10. John Worlidge, *Systema Agriculturae*, p. 26: not in the 1668–9 edition; William Ellis, *The Practical Farmer* (1732), pp. 41–2, 48, 53; Jones, *op. cit.*, pp. 166–7.
11. See Joan Thirsk, 'Industries in the Countryside', in F. J. Fisher (ed.), *Essays in the Economic and Social History of Tudor and Stuart England* (London, 1961), and Joan Thirsk (ed.), *The Agrarian History of England and Wales, 1500–1640* (Cambridge, 1967), esp. pp. 9–15, 417–29.
12. Paul Mantoux, *The Industrial Revolution in the Eighteenth Century* (London, 1928), pp. 208–9.
13. Daniel Defoe, *A Tour through England and Wales* (London, Everyman edn., 1928), II, pp. 195, 199.

14. Jones, *op. cit., passim*, and see Chapters 3 and 4 above.
15. H. Barnard, *The Origin and History of Honiton Lace* (Sid Vale Association, n.d.), p. 1; W. G. Hoskins, *Devon* (London, 1954), p. 141; Charles Freeman, *Pillow Lace in the East Midlands* (Luton, 1958), pp. 10–14; Defoe, *op. cit.*, II, p. 114.
16. W. H. B. Court, *The Rise of the Midland Industries 1600–1838* (Oxford, 1938), pp. 27, 30.
17. *Ex inform.* Mrs. J. B. Donald of Long Crendon.
18. Robin Atthill, *Old Mendip* (London, 1963), pp. 56–8.
19. J. D. Chambers, 'The Rural Domestic Industries during the period of transition to the Factory System, with special reference to the Midland Counties of England', in *Communications*, Second International Conference of Economic History, Aix-en-Provence (1963), p. 432, and *The Vale of Trent 1670–1800*, *Econ. Hist. Rev.* Suppl. no. III (1957), pp. 13–14 and map; W. G. Hoskins, *The Midland Peasant* (London, 1957).
20. Cf. the study by A. C. Chibnall, *Sherington: Fiefs and Fields of a Buckinghamshire Village* (Cambridge, 1965).
21. Jones, *op. cit.*, p. 165, and see Chapter 3 above.
22. But see discussion, *ibid.*, pp. 31–2, and Chapter 4 above.
23. B. H. Slicher van Bath, 'Yield Ratios, 1810–1820', *A. A. G. Bijdragen*, x (1963), esp. p. 16.
24. J. A. Faber, 'Het probleem van de dalende graanaanvoer uit de oostzeelanden in de tweede helft van de zeventiende eeuw', *A. A. G. Bijdragen*, IX (1963), pp. 3–28.
25. For cereal prices see Slicher van Bath, *Agrarian History*, tables pp. 326–7.
26. B. H. Slicher van Bath, 'Historische ontwikkeling van de textielnijverheid in Twente', *Textielhistorische Bijdragen*, II (1960), pp. 21–39, and with H. K. Roessingh's contribution in J. A. Faber *et al.*, 'Population Changes and Economic Developments in the Netherlands: A Historical Survey', *A. A. G. Bijdragen*, XII (1965), *passim*.
27. P. Deprez, 'The Demographic Development of Flanders in the Eighteenth Century', in D. V. Glass and D. E. C. Eversley (eds.), *Population in History* (London, 1965), pp. 611–12, 621.
28. Germaine Veyret-Verner, *L'Industrie des Alpes Françaises* (Grenoble, 1948), pp. 70–5, 105; Rudolf Braun, 'The Impact of a Cottage Industry on an Agricultural Population', in D. S. Landes (ed.), *The Rise of Capitalism* (New York, 1966), pp. 55–7.
29. W. O. Henderson, *Studies in the Economic Policy of Frederick the Great* (London, 1963), p. 140.
30. J. H. Clapham, *The Economic Development of France and Germany 1815–1914* (Cambridge, 1961 edn.), pp. 95–6.
31. E. P. Thompson, 'Time, Work-Discipline, and Industrial Capitalism', *Past and Present*, no. 38 (December 1967), pp. 56–97.
32. Herbert Kisch, 'The Textile Industries in Silesia and the Rhineland', *Jl. Econ. Hist.*, XIX (1959), pp. 555–8, and his 'Growth Deterrents of a Medieval Heritage: The Aachen-area Woolen Trades before 1790', *Jl. Econ. Hist.*, XXIV (1964), pp. 523–32; and A. Klima, 'English Merchant Capital in Bohemia in the Eighteenth Century', *Econ. Hist. Rev.*, 2nd ser., XII (1959–60), pp. 34–44.
33. Eli Heckscher, *An Economic History of Sweden* (Havard U.P., 1954), pp. 150, 172–3; Danish National Museum, *Danish Peasant Culture* (Copenhagen, 1955), pp. 283–5; H. Rainals, 'Report upon the Past and Present State of the Agriculture of the Danish Monarchy', *Jl. of the Royal Agric. Soc. of England*, XXI (1860), pp. 323–4.

34. Eric Williams, *Capitalism and Slavery* (London, 1964), pp. 109–11; R. G. Lounsbury, *The British Fishery at Newfoundland 1634–1763* (New Haven, 1934), p. 191.
35. Quoted by R. W. Kelsey, 'Possibilities of intensive research in agricultural history', *Annual Report of the American Historical Association*, I (1919), p. 381. Rising agricultural productivity in eighteenth-century Pennsylvania depended on remarkably similar innovations to those of southern England, see James T. Lemon, 'The Agricultural Practices of National Groups in Eighteenth-century Southeastern Pennsylvania', *Geographical Rev.*, LVI (1966), pp. 477–8, 481, 483–4.
36. Carl Bridenbaugh, *The Colonial Craftsman* (New York, 1950), p. 46; J. Leander Bishop, *A History of American Manufactures from 1608–1860* (Philadelphia, 1864), I, p. 499; V. F. Barnes, *The Dominion of New England* (New Haven, 1923), pp. 137, 139.
37. Bridenbaugh, *op. cit.*, pp. 5–9, 18.
38. *Ibid.*, pp. 34–5, 53–8; James T. Lemon, 'Household Consumption in Eighteenth-Century America', *Agric. Hist.*, XLI (1967), p. 67, and 'Urbanization and the Development of Eighteenth-century Southeastern Pennsylvania and Adjacent Delaware', *William and Mary Quarterly*, 3rd ser., XXIV (1967), pp. 529–30 and figure VII; Fred A. Shannon, *American Farmers' Movements* (Princeton, N.J., 1957), pp. 34–5.
39. The best source is T. C. Smith, *Agrarian Origins of Modern Japan* (Stanford U.P., 1959).
40. The most helpful sources for this purpose are W. G. Beasley, *The Modern History of Japan* (London, 1963); E. S. Crawcour, 'The Japanese Economy on the Eve of Modernization', *Jl. of the Oriental Soc. of Australia*, II (1963), pp. 34–41; R. F. Wall, *Japan's Century* (London, 1964).
41. See Smith, *op. cit.*, e.g., pp. 163–4.
42. Clapham, *op. cit.*, p. 40; T. S. Hamerow, *Restoration, Revolution, Reaction: Economics and Politics in Germany 1815–71* (Princeton U.P., 1958), p. 41.
43. Jones, *op. cit.*, pp. 28–30, 36–7, and see Chapter 4 above.
44. Significantly, even in the least familiar case, Japan, Professor T. C. Smith concludes his study by stressing that 'for upward of two hundred years the agricultural labour force had been unwittingly preparing for the transition to factory employment ... Few countries have embarked on industry with a superior labor force at hand' (*op. cit.*, p. 212).
45. See especially Braun, in Landes, *op. cit.*

TWO: Agriculture
in the Urban-Industrial Economy

6. Hereford Cattle and Ryeland Sheep: Economic Aspects of Breed Changes, 1780–1870

Herefordshire may justly claim pre-eminence for the establishment of county breeds of both sheep and cattle. The chief competitor would be Sussex, but whereas Sussex cattle, for all their qualities, have disappeared, the Hereford breed has never ceased to be of the first importance. And if Hereford's Ryeland sheep have never challenged the Southdown except as regards quality of fleece, they have at least survived as a local breed. A study of Herefordshire agriculture therefore provides an unparalleled opportunity to disentangle the evidence scattered through a highly technical (and highly partisan) literature as to the economic considerations which prompted sweeping and ineradicable changes in livestock types and distribution about 1800.

I

In examining the place of cattle in the farming economy of Herefordshire it is not necessary to repeat the familiar and sometimes speculative accounts of breed history as such. The ancestry of individual cattle is of rather recondite interest. The work of the great breeders of the past, in fixing breed type and popularizing the Hereford breed, has been dealt with at length by earlier writers, and indeed their extreme concern with the contribution of a few individuals (which had its merely fashionable side and concerned a relatively small part of commercial meat production) has tended to divert attention from the history of the breed and the cattle industry as a whole. Instead, the spread of the Hereford and the underlying causes of its competition with the Shorthorn will be considered here.

Herefordshire was for centuries a rearing county from which cattle were sent along the tracks followed by drovers of Welsh cattle *en route* to the fattening pastures of the Midlands and south-eastern England, which served the London market. In the late eighteenth and early nineteenth centuries cattle of the Hereford breed from farms in Herefordshire and some adjoining counties were sold at various fairs—the biggest being Hereford October fair —to graziers from more easterly parts of England. The biggest stream of animals passed via Evesham and Stratford, some into the hands of Gloucestershire and Worcestershire graziers, but most moving on to Buckinghamshire and Northamptonshire. A second stream crossed the Cotswolds farther south, following the Welsh Way. At Buscot, high up the Thames, some were met by London dealers, although other Londoners were penetrating as far west as Kington to buy stock to fatten on the waste at the London distilleries. Most animals on this second route were fattened in north Wiltshire and the upper Thames valley. The Goddard family of Swindon, for example, bought oxen at Ross, Hereford and Ledbury during the 1780s and after fattening them, drove them on to London, while early in the nineteenth century the Turners of Kelmscot, Oxfordshire, a dozen miles from Swindon, fetched Herefords from Hereford fair to feed by the Thames, choosing them for their ability to travel.[1]

Within Herefordshire the traffic in stock was intricate. The county was not solely occupied by its nominal breed. Cattle were fetched from South Wales for feeding and resale. Occasionally one of the larger estates would feed bullocks of more distant origin, often from Scotland, while in 1813 the Hoptons of Canon Frome experimented by buying '2 small Irish cows to feed'. At the end of the eighteenth century there were still long-horned cattle in the north-west of the county, although they were fast retreating before the Hereford.[2] A further complication arose because of the relatively poor milking propensities of most pure-bred Hereford cows, which meant that the larger estates preferred to stock their dairies with Alderneys (that is, Channel Islanders of some sort) and Yorkshire cows. The Hoptons even had 'a little Scotch cow' in the dairy in 1787 and in 1815 bought an in-calf Alderney direct from Bridport, Dorset.[3]

Despite these interlopers the Hereford breed and within the breed the 'Hereford type'—red and white—predominated, supposedly following the introduction of Dutch blood into the red strain of south-west Midland and Welsh border stock in the seventeenth century. Many colour combinations were to be found, but whereas in 1750 a bullock could be distinguished simply by its white face this was no longer a sufficient description by 1800, when red cattle with 'bald' white faces had come to be the most usual type. The suggestion is that many breeders would select the white-faced animal if this and one of some other colour were approximately equal in other respects. Without concerted planning, at least at this early period, the white face gradually expanded within the breed at large.[4] Complete uniformity of colour was not achieved until well into the nineteenth century, for the earlier breeders had not been fastidious over colour if an animal were satisfactory on more important counts. During the first half of the nineteenth century colour and pattern came to be regarded more seriously and the first herd book, in 1845, portrayed four main types—white-faced, mottle-faced, light grey and dark grey. The contest between these types, although a fanciful affair, turned out for the best when (by the late 1850s) it was resolved in favour of a red body colour and a white face, stamping the breed with an unmistakable trade-mark.[5]

The more immediately useful breed points—good beefing qualities, ability to thrive on poor pasture, and docility in the yoke— were fixed by the late eighteenth century. Published weights of the breed show little improvement between 1786 and 1815. The usual Hereford was large and heavy, worked at the plough until its fifth or sixth year when it was sold to the Midland graziers for fattening on grass. Early in the eighteenth century oxen had often not been fattened until about their tenth year. At the end of that century Hereford fatstock fetched very high prices at the London markets, since it formed an important part of the meat supply for the better-paid urban workers. Much of the breed's popularity was due to John Westcar of Creslow, Buckinghamshire, who bought cattle at Hereford October fair every year from 1779 to 1810 and induced several influential, hobby-farming noblemen to buy there. Besides fetching top prices Westcar's fatstock consistently won prizes at the fashionable Smithfield Club.[6]

The first quarter of the nineteenth century was the heyday of the breed and of the great breeders, Benjamin Tomkins, John Price of Ryall, Smythies and Weyman. Although there was no single, nationally-famous improver, these men and others contrived a fervour about the breed, issuing challenges to show stock for high stakes against the cattle of all comers within or without the Hereford breed. Great attention began to be paid to pedigree and a fetish was quickly made of descent from Tomkins's stock. In consequence of this public relations work extravagant prices could be charged for the hire of a good stock bull. An eminent breeder like Price, who had cultivated customers among the nobility, could realize enormous prices at his sales.[7]

II

The spread of the Hereford from the bounds of its native county which was taking place in the late eighteenth and early nineteenth centuries continued without much change for a few decades.[8] By heavy crossing or actually by ousting local breeds the Hereford became more and more firmly entrenched in the adjacent Welsh counties and in Glamorganshire. Similarly, the Longhorn was being replaced in the west Midland counties. Hereford crosses had become important elements in the dairy stock of several south-western counties, for the heavier stocking per acre which could be reached with them compensated for their poorish milk yields. The rearing herds contained few good milkers, and a really excellent dual purpose herd could hardly have been found. Elsewhere in England, although rarely north of Cheshire, an occasional gentleman farmer kept a Hereford herd.

The established pattern of the traffic in store cattle persisted with little alteration. Grass-fattened Herefords continued to form the bulk of the supply which the Midland graziers sent to the London markets. Leicestershire and some Bedfordshire graziers were fattening more Herefords, though they were never important east of the Welland. The main change in the trade was the decline of the great autumn fairs as a result of anticipatory, private buying by the graziers. Such buying was taking place in the 1820s and by the 1850s the sale at the October fair effectively began on the day of the Herefordshire Agricultural Society Show—the day before the fair —indeed, by then, the dealers had been travelling round the farms for some weeks, buying up the best beasts and dispatching them to London by rail. In 1863 1,000 or 2,000 head fewer were offered at the fair than ten years previously, and the fair was a shadow of its former self as regards the quality of stock offered.[9]

In their home county Hereford oxen had ceased to be used for ploughing before sale for fattening, but Wiltshiremen bought them at the October fair, yoked them in plough teams for a year or two, and resold them to the Buckinghamshire graziers. From the 1820s farmers on the Cotswolds had begun to rear Herefords, working them in the yoke and subsequently selling them at Banbury market to the Buckinghamshire graziers. Herefords had continued their colonization west into Wales. A sizeable export to Australia, Ireland (where there were old-established herds) and some other countries grew up from the 1850s, but although Herefords were first exported to the U.S.A. in 1817, it was not until the pedigree cattle boom of the seventies that they were sent in any numbers to the Middle West. In the 1860s they were the almost exclusive breed of Hereford, Shropshire, Monmouth, Brecon, Glamorgan and Radnor, and an important breed in the remainder of Wales, Worcester, Gloucester, Warwick and Wiltshire. Yet clearly in England (though not in Wales) this distribution was merely a consolidation of the territory held in the first decades of the century. The territorial expansion of the breed had at some point met with a check.

III

The main force in arresting the expansion of the Hereford's province was collision with the dynamic southward spread of the Durham, or, as it came to be known, the Shorthorn. In the first decades of the nineteenth century prominent livestock breeders repeatedly made partisan assertions about the relative merits of the Hereford and the Shorthorn in the national farming press and in local newspapers, and issued challenges—seldom accepted—to show stock in competition.[10] Attempts were made to test the comparative performance of the two breeds but the conditions of the trials usually rendered the results inconclusive and in any case the decision had commonly been arrived at in advance.

The Hereford and the Shorthorn flourished under rather different management regimes. The Shorthorn thrived under the milder range of conditions, the Hereford under the harsher. 'Shorthorn' could in fact mean very diverse types of animal kept for almost any purpose. In Midland and western England Shorthorns were dairy cows of a capacity never attained by pure Herefords; elsewhere they were 'improved' beef animals reared by specialist breeders and fattened, more speedily and economically than Herefords would fatten, on green fodder in the stalls and yards of arable farms. The versatility of the Shorthorn enabled it to become in the nineteenth century more numerous and more widespread than any other breed in England before or since; in 1908 Shorthorns constituted two-thirds of all British cattle.[11] The only potential rival for versatility among English breeds, the smaller Devon, probably the better milker, occupied much the same niche among beef breeds as the Hereford and was unable to oust the Hereford from the Midland pastures. The Devon in practice hardly entered the lists against the Shorthorn. At the end of the 1830s it was observed, 'there cannot be a question but that . . . the competition is between two breeds only—the Hereford and the Durham'.[12] Crosses between these two breeds seemed an excellent idea, but although not unsuccessful for the dairy they were never wholly satisfactory as beef animals.

The real clash between the two breeds as commercial stock came only after the leading breeders on both sides had been wrangling *in vacuo* for some years. In the 1830s Shorthorn herds began to appear in Worcestershire, at that date Hereford country. By the middle years of the century it had become apparent that the position of the Hereford even in its traditional haunts would be endangered if colonization by the Shorthorn continued. Shorthorns and Shorthorn crosses (especially with the smaller beef breeds of Scotland, now pouring south to the London markets) made up the largest component in the nation's meat supply. Over two-thirds of the beasts entering London in 1863–4 were Shorthorns or their crosses.[13] Were the Shorthorn to engross the market for store cattle any further the Hereford breeders might be forced to turn over to fattening their own stock. By the early 1850s Herefords were starting to go out of fashion as national prize stock.[14]

The popularity of the Shorthorn was undoubtedly linked to the prevailing enthusiasm and demand for stock to fatten in the stall on arable farms. For this purpose, feeding high on grain and oilcake to produce both beef and manure for the wheat fields, the essentially pastoral Hereford could not compete. The Shorthorn put on fat more quickly. Nevertheless, over-feeding was threatening to damage the breeding and milking qualities of Shorthorn cows and heifers, and there were complaints that the meat was too fatty and ill-tasting from overmuch oilcake. The Hereford possessed countervailing advantages—the ability to thrive on poor keep and in exposed situations, and as the Midland graziers were well aware, to feed on grass (instead of costly oilcake) outdoors all winter. Under those rigours the highly-bred Shorthorn would 'go back' in condition. These properties preserved the Hereford from eclipse. Its rearing and fattening territories remained more or less intact, although the breed was unable to extend its range. Within a very few years, by 1860, the Hereford had staged a come-back.

The new policy was to fatten Herefords at two or two and a half years instead of three years.[15] The Shorthorns were still ahead, being fattened at less than two years old in the early 1860s, but the reduction in the age of fattening Herefords gave producers of that breed a very necessary boost from the faster turnover of stock and hence of capital. The trend towards earlier maturity for all breeds was a long-term movement, brought about by rising consumer purchasing power and increasing preference for younger and leaner meat. However, the need for farmers to realize capital during the difficult years of the 1820s and '30s, and the need to compete with the earlier maturing Shorthorn in the 1850s, meant that these were two periods of sharp fall in the age of fattening Herefords. The second of these enabled the breed to hold its ground. As Herefords were summed up in 1868, 'if their ramifications are not nearly so wide, and if they have not shown the same peculiar aptitude for crossing as the Shorthorn, it must also be remembered that, as a breed, they have been maintained principally by struggling tenant-farmers, and have not had one twentieth portion of the money expended on them'.[16]

IV

The broad lines of the changes in the nature and distribution of sheep types at the end of the eighteenth century are well known. The events for thirty or so years after 1780, especially the conflict between the interests of mutton and wool production, are crucial to an understanding of subsequent nineteenth-century developments. The price index for mutton was rising almost continuously, from 109·5 in 1780 to 121·6 in 1790 and 246·4 in 1800; by contrast wool prices remained nearly stationary, except when imported supplies of short-stapled clothing wools were endangered during the Napoleonic wars. There was a significant differential between the prices of short-stapled, fine wools and long-stapled, coarse wools: 'Of English breeds the wool of the Ryeland was highest in value at 30d. lb., followed by the related Morfe of Shropshire at 18d. In both these . . . the clip was a matter of 1 to 3d. lb. a head. The long wooled Romney and the Lincoln gave clips of 10 lb. or more of wool worth 6d. and 5d. lb. The profit from wool therefore probably lay in favour of the longwools; and the profit from the carcase certainly did.'[17] These were the prices in 1779, but the differential increased and induced flock-masters to turn to larger, long-wooled breeds, or at least to cross a ram of one of these—

notably of Robert Bakewell's New or Dishley Leicester breed—on ewes of whatever their own local, small, fine-wooled heath breed happened to be.

V

The native Herefordshire breed was the Ryeland. In the eighteenth century this was a small, white-faced, hornless, heath sheep noted for the finest, short-stapled wool of any English breed and almost rivalling in quality imported Spanish Merino wool. Ryeland mutton was lean and 'sweet' and the breed was further notable for its ability to thrive on scanty feed; according to Sir Joseph Banks's aphorism it deserved 'a niche in the temple of famine'.[18] The Ryeland occupied the lower, more cultivated parts of Monmouthshire, Herefordshire, western Worcestershire, the western uplands of Gloucestershire round Newent and the low-lying commons of the Vale of Severn above and below Gloucester. Locally, it was claimed that the Gloucestershire 'Ryelanders' of the Newent district were the true breed, as they had escaped crosses from other breeds since the landowners of the district were absentees. But the true centre of the Ryeland country, where it gave the best-selling wool, was still the Ryelands proper about Ross, where the sheep were kept on the weeds of the fallows and the mown or already-grazed clover of the stubble fields. From here the breed took its name.

The Leominster district, probably the poorer sandstone upland north-east of the town, had traditionally been the source of England's finest clothing wool, 'Lemster Ore', but by 1793 John Lodge considered that 'the finest wool about Leominster is now much inferior to the Ryeland fleece'.[19] Similarly, Leominster had conceded to Ross the first place among the county's wool marts. The deterioration in the quality of wool from round Leominster during the second half of the eighteenth century may have been one of the casualties of agricultural 'improvements'—the extinction of some common arable fields where sheep had been depastured on fallows, the introduction of 'brush' or catch crops on fallows and turnips for sheep in the hopyards, and perhaps also—under the stimulus of rising mutton prices—an extension of the practice of feeding sheep in the rich meadows of the Lugg. The relationship between a richer diet for sheep and a lengthened and coarsened fleece was well known to early writers.[20]

In the usual management of a Ryeland flock wool was the chief object, and usually the only sheep sold were ewes culled at four or five years. The flocks were not folded, 'a striking peculiarity' of Herefordshire farming,[21] since it was thought that this would develop protective and hence coarse fleeces. Instead, by a practice unfamiliar elsewhere in England and just conceivably introduced from the Netherlands, the sheep were 'cotted', that is confined at night in wooden shelters each holding up to 200 head. In the cot they were fed only pea haulm and a little barley straw. This dry foddering was supposed to reduce the risk of rot, while in the absence of folding cotting was 'the only means of collecting their dung; and rendering them most useful in an arable country'.[22] The Ryeland in its type habitat was therefore cheap to feed, but by comparison with long-wooled sheep fattened on turnips it was light both in fleece and carcass. If the breed were not to be replaced by heavier and potentially more profitable sheep these deficiencies had to be remedied. As John Clark observed in 1794, 'the superior quality of the wool, not making a full recompense for the inferiority of the quantity, and the smallness of the carcass, the time seems fast approaching when this breed will be wholly extinct, in order to make way for a more profitable one'.[23]

During the French wars the Ryeland was consequently being transformed, rather than extinguished, by crossing with rams of other breeds. Returns favoured the mutton producer, for example the Hoptons of Canon Frome switched markedly over the winter of 1804-5 from consuming sheep in the house and selling mainly the wool to buying in ewes and selling off the lambs these reared. Gross receipts from the sheep enterprise rose noticeably both on the Hoptons' farm and on Sir George Cornewall's farm at Moccas Court between 1800 and 1815.[24] Successful infusions into the Ryeland of Dorset, Southdown and above all New Leicester blood came to be made widely and all raised the Ryeland's carcase weight. Crosses with Shropshires, Radnors, Cotswolds, Lincolns, were all tried for various purposes. A writer had in 1791 'found that Herefordshire sheep in general were denominated Ryeland, but the only traces of the original sort were to be found upon small obscure farms, in the neighbourhood of Ross', and of one hundred ewes bought from over twenty farms during the following ten years he obtained no more than a score which agreed in form and wool.[25]

The deterioration of Ryeland wool which resulted from crossing with long-wools and from the growing practice of feeding on turnips was lamented because it harmed the only likely English alternative to the Spanish Merino as a source of short-stapled wool sufficiently fine for the clothing industry. The extent of the damage may be gauged from the experience of a Gloucestershire clothier who in 1801 sought the finest-wooled sheep from the best flocks in Herefordshire and found only 'an assemblage of all sorts under the name of Ryelands, and not above one in twenty that I could choose for my use'.[26] Crosses with Leicesters were mainly to blame. Although the Leicester × Ryeland was expected to suit the mutton market, for which many butchers found pure Leicester meat too fat, the cross also spoilt the flavour of Ryeland mutton, the fineness of its fleece, the quickness of the breed in foraging, and its celebrated freedom from abortion and disease. This became apparent only gradually, but by 1801 'farmers ... who six years ago were always boasting how few sheep or lambs they lost, are now ... wondering they lose so many of both'.[27]

Another heath breed, the Morfe, extended from Morfe Common in Staffordshire through Shropshire and Worcestershire into the northern and eastern hills of Herefordshire. The Morfe was horned, black or speckle-faced, sweet-fleshed and fine-wooled (although on none of these counts was it up to the original Ryeland standards) and it was hardy enough to be run on high ground. Morfe ewes were put to fatten only when aged, for the breed was kept for its wool which was second in value only to that of the Ryeland and about 1800 advancing relatively. The Morfe fleece was, however, even lighter and its quality succeeded correspondingly less in balancing the small quantity and the inferior weight of the carcase. The small Herefordshire hill farmers who kept Morfes lacked fodder crops and the breed escaped the attention of 'improvers', so that it retained the characteristics of heath sheep more than did the Ryeland.

The course of alterations in sheep type in Herefordshire is reasonably clear. First landowners, next their more alert tenants and lastly the ordinary run of farmers brought in heavier rams to cross with the Ryeland. There was a great and unprecedentedly swift mingling of breeds 'as the rams have been forwarded and recommended from one neighbour to another, from their respective districts, to every part of the kingdom'.[28] Fine-wooled, small sheep were 'driven, by the introduction of heavier [breeds], into the hands of small farmers', and because these men had few resources and only small lots of wool to sell the dealers were able to offer them very little above the price of coarse wool.[29] Thus the Plain of Hereford was given over to an assortment of cross-breds, Leicester × Ryeland or so-called Ryelands with some long-wool blood. 'There is', it was asserted, 'a fashionable rage in farming as in most other things'[30] but fashion was less easily reversed than started on its course. The constitutions of the Leicester crosses were not strong and sheep mortality rose, while stocking rates and possibly even the total sheep population of Herefordshire fell.[31]

The damage done to the fineness of Ryeland wool became a matter for alarm when imports of short-stapled Merino wool from Spain were threatened by the Napoleonic blockade. Interest in English wools for a time revived, especially among the West of England clothiers. The solution seemed to be to produce Merino wool in this country. A Merino flock had been procured for George III in 1787 and rams from this and other importations (the Hoptons of Canon Frome bought ten Merinos including a ram from Bromsberrow, Gloucestershire, as early as 1785) were distributed among would-be experimenters by the king's circle of aristocratic hobby farmers. The Merino experiment was not a success, for pure Merinos neither thrived nor retained their fine wool in English conditions. The Ryeland, despite its adulteration and the loss of hope that it could by itself meet English fine-wool requirements, was still the natural choice among possible crosses with the Merino. Several flocks of Ryelands were taken from Herefordshire with this end in view. Within Herefordshire T. A. Knight, who had been given a Merino ram by George III in 1799, Col. Scudamore of Kentchurch, two tenant farmers (Mr. Ridgway, who was supplied with Merinos by his landlord, and Mr. Weyman), Sir George Cornewall and the Hoptons all crossed Merinos and Ryelands. But English keep and weather led to poor results: the wool relentlessly coarsened while the carcase improved little.[32]

VI

When the military threat to fine-wool imports subsided the breeders of Merino × Ryeland sheep found that what they had gained so briefly and so dearly in the fleece they had more than lost in the flesh. In addition, long combing wools (rather than short-stapled carding wools) became most profitable in the years after the Napoleonic wars. Mutton continued to be more profitable than wool. Consequently those farmers who had introduced the thin-carcased, short-wooled Merino, faced a slump in fine-wool prices and were obliged to make a painful readjustment. By 1817 in Herefordshire 'many farmers have therefore been under the necessity of changing (at a considerable loss) their whole flock of sheep'.[33]

Merinos lingered on a few farms, but by 1835 only one sample of their wool from a Herefordshire flock was shown at Hereford July fair and that did not sell.[34]

Three main, though overlapping, phases of change in Herefordshire sheep husbandry are therefore distinguishable. The first, in the last two decades of the eighteenth century and to some extent thereafter, was the introduction of long-wools, notably the infusion of so much new Leicester blood. Second, over the turn of the century, was the Merino experiment. Third, from the late 1790s, there was an important introduction of the Southdown. This was a heavier short-wool than the Ryeland, and was an excellent folding sheep while producing a fleece which of all the 'improved' breeds most closely approached the Ryeland in quality while surpassing it in quantity. The Southdown was considered to be in competition with the Leicester, but direct competition was minimized because their habitats were different, the Leicester being best suited to rich pasture and the Southdown to the fold on the ploughland. Ultimately the Southdown, and other down breeds derived from it, greatly influenced the form of the Ryeland.

When the advertisement columns of the *Hereford Journal* specify a breed of sheep which was offered for sale it can be seen that Southdown flocks, although widespread in Herefordshire by 1815, were often kept pure, whereas there were many flocks of Leicester × Ryelands, some pure Leicester flocks, but only a small and decreasing number of allegedly pure Ryeland flocks. As long combing wools continued to hold the best price, crossing Ryelands with more and more long-wools proceeded, and 'Ryeland' wool was thereby increasingly lengthened and coarsened. By 1831 it was Southdown wool, from a Dinedor flock, and not Ryeland wool, which realized the best price at the July fair, the Hereford wool fair.[35] Cotting was discontinued, perhaps because 'Ryelands' now did wear a long, protective, coarse fleece; it was usual round Ross to fold sheep and to fatten them on turnips wherever possible. The triumph of the long-wools in the first quarter of the nineteenth century is evident from the figures of wool production in Herefordshire:[36]

	1800	1828
Short wool	4,200 packs	2,800 packs
Long wool	nil	5,550 packs

VII

The clash of interest between breeders principally concerned with mutton production and those who wished to revive English fine wools gave rise to a considerable literature on the properties and distribution of sheep breeds during the Napoleonic wars. Thereafter information on these matters becomes much scarcer. In addition the distinctions between breeds became increasingly blurred. By the middle of the century it became 'extremely difficult to distinguish the various improved breeds, and far more than even the breeders themselves can do, to determine where one tribe ends and another begins'.[37] The predominant type remained the mongrel Leicester × Ryeland. This type was often called Ryeland, although sale advertisements for important flocks, like specialist writers on sheep, distinguished it from the purer Ryeland flocks (really pure Ryelands survived only in a couple of flocks near Ross) of the Ross district and the poorer hill pastures. There, high-price mutton was produced for the epicures at Malvern. Separate Southdown flocks and some pure Leicester flocks were still kept, but more and more Leicester blood (and in the 1850s and 1860s that of other long-wools, Lincolns and Cotswolds) was introduced into the mongrel Ryelands because prices continued to favour the production of the longer combing wools. Nevertheless, in the middle of the century, Shropshire Downs invaded much of the northern side of Herefordshire; these produced moderately heavy fleeces of a close texture and a fine quality of mutton. They were well suited to the third quarter of the nineteenth century when both wool and mutton prices were good. By way of contrast the so-called Ryeland was undistinguished, and Herefordshire was no longer of special note as a sheep-breeding county, for 'nearly every farmstead shows a different variety of sheep, and size is aimed at instead of quality'.[38] It was only the attention some breeders began to pay to the purer strains of Ryeland at this period which saved the breed's individuality.[39]

There was a good deal which was merely fashionable in livestock breeding. But attempts (such as the Merino experiment) to run counter to what proved to be the long-term demands—for more meat and long-stapled wools—turned out to be short-lived. The cases of both Hereford cattle and Ryeland sheep show convincingly that farmers were predominantly in business for business reasons. They were willing and able to refashion their breeds of livestock to suit the market-place with impressive speed.

NOTES TO CHAPTER 6

1. Farm Account, 1780–91, Goddard Collection 992, Swindon Public Library; J. A. S. Watson and M. E. Hobbs, *Great Farmers* (1951), p. 152.
2. T. A. Knight, 'Account of Herefordshire Breeds of Sheep, Cattle, Horses and Hogs' (dated 1797), *Communications to the Board of Agriculture*, II (1800), p. 176.
3. Hopton Family Farm Accounts, 1779–1815, Hereford City L.C. Deeds 8547, 8550, 8551.
4. See e.g. *Hereford Journal*, 18 November 1847.
5. See e.g. *Journ. Roy. Agric. Soc. Eng.*, 2nd ser., IV (1868), p. 279.
6. See e.g. *JRASE*, XIV (1853), p 450.
7. See e.g. *Farmer's Magazine*, XXIII (1845), pp. 287–9.
8. The following section on the nineteenth-century distribution of the Hereford is based on various sources, notably the prize essays on the agriculture of the English counties appearing in the *JRASE*.
9. Based on the annual fair reports in the *Hereford Journal*.
10. See e.g. *Farmer's Magazine*, 3rd ser., XXI (1862), p. 38.
11. E. S. Simpson, *Geog. Studies*, V (1958), pp. 45, 58.
12. C. Hillyard, *Practical Farming and Grazing* (1840), p. 94.
13. 'The Market Demand and Supply of the different kinds of beasts ... ', *Farmer's Magazine*, 3rd ser., XIX (1861), p. 312.
14. *Farmer's Magazine*, 3rd ser., XIV (1858), p. 372.
15. Besides many statements in the literature, figures of the ages of stock are given in the Herefordshire Tithe Files, Tithe Redemption Commission, 1838–42, and in the agricultural statistics collected nationally from 1866.
16. *JRASE*, 2nd ser., IV (1868), p. 290.
17. R. Trow-Smith, *A History of British Livestock Husbandry 1700–1900* (1959), p. 209; R. M. Hartwell, 'The Yorkshire Woollen and Worsted Industries, 1800–1850', unpublished D.Phil. thesis, University of Oxford, n.d., p. 21.
18. Quoted by William Youatt, *Sheep*, n.d., p. 258.
19. John Lodge, *Introductory Sketches ... Hereford*, 1793, p. 14.
20. See e.g. Isaak Walton, *The Compleat Angler*, n.d. (1st edn., 1653), p. 119.
21. William Marshall, *The Rural Economy of Glocestershire*, II (1789), p. 234.
22. *Ibid.*, p. 236.
23. John Clark, *General View ... Hereford*, 1794, p. 79.
24. Hereford City L.C. Deeds 8547 and 5871.
25. J. Powell, 'Ryeland Sheep', *Annals of Agriculture*, XLV (1808), p. 9.
26. Edward Sheppard of Uley in *Communications to the Board of Agriculture*, VI, pt. 1 (1808), p. 66.
27. Powell, *loc. cit.*, p. 7. This was written in 1801.
28. *Ibid.*, pp. 7–8.

29. *Ibid.*, p. 8.
30. *Ibid.*, p. 8.
31. Knight, *loc. cit.*, p. 175.
32. For a comparable account of the experience of another short-wooled breed at this period see E. L. Jones, 'The Entry of Southdown Sheep into the Wessex Chalklands', *The Laden Wain* (University of Reading Agricultural Club) (1961), pp. 38–40.
33. T. G. Price, *A Treatise on the Difficulties and Distresses of Agriculture ... dedicated to the Gentlemen and Farmers of the County of Hereford* (1817), p. 30.
34. *Hereford Journal*, 8 July 1835.
35. *Hereford Journal*, 3 July 1833.
36. Youatt, *op. cit., passim.*
37. *JRASE*, 2nd ser., II (1866), p. 549.
38. H. G. Bull, 'The Ryeland Sheep', *Trans. Woolhope N.F.C.*, 1867, p. 127.
39. *Journal of the Bath and West Society*, XIII (1865), p. 6.

7. Industrial Capital and Landed Investment: the Arkwrights in Herefordshire, 1809–43

'An Estate is but a Pond, but Trade is a Spring.'
Daniel Defoe

Long before the apparent acceleration of economic growth called the Industrial Revolution the interests and wealth of the law, public office, finance, trade, and industry were entwined with those of the land. Many landowners cashed the industrial potential of their territories, especially where these overlay deposits of minerals; their sons married 'West Indian' heiresses and the dowried daughters of merchants; whilst the juiciest profits of urban enterprise, by a kind of perpetual creaming, sought a final safebank in the purchase and embellishment of landed estates. 'It is hard', writes Professor G. N. Clark of the early eighteenth century, 'to find a class of mere landlords.'[1] Disraeli, not perhaps to be taken literally, but of some weight nevertheless, observed in the Commons that, 'from the days of Sir Robert Walpole to the present moment, with one solitary exception, all those who have realized large fortunes in our great seats of industry have deposited the results of their successful enterprise in the soil of their country'.[2] Political institutions and social values sloughed off their agrarian origins less adroitly than new springs of wealth emerged. Successive waves of self-made men were thus provided with similar motives for assuming the protective camouflage of broad acres.

The existence of circumspect but well-trodden stairways to the established reaches of society, the commingling of new cash and old manners, doubtless averted the cleavage between landed and manufacturing interests which threatened under the strain of more rapid industrialization from the middle of the eighteenth century. The processes of economic growth thereafter threw up more and more vigorous, rich industrialists, whose young trade associations Josiah Wedgwood combined in 1785 in the General Chamber of Manufacturers of Great Britain. Yet although the history books concern themselves most with the divisive issues, where pressure groups of this kind clashed with the entrenched agrarian order, the forces of cohesion ultimately triumphed in England. This was very different from the Continent. In the Netherlands, for instance, with the onset of severe agricultural and demographic depression in the provinces round the Zuider Zee about 1650, the merchants of Amsterdam had ceased to finance reclamation of the meers and had withdrawn from their country estates. Thereafter their rural residence was limited to mere summer houses along the road from Utrecht to Amsterdam, or the gilded wooden cottages of Broek-in-Waterland, where a colony of storks could nest on the close-grouped chimneys.[3] The town houses of Amsterdam had become the permanent bases of almost purely urban and wholly mercantile dynasties. In France an exclusive caste of landed aristocratic drones became encysted in society and was removed only by a violent surgery.

But in England no such gulf yawned between town and country, and no final, disruptive break materialized, not even over the 'Great Debate' on free trade. It is true that in eighteenth-century London there emerged an urban bourgeoisie who were well-to-do, but in the tighter land market of that century could nevertheless not afford the prestige price of the large landed estate.[4] Yet the economic interests of the truly affluent and most powerful in trade, industry, and land did overlap in England. Moneyed interest and landed interest could not fatally bifurcate in a country where so many great landed proprietors were aware that their true roots lay not in coats of arms cash down, as it were, from the College of Heralds, but in discreet remittances from warehouses, mines, or mills, and where, since socially the landed gentleman was king, so many successful manufacturers would aspire to his crown.

The political consequences of the involvement of English trade and industry with land are familiar, the economic consequences less so.[5] The early industrialist was making his way of necessity in a predominantly agrarian society. This environment, it may be supposed, was likely to exert strong pressures on his investment behaviour by swaying his personal aspirations. With his factory in a rural setting, with the ultimate social reference group the great landowners, the successful industrialist had every incentive to assimilate to the existing status structure by buying a large block of land. He had perhaps attained his wealthy eminence by novel means and untraditional attitudes, but to fix his children in the social firmament, as to the manner born, he would have to play by the rules of established, landed society. Few families held out long against its leisured, bucolic delights.

As a starting-point in an examination of the industrial and agricultural effects of the flow of industrial wealth back into landed property, a single case is described here of the acquisition of a large estate by one of the outstanding entrepreneurial families of the late eighteenth and early nineteenth centuries, the Arkwrights, cotton spinners. The study runs from the turn of 1808–9, when Richard Arkwright, Jr., negotiated to buy the Hampton Court estate, Leominster, Herefordshire, until he died in 1843, when his son, freed from papa's financial oversight, began a more generous era of estate management. This account may find a place in the growing literature on estate administration during the eighteenth and nineteenth centuries, for no study of the initial bargaining for a great estate seems to have been published. But so descriptive an essay is offered mainly because of the intense interest in the business methods of the Arkwrights, an interest equalled until recently only by the paucity of documents concerning them. The material which has now come to light and which it seems desirable to make available to other historians consists of the estate records and many scores of letters to Richard Arkwright, Jr., together with drafts of his replies, concerning the purchase and management of the Hampton Court estate. Richard Arkwright's draft letters are indeed a find, because hitherto Arkwright letters have been very scarce.[6] Even this collection is not, unfortunately, complete. There is, for instance, only a single volume of accounts for the period 1809–19, and although thereafter voluminous estate records have been preserved, even these lack overviews of policy and finance. Nevertheless, the economic behaviour and fortunes of such a leading industrial family are worthy of an attempt to squeeze the orange dry. How quickly could a leading industrial family like the Arkwrights succeed in penetrating Hereford county society? What effects did their take-over have on management and agricultural investment on the Hampton Court estate? Did the Arkwrights seek to bring the techniques of the factory floor into the running of landed property? And how does the capital sum they removed into land compare with the growth of capital in the early cotton manufacture?

I

On the industrial scene the first Richard Arkwright, cotton spinner, sometime barber, knight-to-be, had 'arrived' by about 1775. He was soon involved with land purchases and dealings with his landed neighbours. In 1776 he may have bought the lands round Cromford in Derbyshire, only to part with them for a while in order to release capital for further mill building. This possible temporary withdrawal of investment from land may have coincided with a critical doubling of the capital value of buildings and machinery in the cotton industry from £1 m. to £2 m. during 1783–7.[7] Similarly another cotton master, Samuel Oldknow, when he wanted to extend his factories in 1791 mortgaged an estate he had bought (in 1787) in near-by Mellor and Marple to Richard Arkwright, Jr., for £12,000 at 5 per cent. The mortgage did not prevent Oldknow from subsequently buying up farms and land continguous to this estate, all of which finally came into Richard Arkwright's hands in settlement of debts at Oldknow's death in 1828.[8] These transactions do illustrate the fine balance between entry into land and further investment in industry among the leaders of the cotton industry at this time. Probably only exceptional opportunities in manufacturing could induce them to defer the purchase of land, which seemed so desirably safe and prestigious an investment.

In 1789 Sir Richard Arkwright definitely bought, or regained, the land round Cromford and began to erect a residence called Willersley Castle. The house may have reflected the inexperience of the *nouveau riche*; John Byng, Viscount Torrington, who called there during the building in 1790, considered it, 'within and without, an effort of inconvenient ill taste'. Certainly the building was an expensive effort, for a huge rock had to be cleared from the site at a cost of £3,000, road bottoms had to be blasted, grounds laid out, trees planted, a 'prospect' designed. Sir Richard began ostentatiously to build a church at Cromford, and he had already covertly advanced over £6,000 to pay off the gambling debts of Georgiana, Duchess of Devonshire, wife of a local magnate, who still owed the principal to Richard Arkwright, Jr., in 1801.[9] Georgiana was not the only embarrassed member of county society to find attractive the opportunity of borrowing from a rich upstart, as the younger Richard Arkwright was to find again when he bought the Herefordshire estate. The Arkwrights learnt that they had not only to 'buy in' to landed society, but to prop up its weaker brethren. Their ability to

M

do so was a distinct asset in a hostile rural environment. Richard Arkwright faced litigation because his father, Sir Richard, had intruded industry brusquely into the countryside, setting up his cotton mill at Bakewell first and reckoning to negotiate afterwards about the interrupted flow of water to the downstream corn mill and trout fishery belonging to the lord of the manor, the Duke of Rutland. Probably it was the secret loan to the Duchess which persuaded the Duke of Devonshire, another opponent of the arrival of industry in the Derbyshire countryside, not to gang up with the Duke of Rutland to prevent it.[10]

When Sir Richard Arkwright died in 1792 he left his only son, Richard Arkwright, Jr. (b. 1755), the bulk of a fortune estimated at 'little short of half a million' and 'manufactories the income of which is greater than that of most German principalities'.[11] The younger Arkwright completed Willersley on his father's death and moved there from the house next to the cotton mill at Bakewell which his father had given him long before, and where he had founded a semi-independent business fortune. There, still close to the springs of the cotton manufacture, he stayed until he died in 1843, 'probably the richest commoner' in the country.[12] But despite the aptitude and inclination of the younger Arkwright for industrial organization, that he should also wish to acquire extensive landed properties is unsurprising. His friends and business associates, such as Oldknow, the Strutts, and the Cromptons, had done the same; the principal figures of their Derbyshire neighbourhood, the titled proprietors, derived much of their prestige from holding large estates. Arkwright was as rich as, or richer than, any of the manufacturers and could aspire to grander territorial ambitions, even if the narrow land market of the French wars set the price high and obliged him to scatter his estates in unfashionable counties. He himself would not let go the reins of his cotton empire, but his wealth, his milieu, and doubtless the desires of his family all prompted extensive investment in land. After all, in the private opinion of the Duchess of Devonshire, to whom he had been kind, he was a simple, benevolent and rich man, and as such would seek to indulge his sons.

During the wars Arkwright seems to have been seeking means of diversifying his interests. In 1804, for example, he took a partnership in the Wirksworth bank. Similarly, he set money aside to enable his sons to climb into landed circles. Like Sir Robert Peel, Sr., another cotton master, and William Crawshay, the ironmaster, both of whom likewise bought estates, he had large holdings in the funds. This was a sound move for anyone contemplating the purchase of land, for the funds required no management and were easily realizable, and while they yielded less than industry, they earned more meanwhile than land.[13] Thus one of Arkwright's sons was to follow him as Arkwright of Willersley. Another son was installed at Sutton Scarsdale, also in Derbyshire, a third at Mark Hall, Essex, and Normanton Turville, Leicestershire, a fourth at Hampton Court, Herefordshire, while a fifth farmed at Dunstall, Staffordshire. The family exposed its sons to the alternative scholastic embers of Eton and Christchurch or Harrow and Trinity College, Cambridge, and spread their activities into local government, Parliament, the Church, and the law, all most respectable in the eyes of Society. The outlying members of the network were in any case too distant to play an active role in the cotton business, even had they wished. They were to be branches of a landed dynasty.

From July 1808 Arkwright noticed newspaper advertisements offering for sale an estate at Hampton Court, Leominster. He might have balked at buying property in Herefordshire, which was notoriously difficult to develop because of poor communications with the adjacent English counties.[14] Yet in itself the county was fruitful and attractive. The mansion at Hampton Court was set by the River Lugg, in lush meadows between wooded hills, surrounded with all the paraphernalia of a miniature kingdom, and amidst an estate where the notably diverse farming typical of Herefordshire was carried on: breeding Hereford cattle, breeding sheep, growing wheat, barley, pulses, hops, fruit, and other crops. More pertinent, a would-be buyer like Arkwright would have had to search hard to find another seller with an estate of over 6,000 acres to offer like Lord Essex, who had not even visited Hampton Court for a couple of years, had acquired it in the first place only by marrying into the Coningsbys, who preferred his own seat at Little Cassiobury, Hertfordshire, and who moreover was moderately short of ready cash to rebuild his own house. The Coningsbys had encumbered some of their manors with debt charges[15] and Lord Essex would apparently feel relieved to be rid of the estate. He seems to have sold outlying Herefordshire lands during the 1790s and he was selling properties closer in to Hampton Court in 1807.[16] His agent had left no fallows and sown almost no forage crops on the home farm at Hampton Court from 1805 or 1806, which suggests that a plan had been formed about that date to sell the whole estate and to take as much out of it as possible in the meantime.

Not until 5 December 1808 did Arkwright bring himself to act.

He then wrote to a partner in his London bank, Pole, Thornton & Co., to ask him to act as agent in the prospective purchase of the estate. This man, John Smith, was an excellent choice as inter-mediary—as discreet as his name, a thorough worker, and prepared if need be to pump anyone's employees about their master's busi-ness. Arkwright asked him to obtain an assurance from Lord Essex that the estate would not be sold yet awhile, not until Arkwright had viewed it anonymously, for 'of course, you will not mention my name'. Smith quickly discovered that another prospective pur-chaser was actually negotiating for the estate and he suspected (accurately as it turned out) that this was Sacheverell Chandos Pole, who was fortunately a Derbyshire man, too, and whose credit Arkwright was therefore well placed to assess. Arkwright indeed reckoned Pole to be a poor competitor, and he promptly applied for the refusal of the estate himself. Smith had an interview with Lord Essex and reported he had been told,

> that Mr. Pole would be obliged to sell all his Derbyshire property which would delay the payment of the purchase money. I remarked in answer that my friend was quite able to pay for any estate he might contract for, and though I was not authorized to say so I felt confident he would not require many months to pay the purchase of this large property perhaps not many days. Ld E— was very much struck with this remark and said that would be very convenient indeed. His Lordship said that . . . £235,000 included the Timber, and every thing without exception. Wine Books Plate &c &c &c. In short that a Purchaser might go down, and commence Housekeeping the day he arrived.

Arkwright concurred. It would be convenient to step into a ready-equipped country mansion, and he was aware that he would be bargaining from strength in offering to pay on the nail. To avoid tedious manœuvring he would hand over the whole of an agreed price immediately.

Arkwright now thought Pole was no longer a serious or active rival and he therefore set off to view the estate. Having seen it, he was inclined to look unfavourably on the household effects, but still keen enough to buy the entire property. He set about obtaining an accurate valuation, commissioning a surveyor himself, receiving a copy of the valuation made for Pole as a very unusual favour from Pole's surveyor, acquiring two more from potential buyers who had conclusively dropped out of the running, and obtaining a fifth

through Smith, who quite by chance had a hold over another surveyor. When Arkwright came to compare these valuations he found
them unsatisfactory in detail. One surveyor had gleaned his information about rentable values merely from conversations with
tenants, which in Arkwright's eyes 'hardly seems sufficient to enter
an agreement upon'. Nevertheless, the valuations as a body helped
him to a decision, and on the last day of 1808 he offered Lord
Essex £220,000 for the estate, the money to be paid on Lady Day
next on receipt of a completed title. So sure was Arkwright that no
one else would match his offer of instant payment that he set the
price below the totals of the valuations, all of which had assumed
part payment on mortgage over a number of years. He was confident
enough to draft a complete proposal of terms of purchase, and
wrote, 'I do not like dodging . . . I hope the offer will be accepted
or rejected in *one week*.'

What gain did Arkwright anticipate on this outlay? The formal
valuations had ranged from £235,000 to £301,844 for the house, the
equipment of the estate, and approximately 6,000 acres of land.
The valuation which he had himself commissioned was the one to
which he gave most weight. This suggested £261,749, but checking
the property parcel by parcel Arkwright concluded that the true
figure on the assumed values should be £264,444. He preferred his
own arithmetic. On his offer of £220,000 he therefore stood to gain
£44,444 at once on capital value, plus a substantial sum from a
perfectly feasible upgrading of the rent roll. In addition, the estate
would be a social asset and a safe investment for his posterity,
though he did not apparently think that good reason for paying a
fancy price. He was more conscious that the annual cash return
would be less than he was accustomed to from non-agricultural
investments. Indeed, in a fit of depression at one stage of the
negotiations he wrote,

> I feel as if the 11,000£ a year, was quite as snug where it is, as
> if the money was vested in an estate, bringing in with no little
> trouble about half the sum, clear of outgoings.

This implies that he was receiving about 5 per cent in the funds,
whereas the estate would not only cost forty years' purchase and
require an effort of management, but would return only 2½ per cent.

Before Arkwright could receive a reply to his offer he heard from
Smith that Pole, who was, in fact, still in some obscure way com-
mitted to making an offer for the estate, had revealed to Lord Essex
that Arkwright was the anonymous bidder. This Arkwright took to

be a device whereby Pole could escape his own obligation to negotiate. When Arkwright's identity stood revealed, Lord Essex abruptly
refused his offer, while trying to tempt him to advance. And Smith
felt obliged to warn Arkwright that Lord Essex might still obtain
£230,000 or £240,000 if he sold off the estate in small lots.

Outwardly, Arkwright's stand was firm. He would not advance.
Before Smith could convey this rejoinder he had a surprise visit
from Lord Essex's agent to say that an offer of £240,000 for the
estate had been received from a syndicate headed by a wool-stapler
from the Borough. Smith commented, 'I suspect the party in question are hard jobbers who must sell before they can pay'; that is,
speculators who would borrow the purchase price and recoup by
dismembering the estate for resale—exactly the kind of competing
purchasers whom Smith had feared. Arkwright thereupon gave up
all hope of the estate, and on 14 January 1809 he wrote valedictorily
to Smith, thanking him for his services.

At this date winter snows delayed the Derbyshire mails, and for
a space Arkwright heard no more. Nine days later he wrote again
to Smith instructing him to invest £40,000 at 3 and 4 per cent, 'as
I have now a considerable sum of money, for which I shall have no
occasion'. On the very brink of buying land he had been holding
ready cash as a lever in bargaining. He asked wistfully whether the
Hampton Court sale were completed. Smith did not reply at once,
and when another nine days had elapsed Arkwright revealed something of his secret ambitions by inquiring earnestly whether or not
Lord Essex had sold. This produced a reply from Smith to the effect
that the propective sale to the syndicate was hanging fire and that
Arkwright might be well advised to examine the estate again. The
offer of a ready £220,000 was immediately repeated, for Arkwright
remained convinced that this should be an effective bid, but he
agreed with Smith that were it once again to be refused he would
revisit the estate to see if he could not persuade himself to make a
higher offer.

The closing play of the match is revealed in less detail. Lord
Essex once more refused £220,000, but tossed Smith a hint that
£230,000 might be acceptable. Arkwright could not convince himself that the property was of any greater value, but going over the
ground again he found such charm that he instructed Smith to go
up to £225,000 rather than lose it. Soon after, he rose to the required £230,000, at which sum Lord Essex clinched the deal in
February 1809. At the margin considerations other than those of
maximum financial profit clearly motivated Arkwright's action,

although he had acted the hard businessman most of the way. Troublesome, but minor, disputes over the transaction were still to come. Lord Essex and his agent, Mr. Tanner (who occupied the home farm on his own account), both left loopholes in their agreements for subsequent haggling with Arkwright, frustrating his countermoves by withholding necessary information. Long after the sale Tanner was making outrageous demands for further payments on account of livestock which he claimed (without, however, being able to produce a satisfactory list) to have left behind on the home farm. Lord Essex was covering repeated depredations on the library, china room, and portrait gallery at Hampton Court with disingenuous protestations that he had assumed he would be able to return for personal effects. The sourest taste in Arkwright's mouth was left by a subsequent legal battle with Lord Essex over the apportionment of the costs of enclosing common lands at Bodenham, where the enclosure had inconveniently been in progress during the sale. Both Lord Essex and Mr. Tanner overdid their demands, so that at last Arkwright was driven to write bitterly (and revealingly) to their solicitor:

> I shall close this subject for the present, by merely observing to you, that if I had not been accustomed by long habit, to investigate what *some* may call *trifling* matters I should never have purchased H.C.

The last, ludicrous claim was put in by Lady Essex's heirs as late as 1837, when Arkwright was an old man. This claim hinged on a supposed mistake by a copying clerk and was for the value of timber felled between February 1809 and Lady Day that year. Nothing seems to have come of it, and these irritating rear-guard actions apart, Richard Arkwright had been in secure possession of the estate from Lady Day 1809, when some of the farms were re-let on his behalf.[17] At the time of the sale the estate showed signs of recent mismanagement. Tenants were in arrear with their rents, old grassland had recently been ploughed out, young timber had been destroyed by browsing stock. This state of affairs, coupled with the further unreasonable demands of Lord Essex and Mr. Tanner, led Arkwright to seek arbitration for deductions. In the end the price was reduced to £226,535, plus £2,200 to Tanner for stock left on the home farm.

What can be learnt of Arkwright's business attitudes and methods from this account of the transaction? It is hazardous to deduce much about his motives in buying the estate, but it is clear that he was a hard bargainer. Arkwright occasionally displayed his dislike of Lord Essex's languid, unbusinesslike ways. He detested Tanner's dissimulation (though he was not above a trick or two himself) and quickly replaced him with a bailiff of his own from Derbyshire. Arkwright was prepared to take some personal pains, as far as his knowledge of the land allowed, to assure himself of the estate's long-term worth, in contrast with the lackadaisical ways of other would-be purchasers. He employed the best 'professional Gentlemen' to conduct his business—for example, Edward Wakefield, the Pall Mall land agent and father of Edward Gibbon Wakefield, was retained to collect the rents from all his estates. Arkwright demanded order and meticulousness: when Tanner admitted to having no records of the farm stock he observed, 'it is somewhat singular ... Men of business generally take care to have written documents to refer to.' That is what Arkwright was, a man of business. He was able to temper his evident desire to own this particular property with stern calculation. He played by strict, if individual, rules, on the one hand concealing his identity and his wealth and seeking information by the back door, but on the other refusing to beat the price down by denigrating Hampton Court and forbidding Smith to haggle for the lowest price. A shrewd, decisive man, Arkwright was eager to insert himself, or rather his sons, into the higher reaches of landed society, but for him an estate had also to be a fair invest-ment. Arkwright bargained less closely than he would seemingly have done in his industrial role, but far more narrowly than the established country gentleman.

II

Richard Arkwright did not himself settle in Herefordshire, but his family had little or no difficulty in finding acceptance in the society of the county. Former industrial families had already succeeded in penetrating this most rural of shires—the Knights and the Foleys, both ironmasters, had done so. Apparently the Herefordshire landed proprietors were free of the suspicion which the Arkwrights had encountered in their Derbyshire neighbours, the Dukes of Rutland and Devonshire. Certainly the Duke of Norfolk wrote at once from his seat at Holme Lacy to welcome Arkwright to Here-fordshire, inviting him and any friends to dine, and offering a few does to replenish the run-down stock in the Hampton Court deer park. For a manufacturing family the Arkwrights were rather oddly but most conveniently placed, being both Anglican and Tory. John Arkwright, the one of Richard's sons who was installed at Hampton Court in 1819, had been at Cambridge and was sufficiently acceptable to be appointed High Sheriff of Herefordshire in 1831. It was an exceptionally churlish local landowner who in 1833 still referred to Richard Arkwright as 'a tradesman'.[18] Another neighbouring family, the Beringtons, not only mixed socially with the Arkwrights right from the start but were soon to solicit and obtain a loan from Richard Arkwright.

The estate was by no means in the pink of condition. In many ways it was ripe for development. Hampton Court house itself was old, rambling, and built in a motley of styles. As late as 1828 a neighbouring diarist observed that it 'would require a fortune to put into repair, and then would only be fit for a Prince to live in'.[19] Tanner had let the home farm run down. The tenanted farms were out of repair and not always fully equipped to deal with the wide range of products typical of local agriculture. In the 1820s, for example, there was still at Houghton farm 'no Granary except Bed Rooms, no Room for the management of hops after drying except Bedchambers'. To render the estate in full repair would have necessitated a major outlay, to modernize it an enormous one. No improvements other than some petty exchanges of intermixed farmland had been made since a survey of 1786 and 1787 by the London firm of Nathaniel Kent, Claridge and Pearce had uncovered serious defects, notably the small and intermingled nature of the farms. There was an untidy and ill-defined hangover of communal husbandry, such as the surviving Lot Meadows along the Lugg. The whole fixed capital of the estate, Arkwright discovered, the water carriage, flood-gates, fences, field gates, 'indeed everything about the farm, Park &c. have been shamefully neglected, and of course are out of repair'.

The management of the estate from 1809 to 1819, particularly from 1815, turned into mainly a holding operation. At first, not wishing to live there, Arkwright 'determined to reduce the stock of Deer very considerably, and to take other steps to reduce the expenses of the establishment'. He planned to keep the property as a home for one of his sons. Nevertheless, such outlay as he did make was acutely sensitive to the economic draughts which blew in the deflation after 1815, and possibly even earlier, in the manufacturing crisis of 1811. The agent's memoranda from 1820 reveal such a poor state of buildings on the tenanted farms as to indicate that Arkwright had undertaken no general renovation after his purchase.

Early in 1811, when his neighbour Thomas Berington of Winsley pressed him for a loan of £2,000 linked in some way to exchanges of land which would rationalize holdings on their contiguous estates, Arkwright consented only reluctantly, insisted on limiting the loan to twelve months, and added:

> you are, no doubt, well aware that money can not be very abundant, as every one must, more or less, feel the effect of the general distress in the Mercantile part of the community; but . . . I will accommodate you.

By 1815 Berington owed him £2,472 and Arkwright was urgently requesting repayment. In the twenties Berington's estate affairs were in such difficulty that he could still not repay and Richard Arkwright was pressing him very hard, until John Arkwright, now resident at Hampton Court and more sensitive to local social niceties, intervened on Berington's behalf.[20] And in 1815, too, Arkwright appears to have refused to lend £10,000 to his Leominster solicitor, who had been speculating in Herefordshire land and had much left on his hands by the post-war depression of the market. This was a local loan which Arkwright would probably have made in the more buoyant years of war.

Not only did Arkwright become much tighter about lending in the agricultural slump at the end of the Napoleonic wars, but he retrenched expenditure on his own estate, too. In 1811 he had begun to develop the estate, starting with a programme of draining the lands in hand. He had constructed a new water carriage and stepped up the work year by year until 1814. Then in 1815 and 1816 the programme was severely slashed, although renewed in the temporary recovery of agriculture in 1817. Similarly, spending on all estate work had been expanded from the time of purchase until a sudden, sharp contraction in 1815–16, and likewise had begun to recover in 1817 (see Table 1).

Until the end of 1814 (when he gave the land for a new road over Dinmore Hill, 'the formidable obstacle which has so long impeded our communication with the northern parts of the county and the kingdom')[21] Richard Arkwright thus showed a moderate degree of interest in the improvement of his Herefordshire property. But in 1815 and 1816 he drastically pruned even estate maintenance expenditure, although in November 1815 he did pay his tenants' share of the property tax as a concession to their distress.[22] He spent more freely again in the mild optimism of 1817, but by 1820 Edward Wakefield, collecting the rents, was causing general alarm by dis-

THE ARKWRIGHTS IN HEREFORDSHIRE 173

TABLE 1. Expenditure on estate labour at Hampton Court, Herefordshire, 1809–17

	Total expenditure on labour	Expenditure on labour for land draining
	£	£
1809	392	0
1810	517	0
1811	783	42
1812	1,189	68
1813	1,184	95
1814	1,012	208
1815	344	37
1816	351	37
1817	600	261

Source: Constructed from data in Disbursements Book 'A' of Richard Arkwright, Hampton Court Collection, Herefordshire Record Office. 1809 adjusted to simulate a full year of Arkwright occupation. Figures rounded to nearest £.

training a few tenants and taking 'Judgement Bonds' from any who were at all in arrears.[23] Arkwright attempted in addition to cash some of the assets of the estate. In February 1821 he engaged with William Stoveld, timber merchant and banker of Petworth, Sussex, for a big fall of timber at Hampton Court, and £8,000 from this source was in his hands by June. The contract was tightly enough drawn to make Stoveld dizzy with apprehension about what was in essence a perfectly normal transaction; this extreme caution on Arkwright's part may have been due to the uneasiness which his steward, Edward Wakefield, felt about the economic situation that year.[24] But this attempt to enable the estate finances to withstand the agricultural depression came comparatively late.

Other landowners, more involved personally with their petty kingdoms than Arkwright, seem to have been quicker to fell timber or to draw on reserves in order to brace themselves and (through remittances of rent or written-off rent arrears) to cushion their tenants against the shock of the post-war slump. Their expenditure might fall in the prolonged disillusion of the 1820s, but unless they were trapped (as the Beringtons were) between, on the one hand, urban creditors who did not allow for the state of agriculture and on the other the unpaid rents of their farm tenants, landowners usually made some effort to bear the burden of the early slumps themselves.[25] Arkwright was different; he drew in his horns like the more embarrassed of the lesser gentry, not facing the first onslaught of the depression in the generous manner expected of a territorial magnate accustomed to the temporary hesitations and difficulties of agricultural markets. Arkwright's reaction was hardly the result, as it was in cases like the Beringtons', of dire necessity, but presumably he automatically applied the brakes of an industrialist faced with falling returns. His economies, though not severe enough to cripple his tenants, were perhaps inappropriate to agriculture, where tenant farmers with satisfactory stock, credit, and local experience were not easily replaced if once they had been pushed out of farming.

After 1819, when John Arkwright was settled at Hampton Court, local needs were more generously assessed. Richard's son, however, tended to the extreme of personal extravagance in his younger days. His first wish was for a gracious country abode, and in order to improve Hampton Court to his taste he was always asking his father for remittances. From 1819 to 1822 he received sums totalling £40,000, and these were by no means the last. He may, however, have spent this money on trivial decorations, as alterations to the fabric of the house did not begin until 1834 and were then quite modest.

Less cautious than his father, John Arkwright secured from him a much higher investment in the Herefordshire property than Richard, as an absentee landowner, would himself have contemplated. John Arkwright took to employing 150 labourers on an irrigation project during the early 1830s as a way of countering winter unemployment. John also interceded with his father during the 1820s and 1830s on behalf of the hard-pressed tenantry. These men hung on, incapable of improving their farms, late with the rent, waiting for the harvest or the hop sales or the cider-apple picking so that they could pay something on account. They obtained concessions through John Arkwright, who sympathized with them because his own running of the home farm was similarly leaking away his father's money. Abatements of 10 per cent or 15 per cent of the rent were frequent.

Richard Arkwright had become rather reluctant to acquire any more land, at least outside Derbyshire.[26] Against odds, John persuaded his father to bid for the Berington property when, like so many others, it was forced on to the market by the deflationary pressures of the twenties. When the bid failed Richard could not be induced to try again.[27] During the twenties and thirties the Arkwrights bought only a few cottages and isolated fields in Herefordshire, and did not seriously enter the local land market again until 1837, when agricultural prospects brightened. John Arkwright might have influenced his father more decisively had he displayed a more active interest in farming. As it was, until about 1840 he was prepared to keep the estate's agriculture marking time, although even marking time, in the post-war years, required assistance from the landowner's purse. Thereafter John Arkwright became an ardent agricultural 'improver', encouraged by letters from his brothers Charles in Staffordshire and the Rev. Joseph in Essex,[28] and by his brother-in-law Chandos Wren Hoskyns, author of *Talpa, the chronicles of a clay farm*. The wherewithal to quieten the tenantry and increase John Arkwright's comforts, and now the capital for his improvement schemes, came as subsidies from Richard Arkwright's industrial profits.

III

When Richard Arkwright died in 1843 his sons received handsome legacies. John found that the book debt to his father which he had incurred at Hampton Court during the 1820s and 1830s was liquidated and he gained £261,000 in addition. He embarked on a systematic remodelling of the estate, bought land to extend or help ring-fence the property, undertook the subsoil draining which was so fashionable in the forties, and as a result attracted notice as an agricultural enthusiast.[29] He took a house each year for the Royal Show, at Exeter or Norwich or Southampton. He visited the annual Smithfield Show, ending the day with a visit to the opera. On these semi-agricultural, semi-social occasions he met his brothers, his brother-in-law, and old acquaintances like the Strutts and the Cromptons, themselves families which were forsaking industrial interests for rural ones. The Arkwright brothers were certainly becoming detached from the industry which had launched them. Robert, for example, was trying unsuccessfully to sell his cotton mill during the depression of the early 1840s, and was finally obliged to let it at a low rent; he did not contemplate running it himself, being absorbed in improver's work on his estate at Sutton Scarsdale.[30] John himself tended to invest his capital in the funds and railway companies. Soon the most obvious reminder of the *fons et origo* of their wealth was merely the hank of cotton, argent, on the crest of each of the landed brothers. An enormous capital had come with the Arkwrights and their circle out of industry into the less profitable business of administering landed estates.

Richard Arkwright's will had assigned his sons sums of between £40,000 and £100,000 each, besides numerous and substantial bequests to grandchildren and others. His sons in addition received the residue of his assets, so that John Arkwright actually obtained —after his book debts had been liquidated—a total of £261,000. The residue alone of Richard Arkwright's property was sworn to exceed £1 m., at which point the scale of the stamp duties ceased.[31] There is thus no certain means of calculating the true size of his fortune. Nevertheless, John Arkwright actually received over five times his nominal legacy of £50,000 and if the (admittedly hazardous) assumption is made that the real total received by the remaining sons all exceeded their specific legacies by the same factor of five, Arkwright would have left a fortune of over £1½ m. If the value of Hampton Court is any guide, the five or six landed estates included among his assets might have been worth a further £1 m. This estimate is very little more than a guess, but it does seem to establish the general proposition that a very high proportion of Richard Arkwright's industrial profits had already ended up in landed property by his death. Again, if John Arkwright's behaviour were typical of his brothers, much of Richard Arkwright's liquid assets was transferred to his sons' estates soon after his death. Such a flow of capital from industry into land (almost one-quarter of a million pounds on the initial purchase of Hampton Court alone) was very considerable indeed.

The agricultural effects of the Arkwright family's movement into land were at first less forceful than might have been anticipated, partly because they coincided with the post-Napoleonic deflation, but in the main because Richard Arkwright was a reluctant spender on poor agricultural investments. The social ambitions of his sons countered his caution to some extent, but it was only with the new enthusiasm for farming after 1837, and more particularly after Richard's death in 1843, that they were able to spend heavily on fashionable agricultural improvements. There is no sign that in the early days the Arkwrights introduced any novel technology into the farming of their estates, although their estate book-keeping was sophisticated and perhaps owed something to industrial experience. If Richard Arkwright, whose personal interest in farming and in his more distant properties was none too great, had not himself lived so long, and had the post-Napoleonic deflation not intervened, it is probable that agricultural investment by the Arkwright family would have been much more vigorous.

A suspicion may be entertained that his purchases of land were, however, so vast that they restricted the flexibility of Richard Arkwright's whole range of investments. Between the funds and industry he could switch much of his accumulated profit with relative ease, but once into land on a big scale he could not readily withdraw. The Hampton Court estate certainly became a drain, both because of the parlous state of its agriculture after 1815 and through the finance which John Arkwright needed personally to be able to mix with the highest county society. The whole history of Richard Arkwright's involvement with his Herefordshire estate is one of nice balance, or near-conflict, between long-run social ambition and short-run financial interest. He hesitated, and then agreed only with stringent conditions, to lend to Berington in 1811; he would not accept land as security for a loan to lawyer Coleman in 1815; he swiftly retrenched spending on his own estate in 1815–1816; and during the twenties and thirties he would not improve the tenanted farms wholesale or much extend his holding of land in Herefordshire. Only John Arkwright's demands for subventions and pleas on behalf of the tenants led Richard to make irregular investments in his Herefordshire offshoot or to forgo the proceeds, and very occasionally to buy a little land or undertake some agricultural scheme. All in all, Richard Arkwright seems to have lacked the ready policy of investment in his land that one would expect of a rich, new entrant to an estate. He was not so possessed of spare capital, or so abandoned, as to invest freely in both agriculture and industry when economic prospects were temporarily poor.

Beyond this, materials with which to demonstrate the effects on the Arkwright cotton concerns of their phased withdrawal of resources into land are lacking. It seems that Richard Arkwright's sons quietly avoided or gradually withdrew from active participation in the cotton manufacture. If, however, the precise consequences of their withdrawal of capital from industry cannot be calculated, some attempt may at least be made to show how the purchase price of the Hampton Court estate compared with current annual investment in the cotton industry. Available figures on capital formation in British industry at the beginning of the nineteenth century are very approximate, but at least they indicate the orders of magnitude. Accepting the published figures at their face value, it would seem that Richard Arkwright spent on the one fixed investment of Hampton Court a sum equivalent to approximately 30 per cent of the total annual investment in the cotton industry. This is quite apart from any working capital needed at once on the estate and anything he may have been spending on landed properties elsewhere, such as at Willersley Castle. At this date, 1809, cotton was a leading sector of the economy, producing approximately 40 per cent of the declared annual value of all domestic exports.[32] Furthermore, Professor Pollard, who argues that the real problem of the early industrialists was in finding circulating capital to hold stocks and carry work in progress, regards the cotton industry as the one exception in which fixed capital investment was the main component. In the up-to-date cotton mill between 1780 and 1830 fixed capital represented a fraction more than 50 per cent of the total capital invested. The cost of Hampton Court therefore equalled nearly 60 per cent of the annual investment of fixed capital in the entire cotton industry. A comparison of the capital cost of the Hampton Court estate with national investment in the cotton industry is shown in the following table.

TABLE 2.

Final purchase price of the Hampton Court estate	=	c. £229,000
Annual investment in buildings and machinery in the cotton industry	=	max. £400,000
Annual investment in circulating capital in the cotton industry	=	max. below £400,000

Source: Hampton Court Collection; Deane and Cole, British Economic Growth (1962), p. 262; S. Pollard, 'Fixed Capital in the Industrial Revolution in Britain', Journ. Econ. Hist., XXIV (1964), p. 302. Figures for 1809.

The achievement of the period 1780 to 1800, according to Deane and Cole, was a rise in the rate of annual capital formation from 5 or 6 per cent to approximately 7 per cent, although it is doubtful whether this level was maintained during the remainder of the Napoleonic wars and their aftermath. Even that rise was small compared with the major upturn, in cotton as in other sectors, after 1830. As yet, however, there is no special reason to associate the check in the rising rate of capital formation with the maturing desire of 'new men' like the Arkwrights to opt out of industry into land. But in view of the scale of Arkwright's transfer of capital i that direction such a relationship is not impossible.

IV

How widespread was the desire among manufacturers to enter landed society? William Cobbett in his *Rural Rides* rages against the replacement of old-established landowners by merchants, stock-·jobbers, and industrialists. This turnover was, of course, nothing new, but part of what he saw was the flare-up of the land market between 1820 and 1829, when landed proprietors nearing defeat in the depression of arable farming sold out in bigger numbers to men who had made fortunes by speculations and other enterprises.[33] New entrants came from many industries, sometimes acquiring land by marrying into the landed gentry and from time to time into the aristocracy, more often by straightforward purchase. The move was made, 'by the Darbys from iron, Matthew Boulton from engineering, the Peels, Arkwrights, Fieldens and Strutts from cotton, Marshall from flax, the Ridleys, Cooksons and Cuthberts from coal, or Samuel Whitbread from brewing'.[34] The exodus of manufacturers from a single industry, iron-making, during the eighteenth century may be seen in the account given by Professor T. S. Ashton.[35] Two of Ambrose Crowley's daughters married baronets and John Crowley's daughter captured the Earl of Ashburnham. 'The same path was trodden by the Foleys, who became barons in the eighteenth century, by the Wortleys, from whom have descended the Earls of Wharncliffe, by the Hardys of Low Moor, afterwards Earls of Cranbrook, and by the Guests, from whom Lord Wimborne springs; while one of the legitimated daughters of Lord Wilkinson married a Legh and became the mother of the first Lord Newton.' Only the Quaker ironmasters stood aside, for they would not marry 'out of the Society', so that there was for them, 'thus no tendency towards the dissipation of capital'. But once the adherents of freer religious sects had become landowners, 'the ladder of iron by which they had mounted was kicked away', not always without agonizing personal readjustments.

The characteristic industrialist entering rural society wanted to make more of an impression than Richard Arkwright himself did— to seal his new status with new heights of splendour in his residence, extensive landscaping in his park and projects of improvement on his farms. Those for whom some information is available seem to have been more ardent 'improvers' than average established landed proprietors. The 'Society of Agriculture at Manchester' had among its subscribers in 1793 Robert Peel and Samuel Oldknow, both

N

cotton men, and nominally at least James Watt.[36] Mr. Wilkes and the Peel family spent £138,000 of their profits from Manchester cotton manufacture on buying an estate at Tamworth about 1789, installing five steam engines and according to Robert Bakewell, a good enough authority, making 'other improvements better worth notice than at any place I have yet seen'. Samuel Oldknow farmed very lavishly on his Bottoms Hall estate at Mellor and Marple from 1788, and in 1813 was noticed as possessing the only machine-driven pump in Derbyshire for irrigation purposes. He was, in fact, pumping urine from the privies of his factory and apprentice house at Mellor on to his meadows, thus anticipating a practice more commonly associated with the third quarter of the nineteenth century. John Wilkinson, ironmaster, undertook arduous reclamations in Denbighshire and the Lancashire mosses, and early introduced steam threshing machines. Marshall of Leeds bought Patrington in the East Riding and was laying an elaborate tile-drain network there 'under the direction of Mr. Josiah Parkes' in the late 1840s. On a smaller scale Richard Beech left Manchester textiles in 1805 at the age of 36 to retire to Eccleshall, Staffordshire, where he continued to prosper by lending on mortgage to the neighbouring gentry. He also busied himself farming, and experimented with a cultivator on his own land.[37] There are other examples. The essential point is that these men whose wealth originated in the factory or the forge invested heavily in agriculture and pioneered improved techniques on their farms.

Land, however, earned them less than the growth industries. There were respectable rewards for agricultural 'improvement', notably during the high-price period of the Revolutionary and Napoleonic wars, but no one expected the total investment in a landed estate to pay high dividends. Essentially, landed property offered a secure and desirable investment for the man with dynastic ambitions. The price for the social advantages and long-run prospects of landownership was the acceptance of a cash profit 1 per cent or $1\frac{1}{2}$ per cent lower even than investment in the funds or mortgages, and several per cent less than direct investment in industry. An estate did not run itself. As recruits to landed society, therefore, erstwhile industrialists 'managed their property and they spent their incomes, and a history of management and of consumption forms the most important part of their economic history'.[38] Much of the money which passed out of industry into land was squandered on prodigious bouts of port-drinking, on assemblies, race meetings, fox-hunts, pheasant battues. Resources were dissipated on unproductive activities like the gyrations of armies of flunkeys, the sonorities of private chapel building, the ordered informality of landscape gardening, the contrived futility of mock ruins and follies. A share of industrially created wealth constantly disappeared in these bonfires of good living for a small, landed class or was immobilized in their ornaments.

The ultimate industrial consequences of this draining of capital are (without a set of case studies) hard to assess. The selling-out of the great industrialists, or more commonly the severed industrial connections of their descendants, may have caused formerly prominent firms to wither. The men who replaced them, of course, obtained ready-made industrial plant, but this turned them away from founding additional, fresh, and perhaps more modern firms. Instead, the purchase price they gave for the mills of their predecessors permitted the outgoing sons and grandsons to live boldly as landowners. Many founding fathers of industry would have been saddened to learn that family connections with their firms were destined, as Dylan Thomas has it in the rather different context of *Under Milk Wood*, 'to die of drink and agriculture'.

The fate of the individual firm or any one industrial family is of less moment than the overall effect on the supply of industrial capital. Whether or not, outside cotton, there ever was a major long-run problem of providing fixed capital may be less important than the exact timing of investment. Technological breakthroughs or the timely extension of industrial plant required 'lumpy' investments. A few strategically placed entrepreneurs, determined instead to insert their descendants into landed society, might withhold investments of this kind, and retard by a fraction the development of the manufacturing base. No doubt the achievement of the growth industries of the late eighteenth and early nineteenth centuries was to keep up capital formation despite the persuasive attractions of the life bucolic. Nevertheless, the opportunity costs of land purchases like that of Hampton Court were high. Economic growth could surely have come faster without them.

NOTES TO CHAPTER 7

1. *The Wealth of England* (1946), p. 159. In the case of one family whose papers have survived, the Radcliffes of Hitchin Priory, Hertfordshire, one member (a silk merchant in London) sent his brother on the estate a constant flow of advice in the 1720s and 1730s both on what stocks and shares to buy and when to export grain to southern Europe. Delmé Radcliffe Coll., Hertford County Record Office.
2. Quoted by H. J. Habakkuk, *British and American Technology in the Nineteenth Century* (1962), p. 177, n. 2.
3. Sir Ralph Payne-Gallway (ed.), *The Diary of Colonel Peter Hawker*, I (1893), pp. 214, 216.
4. H. J. Habakkuk, 'The English Land Market in the Eighteenth Century', in J. S. Bromley and E. H. Kossman (eds.), *Britain and the Netherlands* (1960), pp. 172–3.
5. Political aspects are treated by G. Kitson Clark, 'The Repeal of the Corn Laws and the Politics of the Forties', *Economic History Review*, 2nd ser., IV (1951), pp. 1–13. Economic aspects are discussed most usefully in Habakkuk, *loc. cit.* I am indebted to a more recent discussion by Professor Habakkuk, his summing-up of the conference on 'The Evolution of the Capital Market' held at Nuffield College on 8 January 1964.
6. R. S. Fitton and A. P. Wadsworth, *The Strutts and the Arkwrights* (1958), Appendix C, printed two communications *in extenso*, 'as so few Arkwright letters have survived'. The letters and other documents mainly used here are in the possession of Mr. D. L. Arkwright, of Kinsham Court, Presteign, to whom I am grateful for research facilities and hospitality. The remainder of the Hampton Court Colln. is in the Herefordshire Record Office, in two sections, the first consisting of further family papers deposited by Mr. Arkwright, the second consisting of ledgers and deeds deposited by Lord Hereford, the present occupant of Hampton Court. No useful purpose would be served by loading the present narrative with references to individual letters, especially as the Record Office Colln. has not been finally catalogued. I am most grateful to the staff of the Record Office for commenting on a draft of this essay and supplying additional information.
7. Fitton and Wadsworth, *op. cit.*, p. 77 (the best source for the Arkwrights' Derbyshire and industrial activities); Phyllis Deane and W. A. Cole, *British Economic Growth* (1962), p. 262.
8. George Unwin, *Samuel Oldknow and the Arkwrights* (1924), pp. 140, 202.
9. Earl of Bessborough (ed.), *Georgiana* (1955),p. 155.
10. M. H. Mackenzie, 'The Bakewell Cotton Mill and the Arkwrights', *Journal of the Derbyshire Archaeological Society*, LXXIX (1959), pp. 62–4, 74.
11. Fitton and Wadsworth, *op. cit.*, quoting *Gentleman's Magazine* (1792), pp. 770–1.
12. *Annual Register*, LXXXV (1843), p. 252.

13. Habakkuk, *British and American Technology*, pp. 72–3.

14. See my 'Agricultural Conditions and Changes in Herefordshire, 1660–1815', *Transactions of the Woolhope Club*, XXXVII (1961), reprinted as Chapter 2 above.

15. Coningsby deeds, Hereford City Library Local Colln. 9218(10).

16. Berington Collection, Worcestershire Record Office, 705:24/1380. Lord Essex therefore found Hampton Court personally uninviting, while he had pulled down his Restoration house at Cassiobury in 1800 and needed to pay for the Gothic mansion by James Wyatt which replaced it. Arthur Ponsonby, *John Evelyn* (London, 1933), pp. 289–90 n.

17. The property into which Arkwright thus entered may be summarized from the abstract of the conveyance to him, dated July 1810, as 6,221 acres in twenty manors, Hampton Court house itself, four advowsons, tithes in several parishes, woods in five parishes, twenty-nine farms, a large number of cottages and houses, some mills and some other miscellaneous buildings proper to a large estate.

18. Select Committee on Agriculture (1833), *Report*, reply to Q.8473.

19. John Biddulph's diary, 2 August 1828, Hereford City Library Local Colln.

20. Worcs. R.O.: 705: 24/1409.

21. *Hereford Journal*, 4 January 1815.

22. *Ibid.*, 8 November 1815.

23. Worcs. R.O.: 705: 24/1393.

24. Contract in Timber Book, Hampton Court Colln.; Wakefield's evidence in Select Committee . . . Agriculture, *Report* (1821) esp. pp. 206–7.

25. Discussion in my unpublished D.Phil. thesis, 'The Evolution of High Farming 1815–65' (Oxford, 1962).

26. In 1821 he had run the risk that if the timber merchant, Stoveld, defaulted on his contract he would have had the additional responsibility of receiving in settlement Stoveld's freehold estates, valued at £12,000, far away in Sussex. In 1826 he bought the Sutton Scarsdale estate in Derbyshire, on which his son Robert settled. J. J. Rowley, 'The Farming of Derbyshire', *Journal of the Royal Agricultural Society of England*, XIV (1853), pp. 34, 49.

27. Worcs. R.O.: 705: 24/1409.

28. Joseph was one of Trollope's originals. A. L. Drummond, *The Churches in English Fiction* (1950), p. 84.

29. *Hereford Journal*, 27 November 1844.

30. Rowley, *loc. cit.*, pp. 34, 49; Mackenzie, *loc. cit.*, p. 69.

31. Annual Register, *loc cit.*, p. 253.

32. Deane and Cole, *op. cit.*, p. 295.

33. *Rural Rides*, Everyman edn., *passim*, but esp. pp. 303–4.

34. F. M. L. Thompson, *English Landed Society in the Nineteenth Century* (1963), p. 21. For more extensive lists of new entrants from industry see *ibid.*, *passim*, and G. E. Mingay, *English Landed Society in the Eighteenth Century* (1963), pp. 102–5.

35. *Iron and Steel in the Industrial Revolution* (1963 edn.), pp. 217–18.

36. Unwin, *op. cit.*, p. 205.

37. H. C. Pawson, *Robert Bakewell* (1957), p. 152; Unwin, *op. cit.*, ch. XIV; W. H. Chaloner, 'The Agricultural Activities of John Wilkinson, Ironmaster, *Agricultural History Review*, V (1957); Alan Harris, *The Rural Landscape of the East Riding of Yorkshire* (1961), p. 110; copy of accounts and diary (1806–33), of Richard Beech, in possession of G. B. Masefield, Department of Agriculture, University of Oxford; Norman Gash, *Mr. Secretary Peel* (Cambridge, Mass., 1961), pp. 15–18.

38. Thompson, *op. cit.*, p. 3.

8. Wheat Yields in England, 1815–59[1]

The Royal Statistical Society's library contains two notebooks, one a copy of the other, containing information on the yield of wheat in England during the first half of the nineteenth century. Their provenance is unknown and they are not catalogued, but they can be identified as containing the record described by Thomas Tooke in his *History of Prices*, Volume V.[2] This record, based on actual crop-cutting data, was started by the Liverpool firm of Cropper Benson & Co. in 1809, and when this firm discontinued its interest in the wheat trade in 1836 was continued by Joseph Sandars, a Liverpool businessman. The last entries in the books refer to 1859; Tooke died in 1858 and Sandars in 1860. One book, which carries a Liverpool label, may have been Sandars's original, while the other, whose paper is watermarked 1853, may have been a copy made for Tooke when he was preparing his history. This latter copy contains copies of memoranda in which the remarkably modern technique of yield estimation is described. There is unfortunately no record of the writer of these memoranda, but he may have been J. Danson, a Fellow of the Society, a letter from whom accompanies them.

The first memorandum reads as follows:

Monday 6th June, 1854.

Mr. Sandars, Corn Surveys

Today I dined at Mr. Tooke's and by appointment met Mr. Sandars of Liverpool, a gentleman largely engaged in the Corn Trade there and who has made in that trade a large fortune. Mr. Sandars gave evidence before the Committee (Commons) on Agriculture of 1836—and has taken a somewhat leading part in most discussions on the Corn Laws during the last twenty years.

It was part of Mr. S's plan of operations in his business to institute Surveys of the Crops in England, a few weeks before each harvest, so as to enable him to judge of the probable result of the harvest.

One of the purposes of the meeting of today was to ascertain from Mr. Sandars the precise mode in which these surveys were conducted.

He said that the plan was to send out from his Counting house at Liverpool at the proper time three or four or more persons of intelligence, each of whom took a prescribed circuit and was provided with introductions to a certain number of farmers on that circuit. The inspector was directed to go into a wheat field on each farm, and to use a small mechanical piece of frame work with which he was provided for the purpose of enclosing within the frame a square yard of the growing corn. He was then to count the number of ears within the frame— and stooping down he was to cut off within six inches of the ground the first ten stalks that came to his hand. These stalks he was to tie up and label and forward at once to his employers at Liverpool. When the stalks were received there they were carefully examined, the number of grains in each ear counted and accurately weighed, so as to give a fair average of the whole, and the results tabulated. The effect therefore of each such inspection was to give as regards the field inspected

(1) The number of ears to the square yard

(2) The average number of grains in each of those ears

(3) The average weight of each grain

(4) And the collected stalks served as a sample of the crops

From these data deductions were worked out as to the yield per acre; and the general results were recorded in a form carefully kept up from year to year.

Mr. Sandars said that in many cases the persons employed knew nothing of the subsequent stages of the enquiry.

He also said that an experience of nearly thirty years had satisfied him that the results obtained from these surveys were very rarely far from the truth.

As will be seen below, the recorded yields are remarkably high, and the second memorandum reports Mr. Sandars's comments on this point. The recorded yield in bushels of 60 lb./acre is found by grossing up the measured yield of one square yard. However, the estimate of the acreage under wheat always included paths, head-

FIGURE 1

Routes taken by the surveyors
— — — — Midland circuit
— · — · — Southern circuit

lands, hedges, etc. and as a result it is suggested that the figures should be reduced in the ratio 50 : 72. From a present-day standpoint it would seem more reasonable to leave the yield figure and to adjust the acreage; no adjustment has in fact been made in the results reproduced below.

FIGURE 2

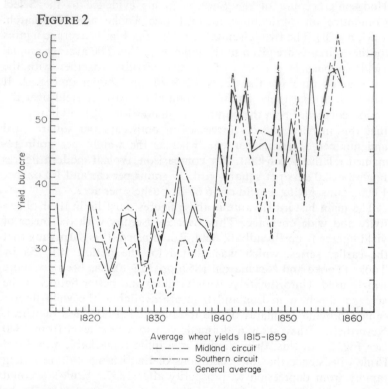

Average wheat yields 1815-1859
— — — — Midland circuit
—·—·—·— Southern circuit
———————— General average

What is completely lacking is any description of the method of choosing the field to be sampled and of locating the sample in the field. From some remarks quoted by Tooke, it is plain that the importance of choosing a 'typical' site and not picking the best of the crop was fully appreciated, but it seems likely that the surveyors visited the more co-operative farms, and that on these the yield tended to be higher than average. It is also well known today from work in India that small crop samples of this kind are liable to substantial positive bias, mainly due to edge effects. For these reasons, the absolute yields may well be too high by an unknown amount. However, the yearly changes are probably quite accurately determined, and the yield components, weight per grain and number of grains per ear, should be free from any substantial bias. Yield figures are given in the books from 1821 to 1859. Yield figures for individual centres start in 1830 and yield components in 1837. Figures of average yield are taken back to 1815 by Mr. David Hodgson's account of the Surveys in his evidence to the Select Committee on Agriculture in 1821 (see Tooke and Newmarch, 1857, p. 121). The two 'circuits' are shown in Fig. 1; average figures for these circuits are given in the table on p. 189. The average annual yields in bushels per acre of the two circuits, together with the national average for the years 1815–20, are shown in Fig. 2. It will be seen that there was a substantial increase in yield over the period covered. From the component figures for 1821–59 it appears that this increase reflects increases in both ears per square yard and number of grains per ear, whereas the weight per grain remained relatively constant. For comparison, typical modern figures might be 320 ears per square yard, 25 grains per ear and 1·4 oz. per 1,000 grains, giving a yield of 56 60-lb. bushels per acre.

The main historical value in these figures must lie in their objectivity and wide coverage. They overlap usefully with the series of yield figures from Broadbalk field, Rothamsted. It is surprising that the earlier series, which was quoted for the period 1815–55 by Tooke (Tooke and Newmarch, 1857, pp. 127–8), has been not more widely used. Unfortunately, without more and better figures of the acreage of wheat in England than are available, the yield figures cannot provide estimates of the total annual production of wheat. Nevertheless, they show a dramatic rise to a new level from 1840 (see Fig. 2). In this, they confirm in a quite remarkable way Lord Ernle's insistence that the conditions of English agriculture swung rapidly from depression to prosperity after 1837.[3] Ernle's account of the suddenness and scale of this transition may seem to be exaggerated, but the figures of wheat yields are consistently much higher in the 1840s and '50s than in the 1820s and '30s. Weather conditions and other short-run variables undoubtedly account for the marked year-to-year differences in average yields in both periods, but the great discrepancy between the two periods as a whole must as certainly reflect the huge increase in agricultural inputs with the rise in farm product prices after 1837. The most important of these inputs so far as grain yields are concerned, the expansion in the application of artificial fertilizers and of dung from the increased store feeding of cattle on oilcake and other purchased feeding-stuffs together with the extension of field-drainage, are mentioned by Ernle. Their effects usually persisted beyond the one season and were able to hold wheat yields at a high level during short periods of severe depression, such as 1849–51, when inputs were curtailed.

TABLE 1. Wheat yields, 1815–59

	Midland circuit				Southern circuit				
	Ears per sq. yd.	Grains per ear	1,000 corn wt. (oz.)	Yield (bu/ acre)	Ears per sq. yd.	Grains per ear	1,000 corn wt. (oz.)	Yield (bu/ acre)	General mean yield (bu/acre)
1815									37·0
1816									25·3
1817									33·4
1818									32·6
1819									27·7
1820									37·3
1821				36·2				29·6	30·9
1822				32·0				30·6	30·9
1823				29·0				25·0	25·8
1824				34·1				27·7	29·0
1825				31·7				35·7	34·9
1826				29·7				36·7	35·3
1827				30·7				35·7	34·7
1828				23·1				28·1	27·1
1829				27·7				27·7	27·7
1830				22·7				36·3	33·6
1831				26·8				31·2	30·3
1832				22·3				39·1	35·7
1833				23·4				37·1	34·3
1834				31·1				44·1	41·5
1835				31·2				33·2	32·8
1836				28·4				38·8	36·7
1837	175·1	23·3	1·563	31·8	169·8	25·0	1·626	34·6	34·0
1838	166·7	21·8	1·546	28·2	157·7	27·7	1·566	34·3	33·1
1839	174·3	25·3	1·415	31·3	161·9	26·5	1·394	31·2	31·2
1840	178·7	28·8	1·536	39·8	192·8	30·5	1·541	46·4	45·1
1841	176·0	27·0	1·535	36·6	190·1	27·9	1·519	40·5	39·7
1842	177·6	30·8	1·661	45·8	205·7	32·8	1·681	57·0	54·8
1843	207·1	33·1	1·526	52·6	210·5	31·2	1·482	49·3	50·0
1844	186·3	30·4	1·626	46·3	215·3	32·7	1·593	56·6	54·5
1845	191·1	30·9	1·434	42·7	199·8	29·5	1·526	45·4	44·9
1846	158·6	28·5	1·559	35·2	199·0	29·9	1·605	48·3	45·7
1847	167·5	29·1	1·598	39·4	220·6	29·7	1·466	48·1	46·4
1848	163·0	23·9	1·590	31·1	209·7	29·0	1·535	47·4	44·1
1849	199·0	28·9	1·707	49·4	214·0	31·2	1·745	58·9	57·0
1850	192·0	28·6	1·506	41·9	194·8	29·5	1·460	41·8	41·8
1851	196·6	28·1	1·596	44·2	203·1	30·2	1·621	50·1	48·9
1852	215·2	34·1	1·459	53·8	203·7	31·7	1·314	42·8	45·0
1853	162·6	28·7	1·560	36·5	178·4	28·4	1·483	38·2	37·9
1854	191·9	37·3	1·642	58·9	208·9	32·8	1·651	56·9	57·3
1855	187·9	31·4	1·493	44·2	192·2	31·9	1·516	46·8	46·3
1856	193·0	34·0	1·542	50·7	201·6	33·1	1·582	53·2	52·7
1857	190·6	35·1	1·514	50·8	195·5	36·7	1·626	58·9	57·3
1858	232·1	35·2	1·553	63·7	213·8	34·2	1·533	56·5	57·9
1859	200·8	36·9	1·518	56·9	213·5	35·6	1·427	54·6	55·1

Note: The general mean yield is obtained by weighting the Midland and Southern circuit means in the proportions 1:4, following a suggestion by Tooke.

NOTES TO CHAPTER 8

1. Written in collaboration with M. J. R. Healy.
2. T. Tooke and W. Newmarch, *A History of Prices*, vol. v (London: Longman, Brown, Green, Longmans & Roberts, first published 1857, facsimile edition 1928), pp. 53–4, 118–33. We are most grateful to Mr. J. A. King, the Royal Statistical Society's librarian, for showing us the books and for directing us to the references to them in Tooke and Newmarch.
3. Lord Ernle (R. E. Prothero), *English Farming Past and Present* (London: Longmans, Green, 1961), pp. 349–76.

9. The Changing Basis of English Agricultural Prosperity, 1853–73[1]

Most historians are familiar with the essential topography of English agricultural prosperity—or adversity—during the nineteenth century. This comprises a peak during the Napoleonic wars, a deep trough for twenty years thereafter, another peak rising steeply from 1837, after which the line dips once or twice during the forties, sags at mid-century, rises in a booming curve through the fifties and sixties, until it crashes down some time in the seventies. To the more sophisticated the line begins to rise again, a little, from 1894.

This stark outline, treating agriculture more or less as a single entity, owes most to the work of Lord Ernle, which for years was slavishly followed.[2] A renewal of interest in nineteenth-century agriculture is now evident, and, as Marc Bloch would have put it, we are again keeping faith with Ernle by striving to modify his findings. The single line, firm but very generalized, with which Ernle drew the depression of the last quarter of the nineteenth century, has already been split into two divergent paths, representing the fortunes of cereal growers and livestock producers, by Mr. T. W. Fletcher.[3] Similarly, two or three regional studies have suggested that the depths of the depression after 1815, which Ernle described so vividly, were plumbed only in restricted localities and for only two or three short spells. The topography of this depression is likely to be reshaped at the hands of the next serious student to treat it as a whole.

The most conspicuous hump in the line is formed by the period from the early 1850s to the early 1870s. These years are usually passed over lightly as a time of prosperity, and in marked contrast to the succeeding period as one of prosperity for the grain grower. My intention is not to try to invert this period into one of depression, for although the accounts of prosperity could be made much more precise than they are at present, its general character is plain. Mr. J. R. Bellerby's figures of farmers' incentive income, obtained by deducting estimates for net rent, wages, and interest on occupier-capital from an estimate of the total factor income of agriculture, and therefore showing the reward for management and risk, are:

in 1851	£21·4 million
in 1870–3 on average	£43·9 million

Incentive income per man-week per farmer:

in 1851	£0·514
in 1870–3	£1·038

Incentive income relative to that for industrial occupations:

in 1851	49·5 per cent
in 1870–3	77·3 per cent[4]

These statistics cannot be used to show the differing experience of various groups of producers, although the different trends might be elucidated by a study of contemporary farm accounts.

My intention here is to examine the agricultural basis of this overall rise in the prosperity of the farmer. Ernle, I think, tended to over-emphasize the role and prosperity of the cereal grower during the years in question, although he did recognize the growing importance of livestock. Not every subsequent writer has remembered this caveat, and some have depicted the period primarily as one of prosperity for the specialist grain producer. I think it fair to say that the fifties to the seventies form a sort of base period in the minds of agricultural historians and agricultural economists, as the persistence of the term 'Golden Age' would suggest, when the wind was set fair for arable England. A heartening number of writers do mention that there were far-reaching changes in the pattern of agricultural production at this time—'down corn, up horn', as Ernle said[5]—but this movement is over-shadowed by the swing towards livestock production during the Great Depression, and its implications have not been much explored.

I

The expression commonly used for the agriculture of the mid-nineteenth century is 'high farming'. The economic and technical connotations of this term have often been confused. I prefer to restrict high farming to the economic sense in which it was used, loosely, by Caird and those who agreed with him, that is, the increase of inputs to farming in supposed attempts to offset falling prices by an increased output. In the technical sense, which is perhaps the commoner and with which we are concerned here, high farming is an extension of mixed farming, that is of any system which interlocks the growing of cereals and the keeping of either or both sheep and cattle. This was epitomized by the Norfolk four-course system, with its close-knit cycle of fodder and grain crops, its arable flock, and its yard-fed bullocks. What high farming adds —and here I prefer to use Philip Pusey's alternative term 'high feeding'[6]—is intensity of operation, the feeding of purchased oil-cake to the livestock on a lavish scale, to produce both meat and dung; the latter with purchased artificial fertilizers, in turn lavished on the arable land to promote high yields of grain, and of fodder crops for the stock. The greater the scale of feeding farm-grown and bought-in fodder and the heavier the applications of farm-produced and purchased fertilizer, the more the saleable produce and the more manure for the next round of cropping, that is, the higher the farming. This was the 'expanding circle' which Mechi advo-cated.[7]

Professor A. H. John has drawn attention to William Ellis's de-scription of East Anglian farming in the early 1740s as having shown 'many elements of what was subsequently called "high farming" '.[8] Turnips were sown before barley and fed to fatting cattle, which returned so much dung that the yields of barley were on the increase. Mixed farming of this type will undoubtedly be found to have been a development of the seventeenth century, when the requisite root-break and hay from rotation grasses became available. An increased yield of grain was usually held to be the *raison d'être* of such systems. This was the case in the 1840s, when Pusey stated that the practice of fattening cattle on arable farms was continued 'not from a view to profit in the sale of meat, but for the production of dung, and the consequent increase of the corn crop'.[9] To Pusey the liberal feeding of oilcake to stock for the sake of extra manure for the land under cereals was the 'great distinction of English agriculture, and constitutes what is called high farming' and what he called alternatively high feeding. The principle was worked out in different ways, typically in the eastern counties by the winter-feeding of oxen bought-in at the autumn fairs, but in the southern counties, where a feeding-house of cattle was a rarity, by giving supplementary oilcake to sheep hurdled on turnips.

On soils derived from chalk, limestone, or sands, high feeding possessed great advantages for the cereal grower. Such soils tend to be very deficient in potash, and although easy to cultivate are 'puffy' and need to be consolidated. Before, and indeed long after, adequate supplies of imported potash became available (from the Stassfurt mines in 1861) and while the only consolidating implement was a light roller, these needs were met by a hurdled flock. Potash was transferred from the subsoil to the topsoil in the dung of sheep fed with turnips, the roots of which had tapped the subsoil supplies of potash. Moisture was retained in the soil in dry seasons in the crumb structure built up by the treading of the sheep in the fold. Sheep and bullock dung acted as the nitrogenous fertilizer and provided humus, which the one course of 'seeds' did not fully supply, for the course of wheat in the Norfolk-type rotations which predominated on these soils.[10] Clearly, the richer the feeding of livestock, the better the dung and the heavier the crops of grain which might be expected.

II

For a score of years after the Crimean war the price of wheat, apart from short-term fluctuations, showed no tendency to rise. There was now a large import every year. On the other hand the general level of prices and the prices of livestock products in particular rose with little pause.[11] This rise in the value of livestock products compared with the value of wheat became marked from 1857 and could not but affect the working of high feeding systems in which livestock and cereal enterprises were nicely combined. The proportions of cost to be ascribed to and of profit accruing to, the meat- and grain-producing enterprises are the subjects of contemporary assertions which are not easy to evaluate, the more so because the nature of high feeding varied according to locality and changed as the balance between the prices for grain and livestock products shifted. Nevertheless an arrangement in chronological order of the statements about the profitable end of high feeding sheds some light on the changing relation between grain and livestock production.

Until the 1850s it was held that the cost of stall-feeding oxen through the winter was not recovered from the sale of fatstock in the spring, but only by charging the grain enterprise for the dung which had accumulated from the beasts. This, and the fact that wheat was stall-fed on a wide scale only when it was exceptionally cheap, as in 1835–6, suggests that before the Corn Laws were repealed wheat production was not as unprofitable as many of the producers claimed. It is probable that fatstock prices were inadequate to cover the purchase of store beasts and oilcake, and leave a profit, and that stall-feeding in many areas was only practised because in addition the price of wheat was high enough for it to pay, in effect, a good sum for the rich bullock dung. The differential of 1d. per lb. more for meat in spring than in autumn, of the days when the supply of beasts fattened on summer grass was much in excess of those winter-fed, had disappeared. The meat and hides of stall-fed oxen were directly profitable only when farm-grown fodder was used as a substitute for expensive purchased feed.

In the Welsh Marches it was worth while to winter stores on turnips and straw 'chiefly for their manure', although this was not common practice. It was usual in eastern England. Lincolnshire farmers were prepared to winter other men's beasts on straw free of charge, although the stock-owner had to provide the oilcake, simply in order to acquire the dung. On thin, arable soils in Norfolk and on Lincoln Heath the dung was needed to turn the straw crop into good manure, and as C. S. Read added, 'on the poor chalk hills, the hungry greensands, and the thin stonebrash, high farming is as necessary as in West Norfolk'.[12] According to Clarke's essay on Lincolnshire farming in 1851, 'the Grounds of the present practice of consuming the Straw with Oilcake given to Beasts on light Arable Farms ... are ... simply the natural infertility of the land and the expectation of bountiful crops from the ample investment of capital in manures'.[13]

Equally, the dung seems to have been the justification for feeding extra oilcake or grain to sheep hurdled on turnips on the chalk uplands, where according to Pusey the effect was 'distinctly seen along the line where the hurdles had stood in the following crop of barley, marking the efficacy of high feeding', while in east Berkshire one farmer would give another his turnip crop if the latter would put his sheep in to consume it in the field.[14] The heavy demand for manure for hop-growing alone justified the generous feeding of cattle in parts of Kent.[15] The conversion of their straw into manure kept up the practice among Nottinghamshire farmers even when meat prices were low: 'they calculate', wrote Corringham in 1846, 'how they shall use the greatest amount of cake, which they regard as an indispensable in good farming—at the least possible loss; for as prices both of beef and mutton have of late been, they must necessarily incur a loss if they expect their remuneration from the livestock, instead of from the land', and he repeated Pusey's

o

aphorism that as in Lincolnshire cattle were 'machines whereby to make manure'.[16]

In Cumberland, by way of contrast, the farmer who fed cattle 'reckons it an unprofitable season if any part of his profit requires to be charged to the dung-heap',[17] but the basis of the Cumberland feeding system was the swede and not costly oilcake. In more easterly arable areas, where a farmer might buy several hundred pounds' worth of oilcake each winter but sell his bullocks in spring for £1 or £2 per head less than they had cost the previous autumn, stall-feeding was only practised as an adjunct to cereal production.[18] In 1851 the four principal farmers of Borough Fen, Northamptonshire, who were lavish feeders of oilcake, agreed that two-thirds of its cost were returned by the manure from cattle and only one-third from the sale of beef, one-third by the manure from sheep, and two-thirds from the mutton.[19] It was this sort of ratio which led Pusey to regard the production of plenty of rich manure as 'the whole object of all feeding'.[20] While Protection lasted, the price of cereals covered losses on meat production by stall-feeding; afterwards they did not, yet mixed farming as a whole continued to be profitable.[21]

In 1851–2, 1858, and the mid-sixties wheat was cheap enough to be fed to bullocks and pigs on a large scale, in the hope of a compensating return from fatstock. The prices for fatstock were high when the price of wheat was low. In this situation, the receipts from grain and livestock products helped to balance one another, and in 1864 when grain prices were low and prices for stock and wool high a correspondent in the *Farmer's Magazine* observed that in consequence the farmer's 'business position would be about an average one'.[22] The complementary nature of the two groups of enterprises is revealed by the unusually frank account of a farmer as to the effects of the bad harvests of 1856 and '57 in Scotland. Sprouted grain was fed to the stock and potatoes were sold for seed instead of human consumption, so that on balance profits were almost if not quite what they might have been had the harvests been good.[23] The inverse movement of the prices and profitability of grain and sheep is further borne out by C. S. Read's comments on the relative fortunes of sheep farmers on the Norfolk heaths and grain growers on the dearer-rented Norfolk soils. It was held at the time a distinct advantage of mixed farming that when grain prices were poor, the crop or some part of it could be fed to the fatting stock.[24]

It is noteworthy that in the East Lothians oilcake and grain were fed liberally when grain prices were good in the early 1840s, were sharply curtailed when grain and stock prices were low at mid-century, and fed freely again in the mid-1860s when grain was cheap but stock fetched a good price.[25] In 1858 oilcake was being fed in Norfolk on a scale which grain prices did not warrant.[26] In other words, in the 1850s and '60s prices for livestock products were sometimes high enough to induce high feeding regardless of unremunerative prices for grain. Low grain prices of course meant low feed costs. As P. H. Frere noted in 1860, 'whereas of old the bread consumer had to pay in part for the supply furnished to the consumer of meat, now, each kind of produce must in the main defray its own cost of production', and at times the production of meat became the mixed farmer's chief aim.[27] The manure from stall-feeding was thought of as devoted not to the wheat crop, as it had been in the past, but to the roots as further feed for the livestock. There are plenty of signs that this new relationship was widely recognized by the mid-1860s.[28]

This account has been somewhat simplified for the sake of clarity: the proportions of profit due to grain and livestock cannot be learnt in detail since few farmers could make the distinction themselves. A Norfolk farmer told Sir Daniel Hall early this century that 'it is impossible to show that any single operation on a farm pays by itself, it is the whole system taken together which succeeds or fails', and in the early days of cost accounting, as Hall agreed, this was not an entirely unreasonable position, because decisions about how to apportion costs and receipts in the Norfolk system are necessarily very arbitrary.[29] Nevertheless, a general change in the profitable base of high feeding systems from about 1850 does seem to be indicated.

III

The long-term movements of product prices had been foretold by Caird as early as 1849, although he had exaggerated their immediacy.[30] Caird expected the price of grain (except malting barley, of which the British sorts were superior) to fall as imports increased, while with the growth of population he anticipated that prices for butcher's meat, dairy produce, vegetables, wool, and hides would rise. In consequence, he advocated turning attention to green crops which could be fed to livestock, partly for the saleable products and partly for manure to increase the yields of the grain crops. Caird was by no means the only one to recognize this trend, which became a source of general comment,[31] but he was the most constant in stressing the need to adjust the pattern of mixed farming to meet it. He returned to the topic in 1868 and pointed out how accurate his prognosis had been. 'Since 1850 the price of bread on the average, has remained the same,' he wrote, 'while that of meat, dairy produce, and wool has risen fifty per cent . . . This and the steadily advancing barley, to which I then referred, is the true explanation of increasing rents and agricultural prosperity, notwithstanding increasing receipts of foreign corn.'[32] Professor Clapham came to the conclusion from price data in the *Economist* that the rise in wholesale prices for meat and dairy produce was nearer 40 per cent, although it was calculated in the '70s that the price of beef in the Metropolitan market advanced 58 per cent and that of mutton 85 per cent between 1853 and '73.[33] Obviously the lowest of these figures is large enough to have brought about very considerable changes in the structure of agriculture. Caird's analysis in 1878 is probably the best formulation of his oft-repeated views and deserves to be quoted at length. 'Thirty years ago', he says, 'probably not more than one-third of the people of this country consumed animal food more than once a week. Now, nearly all of them eat it, in meat or cheese or butter, once a day. This has more than doubled the average consumption of animal food in this country . . . The leap which the consumption of meat took in consequence of the general rise of wages in all branches of trade and employment, could not have been met without foreign supplies, and these could not have been secured except by such a rise in price as fully paid the risk and cost of transport. The additional price on the home-produce was all profit to the landed interests of this country.'[34] Before considering further the nature of these changes, it is worth examining how the disturbance in the relative values of farm products has usually been treated.

The accident of the long-delayed date when national agricultural statistics were first collected has imparted a somewhat false sense of discontinuity in agriculture about 1870. Many authorities take 1870 as the first year in which the statistics are reasonably complete and reliable, and many of them start with this date when tracing the development of present-day agriculture. As a result, the early 1870s are often made to appear as the high-water mark of the 'Golden Age' as regards cereal acreages and production. The increased concern with livestock production from 1873, or '75, or '79 (the utter lack of agreement about the onset of the Great Depression in agriculture itself suggests that the change was not sudden, but part of a cumulative process), has thus been exaggerated at the expense of the more gradual, but fundamental, shift in the pattern of farming from the 1850s. That the alteration in the balance of prices could be and was met by adjustments within mixed farming systems, and only at comparatively late dates by a switch to the grassland production of livestock, has tended to conceal the extent of the transition. The years 1870–3 might more properly be regarded as marked by the final wave, apart from the brief surge in 1878, of high prices for grain and hence big acreages of cereals.

Some recent writers, notably M. Olsen and C. C. Harris in the *Quarterly Journal of Economics* for 1959,[35] deny the growing emphasis on livestock as the profitable end of farming during the 1850s and '60s, and stress the importance of wheat. Their conclusions are based largely on the post-1866 acreage statistics, which cannot of themselves reveal which were the most profitable enterprises in close-knit farming systems, nor even which products were destined for sale and which for farm consumption, nor point to the considerable year-to-year changes in output per acre. The acreage statistics seem to have diverted attention from changes in production which took place without correspondingly large changes in land use. Since there was no clear increase of rotation grass and only a steady, slow expansion of permanent pasture during the '70s, the growing importance of livestock has been minimized.[36] Yet the value of the gross output of United Kingdom agriculture, as recalculated from E. M. Ojala's figures by T. W. Fletcher, was

	1867–9	1870–6
Arable products	£104·17 million	£94·99 million
Livestock products	£126·76 million	£154·87 million[37]

Earlier estimates of cereal acreages collected by Lawes and Gilbert[38] and Drescher,[39] and the figures of 'British corn sold' from 1849 to '72 given by Hasbach[40] show that the peak of arable expansion in the early 1870s was a temporary upswing after a contraction which had begun to set in during the later '50s. The increase in the total cultivated area of England and Wales which is usually said to have occurred between 1851 and '71 is not necessarily inimical to the view that the cereal acreage, especially the wheat acreage, was at its peak in the mid-1850s. In 1868 Lawes and Gilbert referred to 'the general opinion ... that the area under wheat has diminished during the last 15 or 20 years', and agreed that this was the case, especially in Scotland and Ireland.[41] All the signs point to a contraction of the wheat acreage in the less suitable northern and western areas, including parts of England, during those years, while there is additional confirmation that arable clays in England were being laid down to permanent pasture in the mid-1860s, as might be expected from the movement of wheat prices.[42] Olsen and Harris, taking the opposite view, say that 'from the attention lavished on the repeal of the Corn Laws one might assume that all that was important in British agriculture ended in 1846. But it would be more appropriate to say that the downfall of British agriculture began, not in 1846, but in 1873.'[43] Disregarding the emotive word 'downfall', it can be shown that after the Repeal the altered relative value of wheat and livestock products, due to imports which prevented a rise in the price of wheat, the growth of population, and rising real incomes of which an increasing proportion was spent on livestock products, led to considerable modifications in the structure of farming.

IV

Greater production of livestock was attained primarily by increasing output from arable farms. In the 1850s and '60s stall-feeding and yard-feeding of cattle was intensified in mixed farming regions, and spread into districts such as the dairying parts of Cheshire and Gloucestershire, where it was hitherto unknown, on to chalk and limestone uplands where until the 1840s sheep had been almost the only stock, and into parts of Cornwall and Cumberland where the entire dependence had previously been on grain.[44] The spread of mixed farming and high feeding from its original homes in eastern England and on the chalk and limestone uplands was stimulated by the development of artificial fertilizers which were important to the root-break, and by the completion of a railway network by which oilcake and artificials could be carried quickly and cheaply all over the country. It was soon realized that yard- and stall- or box-feeding enabled more and better manure to be collected, and fatstock to be produced in more rapid succession than did feeding in the fields. A further impetus to high feeding came from the high prices of the Crimean war, which prompted the conversion of large acreages of the remaining remote downland, which could not be reached economically with the dung cart, to arable land fertilized by folded flocks.[45] The extension of systems involving hurdled sheep and stall-fed cattle did not, however, mean the end of fattening on the better permanent pastures. Lavergne was exaggerating the trend of the times when in 1855 he bade 'adieu, then, to the pastoral scenes of which England was so proud'.[46]

Nevertheless, the increased importance of livestock on arable farms is obvious. This is brought out neatly when the principal items of expenditure and receipts for a 'mixed soil farm' of 590 acres in east Suffolk and a 'heavy land' arable farm of 230 acres in west Suffolk are compared for the periods 1839–44 and 1863–7. Both farms show the trend, and taking them together between the two periods receipts from wheat fell slightly, whereas receipts from barley, peas, oats and beans, cattle, sheep, and pigs all rose markedly. The bill for feed for livestock nearly trebled and became the largest single item of expenditure in the latter period.[47]

Since the price of wheat did not fall catastrophically until the late 1870s, the joint production of cereals and meat was favoured in the meantime: if the grain enterprise were *given* the manure from the livestock, it could pay its way. On the other hand there were serious obstacles in the way of increasing the grassland production of livestock. Pasture of a sufficient quality to fatten stock was too scarce to provide the whole supply of meat for which there was a demand and could not in any case have provided an all-year-round supply. The three- or four-year leys which contemporaries were able to sow were said to be only half as productive as the 'artificial' feeding on arable farms.[48] As Frere argued in 1860, the additional supply had to come from feeding in the stall or the yard, and the cost of this would *regulate the cost of the whole supply*'.[49] As grain-growing could no longer bear the cost of stall-feeding for the sake of the manure, 'artificial' feeding had to be made directly profitable, and with existing methods this meant that the price of beef would gradually have to rise. But as long as receipts from mixed farming as a whole were adequate, only the economically more astute farmers, in districts where grass grew well, would lay land down to grass and specialize in what were becoming the most profitable farm enterprises, finishing cattle and sheep on pasture with oilcake.[50] High feeding was not inflexible, since high inputs of oilcake were justified by reasonable prices for either grain or fatstock even if the price of the other happened to be low. The system was sufficiently viable, economically and technically, for the emphasis on the various products to be altered within wide limits before the grassland production of beef became a more attractive proposition for the arable farmer.

It might be expected that the increasing profitability of livestock would have led to a marked numerical increase of cattle and sheep. This, however, was offset by severe losses among breeding ewes in hill flocks during the hard weather of early 1860, by losses and liquidation sales in the summer droughts of 1864 and 1868, and by the rinderpest among cattle in 1865-6, which drew attention firmly to the short supply of fatstock. The demand for meat continued to grow, with the supply unable to keep pace.[51] In 1865 it was thought that meat would have become scarce sooner 'had it not been for the war with Russia in the Crimea, which caused corn to rise to a high price, and capital therefore to flow back into the hands of farmers, which enabled them to hold their live stock and increase it, instead of forcing it into market half-grown and half-fat at certain seasons that they might meet their fixed expenses'.[52] Prices and costs favoured the expansion of sheep more than cattle production, but diseased turnip crops and consequently dear feed were alleged to have brought about a decline in the average weight of sheep. It seems likely that cattle were retained on free-draining land where sheep might have brought greater financial rewards because they were more efficient at converting straw into manure. On upland farms the quantity of straw was embarrassing and the insistence of landowners that it should not be sold off the farm was thought a great nuisance.[53] Contemporaries were divided about whether or not sheep numbers rose during the '50s and '60s; the most cogent among them argued that a rise was taking place.[54] The official agricultural statistics for England and Wales between 1867 and 1875 show a rise of approximately 21 per cent in cattle numbers, some of which may have represented recovery from the plague of 1865-6, although a negligible increase in sheep. Earlier maturity, with a quicker turnover of stock and perhaps heavier killing-out weights of cattle, probably increased the quantity of meat marketed still further. The capital value of the livestock of the U.K. increased almost 80 per cent between 1853 and 1878 according to Caird.[55]

Prices moved strongly against wheat in the mid-1860s and at that time the poorer clayland arable was laid to grass in many districts. Much opinion was as yet against this expedient, although that enthusiastic M.F.H. the Duke of Beaufort remarked prophetically in 1861 that 'the next generation will have much more grass to ride over than the present'.[56] The change was slow. Many farmers regarded the wheat crop with an almost mystical reverence, and in public, at least, many of them took the price of wheat to be the index of agricultural fortunes. Frere in 1860 remarked, in rather muddled language, that 'though all are conscious that we can no longer rely on the corn-crops for paying the rent, perhaps none of us have been able sufficiently to throw off the trammels of custom and association, which led him to look for profit first to the stack rather than to the stall'.[57] A reason which was put forward in 1873 for the persistent emphasis on arable cultivation was that returns came in to the arable farmer throughout the year; 'in short, he can as it were, live from hand to mouth on a comparatively less capital. It is not so however with a general stock farmer, who has necessarily to lie [*sic*] out his capital for extended periods.'[58] Most farmers were in any case conditioned to act by the knowledge that a greater physical production of grain and meat could be obtained by feeding stock on arable farms than on grass, and they therefore sought the most profitable combination of stock and grain production.[59] In 1866 it was noted that 'the fact that grass will pay, and pay much better for manure applied, than corn at its present selling price, is as yet recognized by a limited number of the agriculturists of the country'; the same observation had been made in 1858, another year in which grain prices had been especially low.[60] Capital and manure continued to be spent on the ploughland at the expense of all but the best pastures. All except the supreme fattening pastures and the dairy pastures of Cheshire, which were properly drained and fertilized with bone dust, seemed to contemporaries less profitable than they might have been, through continual mowing and depasturing by dairy cows and young growing stock which took more out of the land than they returned in manure. Such pastures were thought to be in a gradually deteriorating state.[61]

Conversion of arable land to permanent pasture was probably delayed by the rise of grain prices to a peak in the early 1870s, but by this time informed opinion was in favour of fattening stock on grass and finishing the beasts with oilcake. This ensured that the pastures were adequately manured, and besides being a cheaper mode of production than yard- or stall-feeding enabled the fatstock to be sold in June or July, when the price of beef was higher than at the end of summer. 'The great difficulty', as it was seen in February 1872, 'is in making a beginning. The routine of years, possibly handed down for generations, cannot be broken through without a pang; but such pangs seldom outlive the first favourable balance-sheet, and it may be confidently stated that for some time past the farmers who have made most money are those who have paid as much attention to the improvement of their grass as to the growth of fine crops of corn or roots.'[62] Even later the trend was on occasion reversed for a brief spell, but the successive peaks of wheat and barley prices and acreages were lower and lower in the '70s and were looked on as transient. For example, at Aldbourne, Wiltshire, where in 1878 'corn growing superseded the making of meat', this was regarded as 'a state of things which cannot last long',[63] and indeed it did not last, for this was where Henry Wilson allowed a large acreage to go down to grass for the stock in which he was dealing, and where as a result the hamlet of Snap was eventually deserted.

There are signs that the growing profitability of mixed farming and the weakening position of the specialist cereal grower were not without influence on the size and type of farm holdings. The census returns of 1851 and '61 show a decrease of 6,132 farms below 300 acres, and an increase of 229 in those between 300 and 1,000 acres, for the ten very diverse counties for which figures are available for both dates. This change was explained as the engulfing of the smaller holdings, which had been occupied by men of little capital, 'who were very much dependent upon corn crops for their living, and, at the present prices of grain . . . not having stock to back them up, cannot make farming remunerative'.[64] In Cumberland in 1874 the growing number of livestock was attributed to the improved quality of the pastures more than to the increased acreage of grass, although many clayland farms which a few years earlier were heavily cropped to afford a precarious livelihood had been drained and converted into good grazing farms.[65]

V

High feeding had been so much extolled as the salvation of the farmer at mid-century (even Fred Vincy in *Middlemarch* was supposed to have written on the 'Cultivation of Green Crops and the Economy of Cattle Feeding')[66] that the shift of advanced opinion in favour of grassland fattening by the early 1870s comes as some surprise. According to Clapham, although lease covenants were in practice winked at, cropping changed in no essential way between 1850 and 1886.[67] But the agitation for more flexible rotations was so strong in this period that had lease covenants been so uniformly a dead letter, there would surely have been major cropping changes. In 1863 the [London] Farmers' Club was discussing how to meet the growing demand for meat and wool, 'without materially disarranging our order of management, so objectionable to land-agents'.[68] The summer droughts of the following year and of 1868, when the root-crops were severely damaged, brought home the need for freedom to amend cropping plans to meet contingencies of this sort,[69] quite apart from the desirability of tailoring rotations to suit the trends of prices. The agitation against cropping restrictions, although perhaps as Professor Ashworth claims in part a rationalization of antagonism to the continued political influence of land-owners,[70] was underpinned by genuine economic considerations. It seems that the growing incentive to produce livestock could account for much of the uneasiness in landlord–tenant relations, in particular the demands for freedom to alter cycles of fodder crops and to insert catch crops of cereals, according to the swaying state of the markets, and for more livestock housing, without which no big increase of stock was possible.

With rising livestock prices as the attraction, fodder crops were at first extended at the expense of grain. On the clays the mangel acreage increased throughout the 1850s, but by 1865 farmers in many clayland districts were finding it cheaper to feed stock on purchased grain than to grow roots.[71] In Worcestershire in 1867 mangels were still being extended on the clays, 'from the high price of meat', and it was observed of Cumberland in 1874 that 'the majority of skilled agriculturists do not go in solely for producing wheat; they would much rather sow the land with oats and barley than forgo the turnip crop, which is now looked on as the mainstay of arable farming'.[72] But in the drier eastern counties, where roots, although more difficult to grow, occupied a larger proportion of each farm than in the west, the root-break had come to be viewed with a jaundiced eye by the mid-1870s. By that time, as Lawes showed, stock could beyond doubt be fattened more cheaply on grain and cut-straw than on roots. The insistence of landowners that 25 per cent of the farm acreage must be kept under roots, according to the dictates of the four-course system, was a source of some bitterness.[73]

VI

The retention of mixed farming systems in which livestock were replacing grain as the most profitable elements had in the 1850s and '60s been a reasonable adaptation to prices, which favoured now the one side, now the other, while gradually swinging farther and farther to the livestock side. Mixed farming was less well suited to the conditions of the '70s. The fall in the price of wheat was uneven and the temporary peak of the Franco-Prussian war period dissuaded grain-conscious farmers from a wholehearted change to fatstock production on grass, but after 1873 hesitation in following the trend of the previous twenty years evaporated. However, the persistence so late with cereal growing under the shelter of mixed farming and high feeding must have intensified the distress when bad harvests and the landslide in grain prices occurred at the end of the '70s. Until then, since mixed farming's strength lay in stabilizing income through the sale of several commodities, short-term, out-of-phase fluctuations in the prices of its various products could be accommodated. The collapse of grain prices and thus one whole side of the system was needed to effect the break-up of mixed farming. Even so, as has been shown from the income tax assessments, the rise in rent between 1851–2 and 1878–9 had been greater in the pastoral north and west and in the grazing counties than in the arable east of England. Indeed, in arable districts, especially on the chalk and sands of the drier counties where grass does not thrive and leys are difficult to establish, and above all on the poor clays where expenditure by landowners may have been highest, there may have been a fall in real rent over these years.[74] This is a final indication that profits from livestock rather than grain had become increasingly the basis of agricultural prosperity. The structural changes in English agriculture during the Great Depression, which made livestock production far more prominent than cereal growing, had been foreshadowed by the transformation of mixed farming.

NOTES TO CHAPTER 9

1. I am indebted to J. R. Bellerby and J. W. Y. Higgs for commenting on a draft of this paper, which was read at the December 1961 conference of the British Agricultural History Society.
2. Most notably *English Farming Past and Present* (1912).
3. T. W. Fletcher, 'Lancashire Livestock Farming during the Great Depression', *Agric. Hist. Rev.*, IX (1961), pp. 17–42, and 'The Great Depression of English Agriculture 1873–1896', *Econ. Hist. Rev.*, 2nd ser., XIII (1961), pp. 417–32.
4. J. R. Bellerby, 'National and Agricultural Income 1851', *Economic Journal*, LXIX (1959), p. 103.
5. R. E. Prothero (Lord Ernle), *The Pioneers and Progress of English Farming* (1888), p. 106. See also J. H. Clapham, *An Economic History of Modern Britain*, II, p. 278; J. R. T. Hughes, *Fluctuations in Trade, Industry, and Finance* (1960), p. 224; William Ashworth, *An Economic History of England: 1870–1939* (1960), pp. 47–8. On the other hand O. R. McGregor has recently asserted that rotations were 'unalterable' and 'majestically though profitably insensitive to shifting market demands'—Introduction, Part II, p. CXVIII, to Lord Ernle, *English Farming Past and Present*, 6th edn., 1961.
6. Philip Pusey, 'On the Progress of Agricultural Knowledge during the last Four Years', *Journ. Roy. Agric. Soc. Eng.* [hereafter *JRASE*], III (1842), p. 205.
7. J. A. S. Watson and M. E. Hobbs, *Great Farmers* (1951), p. 90.
8. A. H. John, 'The Course of Agricultural Change, 1660–1760', in L. S. Pressnell (ed.), *Studies in the Industrial Revolution* (1960), p. 146, n. 1.
9. Pusey, *loc. cit.*, p. 205.
10. Viscount Astor and B. Seebohm Rowntree, *Mixed Farming and Muddled Thinking*, n.d., pp. 55, 58.
11. W. T. Layton and G. Crowther, *An Introduction to the Study of Prices* (1938), p. 75, n. 1. I am indebted to Professor A. H. John for a copy of his graph of wheat, barley, and beef prices from 1816 to 1870.
12. C. S. Read, 'Farming of Oxfordshire', *JRASE*, XV (1854), p. 258.
13. J. A. Clarke, 'Farming of Lincolnshire', *JRASE*, XII (1851), pp. 398–9.
14. Pusey, *loc. cit.*, p. 206; James Caird, *English Agriculture in 1850–51* (1852), p. 100.
15. G. Buckland, 'Farming of Kent', *JRASE*, VI (1846), p. 273.
16. R. W. Corringham, 'Agriculture of Nottinghamshire', *JRASE*, VI (1846), pp. 20–1.
17. W. Dickinson, 'On the Farming of Cumberland', *JRASE*, XIII (1852), pp. 256–7.
18. Philip Pusey, 'Some Introductory Remarks on the present State of Agriculture as a Science in England'. *JRASE*, I (1840), p. 18; A. Huxtable, *The 'Present Prices'* (1850), p. 13.

19. W. Bearn, 'On the Farming of Northamptonshire', *JRASE*, XIII (1852), p. 71 (dated 23 February 1851).
20. Pusey, 1842, *loc. cit.*, p. 207.
21. This was stated categorically by T. J. Eliot, *The Land Question ... as illustrated by twenty-three years' experience on the Wilton House Home Farm*, n.d. [1884], esp. p. 37.
22. 'The Present Position of the British Farmer', *Farmer's Magazine*, 3rd ser., XXV (1864), p. 207; see also 'The Causes of the Decline in the Price of Corn', *Farmer's Magazine*, 3rd ser., XIII (1858), p. 251.
23. A. Simpson, 'High Farming with Profit', *Farmer's Magazine*, 3rd ser., XVIII (1860), p. 239.
24. 'The Present State and Prospects of the Farming Interest', *Farmer's Magazine*, 3rd ser., XXV (1864), p. 193; C. S. Read, 'Recent Improvements in Norfolk Farming', *JRASE*, XIX (1858), p. 271.
25. R. S. Skirving, 'Ten Years of East Lothian Farming'. *JRASE*, 2nd ser., I (1865), pp. 105–6.
26. Read, *loc. cit.*, p. 287.
27. P. H. Frere, 'On the Feeding of Stock', *JRASE*, XXI (1860), pp. 233–4.
28. See e.g. J. Coleman, 'The Breeding and Feeding of Sheep', *JRASE*, XXIV (1863), p. 623; 'Oilcake and Grain for Cattle', *Farmer's Magazine*, 3rd ser., XXV (1864), p. 216; H. Evershed, 'On Sheep', *JRASE*, 2nd ser., I (1865), pp. 332–5; 'Are the Present High Prices of Stock Likely to continue?', *Farmer's Magazine*, 3rd ser., XXX (1866), p. 104. The opposite view taken by J. J. Mechi in 1867 and quoted by T. W. Fletcher, *Econ. Hist. Rev.*, 2nd ser., XIII (1961), p. 422, is exceptional, as Mechi's views tended to be.
29. A. D. Hall, *A Pilgrimage of British Farming 1910–1912* (1914), pp. 83–4.
30. *High Farming, under liberal covenants ...* (1849), pp. 6–7, 25–6.
31. See e.g. 'On the Peculiarities of the Management of Farms', *Farmer's Magazine*, XXII (1850), p. 396; 'The Wool Trade and Meat Trade—foreshadowing the change that must be made in our Agricultural System', *Farmer's Magazine*, 3rd ser., III (1853), pp. 8–9; C. S. Read, 'Farming of Oxfordshire', *JRASE*, XV (1854), p. 256; 'Shall we cultivate corn or cattle?', *Farmer's Magazine*, 3rd ser., XIX (1861), p. 411; H. S. Thompson, 'Agricultural Progress and the Royal Agricultural Society', *JRASE*, XXV (1864), p. 35: 'The breeding and feeding of livestock have thus become such profitable operations that the growth of corn, *as a sequence to stock-farming*, has also become profitable, even at present prices.' A Cumberland Landowner, *A Few Hints to Landowners & Cultivators, Horn or Corn. Which pays best* (1873), *passim*; T. Farrall, 'A Report on the Agriculture of Cumberland, chiefly with regard to the Production of Meat', *JRASE*, 2nd ser., X (1874), p. 429.
32. J. Caird, *Our Daily Food* (1868), p. 33.
33. J. H. Clapham, *op. cit.*, II, p. 278; J. A. Clarke, 'Practical Agriculture', *JRASE*, 2nd ser., XIV (1878), p. 476.
34. J. Caird, 'General View of British Agriculture', *JRASE*, 2nd ser., XIV (1878), p. 289.
35. 'Free Trade in "Corn" ', in LXXIII, pp. 145–6, 165–8. For another account based on the acreage figures and minimizing the importance of livestock before the mid-1870s see J. T. Coppock, 'The Changing Arable in England and Wales 1870–1956', *Tijdschrift voor Economische en Sociale Geografie*, L (1959) pp. 122–3.
36. It was generally agreed in the 1860s that most of the increased production of meat came from turnips, clover, or sainfoin on land where intervening grain crops were taken and not from grass. See e.g. 'W.W.G.',

'The Outcry about Meat', *Farmer's Magazine*, 3rd ser., xxviii (1865), p. 134.

37. T. W. Fletcher, *Econ. Hist Rev.*, 2nd ser., xiii (1961), p. 432.

38. J. B. Lawes and J. H. Gilbert, 'On the Home Produce... of Wheat, 1852–3 to 1879–80', *JRASE*, 2nd ser., xvi (1880), table V.

39. L. Drescher, 'The Development of Agricultural Production in Great Britain and Ireland from the Early Nineteenth Century', *Manchester School Econ. & Soc. Studies*, xxiii (1955), Graph 1, p. 155.

40. W. Hasbach, *A History of the English Agricultural Labourer* (1920), p. 255, quoting *Statistical Abstracts Report*, xx (1858–72).

41. J. B. Lawes and J. H. Gilbert, 'On the Home Produce... of Wheat', *JRASE*, 2nd ser., iv (1868), pp. 365, 390.

42. Anon., 'On the Price of Butcher-meat, and the Increase of Home Supplies of Cattle and Sheep', *Jnl. of Agric.*, xxv, n.s. (1865–6), p. 362; W. J. Moscrop, 'A Report on the Farming of Leicestershire', *JRASE*, 2nd ser., ii (1866), p. 326; H. Evershed, 'Agriculture of Staffordshire', *JRASE*, 2nd ser., v (1869), p. 268, and 'Agriculture of Hertfordshire', *JRASE*, xxv (1864), p. 283.

43. Olsen and Harris, *loc cit.*, p. 168.

44. L. de Lavergne, *The Rural Economy of England, Scotland, and Ireland* (1855), p. 185; Read, *loc. cit.*, p. 222; L. H. Ruegg, 'Farming of Dorsetshire', *JRASE*, xv (1854), p. 412.

45. See e.g. J. B. Spearing, 'On the Agriculture of Berkshire', *JRASE*, xxi (1860), p. 16.

46. Lavergne, *op. cit.*, pp. 54, 187.

47. Royal Commission on Agriculture, *Particulars of... Farm Accounts* (1896), pp. 167–8.

48. 'The Outcry about Meat', *Farmer's Magazine*, *loc. cit.*, p. 135.

49. Frere, *loc. cit.*, p. 234.

50. W. H. Heywood, 'The Comparative Profit from Making Cheese or Butter, Selling Milk, or Grazing', *JRASE*, 2nd ser., i (1865), pp. 342–3, considered grazing even more profitable than milk-producing. Country milking received a tremendous impulse, much of it lasting, when the rinderpest of 1865–6 half-emptied the London cow-houses, but the milk was diverted from the less profitable business of cheese or butter making and no great increase of cows was necessarily involved—J. C. Morton, 'Town Milk', *JRASE*, 2nd ser., iv (1868), pp. 95–7.

51. On the increased demand and high prices in the fatstock markets see Robert Herbert, 'Statistics of Livestock for Consumption in the Metropolis', *JRASE*, xix (1858), pp. 496–500, and annually thereafter.

52. 'The Outcry about Meat', *Farmer's Magazine*, *loc. cit.*, p. 134.

53. Clement Cadle, *On the Management of a Breeding Herd of Cattle, on an Arable Farm...* (1863), pp. 3–4.

54. W. Wright, 'On the Improvements in the Farming of Yorkshire', *JRASE*, xxii (1861), pp. 129–30; J. D. Dent, 'Agricultural Notes on the Census of 1861', *JRASE*, xxv (1864), p. 321.

55. Caird (1878), *loc. cit.*, p. 290.

56. James Stratton, *A History of the Wiltshire Strattons*, n.d., p. 79 n.

57. Frere, *loc. cit.*, p. 219.

58. A Cumberland Landowner, *op. cit.*, p. 11.

59. See e.g. 'Stock versus Corn; or rather the most profitable conduct of farming', *Farmer's Magazine*, 3rd ser., xxiii (1863), p. 142.

60. Moscrop, *loc. cit.*, p. 337; H. Tanner, 'The Agriculture of Shropshire', *JRASE*, xix (1858), p. 38.

61. Anon., 'On the Price of Butcher-meat', *loc. cit.*, pp. 363–4; J. C. Morton,

'On the Management of Grass Lands', *Jnl. of the Bath & West Soc.*, XIII (1865), pp. 62–4, 68–9.
62. H. S. Thompson, 'On the Management of Grass Land...', *JRASE*, 2nd ser., VIII (1872), p. 179.
63. *Agric. Gazette*, n.s., VIII, 18 November 1878, p. 463, quoted by F. M. L. Thompson, 'Agriculture since 1870', *V.C.H. Wilts.*, IV (1959), p. 97.
64. Dent, *loc. cit.*, pp. 323–4.
65. Farrall, *loc. cit.*, p. 407.
66. George Eliot, *Middlemarch* (1947 edn.), p. 889.
67. Clapham, *op. cit.*, II, pp. 275–6.
68. 'Stock versus Corn', *loc. cit.*, pp. 142–3.
69. J. C. Morton, 'Some of the Agricultural Lessons of 1868', *JRASE*, 2nd ser., V (1869), pp. 54–5.
70. Ashworth, *op. cit.*, p. 50.
71. P. D. Tuckett, 'On the Modifications of the Four-course...', *JRASE*, XXI (1860), p. 262; H. Evershed, 'On Sheep', *JRASE*, 2nd ser., I (1865), p. 335.
72. C. Cadle, 'The Agriculture of Worcestershire', *JRASE*, 2nd ser., III (1867), p. 452; Farrall, *loc. cit.*, p. 407.
73. F. Clifford, 'The Labour Bill in Farming', *JRASE*, 2nd ser., XI (1875), pp. 123–4, and citing J. D. Lawes in *JRASE*, 2nd ser., IX (1873), pp. 373–4.
74. Clapham, *op. cit.*, II, pp. 278–9; Caird (1878), *loc. cit.*, p. 315.

10. The Agricultural Labour Market in England, 1793–1872

Some few years since every department of trade was not only in a flourishing, but in an inflated condition . . . and so, tempted by higher wages, the agricultural labourer migrated from the villages to large centres of population, where they at least got a considerably large nominal increase of wages. Consequent upon this the farm labourers rapidly decreased, and as labour, like every other commodity, is regulated by supply and demand, wages gradually rose to the extent of 25 per cent. In this state of things agitators sprung up in every district as thick as blackberries . . .

James Buckman, *The Agricultural Crisis*, 1879, p. 10

This essay presents a highly compressed analysis of the market for agricultural labour from the 1790s to the emergence of Arch's union in 1872. In particular an attempt is made to modify the orthodox view that during the third quarter of the nineteenth century agriculture was characterized by an over-supply of labour, and to examine the implications for the history of the farm worker's welfare of a slightly more sophisticated model of the labour market. Instead of the customary view, and in amplification of some suggestions previously made in print,[1] it is urged that a crucial change from conditions of glut to a partial, but structural, shortage of labour took place during the 1850s. The effects of this transformation on social attitudes towards labour, on employment policies, on the rewards of farm work, and on labour agitation and early trades union activity are discussed.

Existing work in this field is, in the writer's view, too much taken up with incident rather than with a thoroughgoing analysis of the supply, demand and rewards of labour. Failure to appreciate the intense seasonality of farm work has clouded assessments of long-run

P

trends in the labour market. The lack of a systematic approach means, for example, that there is much more information to hand on the events of 1830 or 1834 and of 1872 than on the whole of the intervening span. Furthermore, although in the third quarter of the century there were both 'optimists' and 'pessimists' about the standard of living of the agricultural labourer, subsequent historians have almost invariably adhered to the latter camp. It is not the intention here to raise up an 'optimist' school, yet even a detached observer must deplore, first, the insistence that the apparent absence of collective bargaining was in itself a sign of unrelievedly poor conditions for farm hands, and second, the exaggerated concern with the details of the welfare of labour to the exclusion of its function as a factor of production. Some improvement in welfare might, *a priori*, be expected as a result of the prosperity and demand for foodstuffs in the industrial sector during the mid-Victorian boom, but labour historians do not seem to have gone out of their way to seek evidence of such an amelioration. Alternatively, no coherent explanation has been put forward of the supposed failure of the rising return to agriculture to reach the labourers. All that is available are utterly sombre pictures of the labourer's life, painted from instances of distress and victimization which were on the decrease and which in any case were restricted to particular situations and seasons. In the conventional view better conditions came only with the mushrooming of Arch's union in 1872, an event which has itself been inadequately explained.

I

During the Revolutionary and Napoleonic wars the agricultural economy was disturbed by a scarcity of labour. The quantity and quality of labour were both affected. The armed forces and the war industries drew away from land work a large body of men, including a disproportionate share of the young and able-bodied. According to J. G. Cornish, for example, the tradition persisted on the Berkshire Downs a century later of the 'petticoat harvest' during the Napoleonic wars, when the women got in most of the grain because the men had gone to war.[2] According to John Duncumb at the time, the male population was 'so much thinned by the levies and operations of war, that the farmer in particular, has but little opportunity of selection'.[3] Contemporary accounts confirm that hiring agreements made at the mop fairs were more and more often broken by men who having obtained the farmer's shilling 'earnest money' would run off to take the king's shilling too, or to enter a better-paid job with another farmer or in a non-farm occupation. The canal mania of the early 1790s was another heavy drain on labour. A canal promoter in 1793 felt obliged to defend canal building against the objection raised in parliament to 'the taking off the Hands in time of Harvest destroying the Cultivation of the Land. From the Immense Numbers of Canals now coming on and the not only absence of a Multitude of the Labouring Class abroad in the War but the vast suppos'd Diminution that there will arise from the Destruction in it, a great Scarcity of Hands for the Cultivation will be found at the End.' The promoter observed in reply that the Irish annually supplied many harvest hands, 'from Chester to Dover', and navvies for canals all over England, and recommended encouraging the supply, which was in any case cheaper than English labour.[4]

At the same time investment in agriculture and the demand for agricultural labour were mounting in response to rising farm product prices. Hands were needed to reshape the physical capital of farming—hedges, roads, buildings, drains—after each of a growing number of enclosure acts; to push the margin of cultivation up the hillsides and on to the commons, sometimes to places which no later ploughing campaign has reached; and to extend the growing of labour-intensive fodder crops in attempts to offset the ploughing of permanent grass. According to Robert Southey, for instance, the harvest on recently broken-up downland in Hampshire had by the earliest years of the nineteenth century come to depend on a seasonal influx of workers from the western clothing districts.[5]

In consequence money wages in agriculture rose,[6] and although there was distress when contracting work opportunities and scarcity prices for provisions coincided in a few bad winters, on balance real wages rose too. The rising cost of labour was sufficient to prompt farmers to take every advantage of the limited possibilities of mechanization. Winnowing, chaff-cutting and above all threshing machines were quickly adopted during the war, although as yet haymaking and harvesting defied the inventor and at these seasons any extra labour was sure of a welcome. Troops stationed as far apart as Hampshire and Cumberland were gladly taken on to help reap the wheat. In the latter county a company of Welsh militia quartered in Whitehaven, mostly rural labourers in origin, 'were permitted to go into the country during harvest, and to use the scythes they providently brought with them. Wages being high through a deficiency of hands, they cut a considerable breadth of corn on various farms.'[7] Had so many harvests of the war years not been notoriously scanty the labour troubles of farmers might have interfered seriously with output. As it was, shortages at hay-time and harvest put the men for the time being in a strong bargaining position and enabled them to force up wages and also (as in one of the following instances) to enjoy their leisure preference: 'I spoke to your Lordship at Cambridge for some money to pay the Workers I wish to keep . . . ', wrote the Earl of Hardwick's agent at Wimpole, Cambridgeshire, to his employer on 24 April 1797, 'as your Lordship knows that when the Hay Begins we can have no men but at high weages', and again on 8 September, 'we have Reather been Skearse of hands in this Country   the Consequence was that the men have behaved very badlie in many places   there went 14 of your Lordships men one Afternoon of the field to the Alehouse altho I desired them not—it was a very fine afternoon and they had not don so weel as I would have wished them some times before that . . . I have never had so troublesom a hay and Harvest . . . one Reason . . . was that the men that was early engadged for the harvest was at the last Years price   but they afterwards rose to four Guneas and their Board   the Common price $2\frac{1}{2}$ Guneas and their board.'[8]

In this way the dichotomy in the employment available through the year in arable farming was accentuated, especially in the newly reclaimed and comparatively unpopulated districts. The main winter occupation, threshing, was becoming mechanized, reducing the demand for labour at the slackest season, although while the war lasted this does not seem to have caused much unemployment, presumably because the machines had been introduced chiefly on the large farms of the newly reclaimed districts. The times of maximum demand, hay-time and harvest, saw exactly the reverse trend, the development of shortages which placed bargaining power on the men's side, although formal labour combinations failed to appear. This interpretation is strengthened in that the only significant reversal during the war period occurred with the Peace of Amiens (March 1802 to May 1803). There was then a backwash of servicemen seeking work and complaints arose at harvest-time in 1802 that the farmers were unwilling to employ the labour available. According to the generalized series of wages to hand, average weekly earnings did not fall during the Peace, although with the return of war a markedly steeper upward trend of wages is seen. Had grain prices not fallen from their 1801 heights, however, the Peace of Amiens might have been accompanied by severe distress for farm workers.[9]

II

The wartime reinforcement of the natural periodicity of arable farming was abruptly swept away in 1815. Four hundred thousand men from the armed forces and another considerable body from ancillary occupations and industries geared to war production were thrown on to the labour market. The resultant dislocation in 1815–16, at a time of wider economic disruption, is well known. There was severe unemployment; unprecedented numbers sought poor relief; there were riots in East Anglia.

The experiences of rural labourers during the following twenty years are the best-known of the century, owing to the studies which have been made of the post-war impact of the Speenhamland system, the riots and machine-breaking of 1830, the Tolpuddle martyrdom, and the New Poor Law. During this period agricultural output kept pace with the substantial growth of population and hence of demand for foodstuffs. This was achieved partly by a greater input of labour, but mostly by a rise in productivity per man, presumably as a result of better methods such as the application of bone-dust fertilizer and the use of improved, iron implements. Whereas the per acre yield of wheat, for instance, rose by 16 per cent from 1815/19 to 1832/6, the labour force in agriculture grew at most by 2·7 per cent.[10] The increased employment was insufficient fully to absorb the continued growth of a remarkably static rural population, and the emergence of a serious, although mainly seasonal, surplus of labour which depressed the average annual wage to distressingly low levels hardly needs to be rehearsed. Arable farmers trapped by a faster fall in product prices than in costs became intent on reducing wage-rates, so that the growth of the rural population seems to have produced a less than proportionate increase in the demand for food, and hence (coupled with increased productivity per head) in the demand for labour to grow it. The problem and the resultant strain on systems of poor law administration was most severe in the south and east, where the gradual extension of the use of threshing machines, although slowed by the cheapness of labour for threshing by flail, enabled farmers to stand off more and more of their men for longer and longer through the winter, just when the men's needs for fuel, food and clothing were greatest.

Ironically, labour tended to remain in short supply in arable districts at times of cultivation and more especially at haymaking and harvest, including the lesser—but locally important—harvests of hops and apples. The reclamation of arable land in the Fens and on the Wolds during and after the 1830s produced a heavy demand for labour which the gang system was developed to supply, particularly after 1834 when out-relief largely ceased and the earnings of women and children were essential if family incomes were to be maintained. The gang system was also partly the outcome of the shortage of dwellings in newly reclaimed areas, a deficiency which employers were reluctant to remedy by building new cottages and thereby risking some future increase in the poor rates of their own parishes. Many landowners and farmers, not only in these districts, actively discouraged settlement in 'closed' parishes by pulling down cottages and obliging the inhabitants to congregate in neighbouring 'open' parishes. The cheapness of the hands recruited by the gang-masters in these pools of labour, to work miles away in 'closed' parishes, doubtless reduced the incentive to mechanize cultivation. And the shortage of labour at hay-time and harvest was offset by an annual influx from Wales, Scotland and above all Ireland, so that the wages of the English farm worker did not rise in due proportion to his seasonal scarcity.

On a closer view the twenty years after Waterloo are seen to be marked by a series of slumps and recoveries within the general deflation. During the spells of very low prices for farm products farmers tried to economize the volume of labour they employed, and more strenuously the rate at which they paid for labour. The Select Committee on Agriculture of 1833 was convinced by the detailed evidence that farmers had 'lately' spent less on labour for cultivation. Bargaining power lay in the farmers' hands and some of them were in addition able to exploit the 'roundsman' system (whereby men on parish relief were sent round to work for each ratepayer in turn) at the expense of non-farming ratepayers. Consequently employment was comparatively high at the peaks of prices in 1818, 1824 and in the recovery of the late 1830s and early 1840s, but was at a low ebb in the troughs, such as 1815–16, 1822–3, in the late 1820s, and during the mid-century slump. These movements are mirrored to some extent in the index of average weekly earnings. But the ceaseless growth of the rural population ate away the long-run expansion in employment opportunities and ensured that even at the best of times some men were stood off in winter.

Some landowners, motivated by humanity or by a desire to avert public disorder, attempted to counter the cycles in the employment offered by farmers. Thus in the early 1830s John Arkwright learnt

that employing 150 men on an irrigation project on his Herefordshire estate was 'an excellent way of finding winter work for my
Neighbours' and John Biddulph, another Herefordshire landowner,
confessed to his diary, 'I most heartily wish all our improvements
were finished, as they are dreadfully Expensive, but the labouring
Class must be Emp^d. Especially in the Winter Months, or they will
Poach or go upon the Parish.' In Nottinghamshire the large landowners deliberately engaged men on road-mending and land-drain-
age when trade was slack.[11] These efforts could, however, only
scratch the surface of a problem which tended to worsen with the
growth of the rural population and the rise in *per capita* output
in agriculture. The recurrent spells of winter unemployment, although they varied in scale, duration and (according to the price of
bread and the inclemency of the season) in impact, were marked by
rick-burnings and other disordered symptoms of protest—before
and long after the most serious of the outbreaks, the 'perfect fury of
fires' in 1830.[12]

In the early 1840s the national press again reported three or four
fires each week, 'not as formerly until the spring only, but far into
July and August'.[13] There were more open manifestations of discontent. At a meeting near Blandford, Dorset, in November 1838 a
'working man' called Philips had attacked the farmers for oppress-
ing their labourers. One thousand labourers met at Wootton Bassett,
Wiltshire, in January 1846, 500 near Gosport, Hampshire, in February, some Dorset labourers addressed a protest letter to a local
landowner in May, while occasional bold spirits, among them Joseph
Arch's father, brought retribution on their heads by refusing, stub-
bornly and perhaps irrationally, to sign their masters' petitions
against repealing the Corn Laws.[14] These murmurings and their
sympathetic airing in *The Times* in 1846 brought no redress. It
seemed inevitable that the return to agricultural labour as a factor
of production should be low, as indeed by later standards it was,
just as its use by farmers was by later standards lavish. The position,
at least throughout southern England, between 1815 and the 1840s
and 1850s was seldom very different from that described at a West
Herefordshire Agricultural Society meeting in 1842: 'we have a
sufficient number of labourers resident in every parish for all the
agricultural work in it (harvest perhaps excepted)'.[15]

III

The first major reversal of this situation was the shortage of farm

labour produced in many districts by the sudden demand for navvies to build the railways in the 1840s. This shortage was of course
felt mainly at hay-time and harvest. As an illustration, at the end of
July 1846 much hay was still standing in Herefordshire because of
'the difficulty of procuring labourers at almost any price ... as
much as seven shillings per acre has been asked by mowers, the
ordinary rates being 3s. 4d., 3s. 8d., and 4s.'[16] Nevertheless, winter
employment was still slack and the shortages passed with the railway construction slump. Employment and wage-rates fell during
the agricultural depression at mid-century; there was a spate of
rick-firing and, with provisions cheap, a brief resurgence of the
practice of boarding labourers in the farmhouses.

Lasting and general change awaited the 1850s and 1860s. Only
then did 'improved cultivation, more general and thorough management of root-crops, the extension of sheep-farming, and winter
feeding of stock ... increase employment' sufficiently, when added
to the forces of migration and emigration, to disperse the glut of
farm labour.[17] C. S. Read was convinced that the intensification of
farming methods and not the decrease of population accounted for
the scarcity of labourers which developed in parts of west Norfolk.[18]
The enlarged demand for labour to hoe and lift potatoes and turnips, to mow the hay and reap the grain, was met by a revived
growth of the gang system in some intensively farmed arable districts such as the Fens.

The growing demand for farm labour and the resultant shortages of hands at this period have not been widely acknowledged.
The change was not dramatic, although the Crimean war years
represent a sharp peak in the average earnings in agriculture, and
the shortage admittedly did not apply with equal force to all types
of farm worker. The absolute decline in the rural population is however well known, but does not fully reflect the alteration in the
market for agricultural workers. By 1850 the railway network was
essentially complete and had begun to exert its influence on the
sedentary population of the southern half of England. In the Midlands, for example, a fall in population first became evident in
parishes contiguous to the main line of the London and North-
Western Railway. Migration to the towns speeded up and took
place over longer distances. The gold rushes stimulated emigration,
the expansion of trade in the larger towns, the multiplication of
mills, breweries, sewage works and paving improvement and gas
companies in the market towns all encouraged townward migration.
All these commercial concerns, together with the police, the rail-

ways and the army, which recruited from farm workers, offered higher wages than the land. The rise in real wages in industry pulled up in absolute terms the floor of low wages in agriculture, although farm wages remained on average about 46 per cent of industrial wages.[19] The inducement to leave agriculture, despite the improvements, therefore remained considerable for those young men who possessed the good eyesight and steady hands needed for work at factory machines.

In 1851 the workforce of British agriculture was at its peak and agriculture was still the biggest employment industry, a position it had lost to both commerce-and-finance and domestic service by 1871. Although the country's population continued to rise, the 1861 census registered a reduction in the number of hired workers in agriculture (although there was no corresponding fall in the number of farmers). The fall in the female workforce was greater than that of the male. Between 1851 and 1861, for the first time in the century apart from a fall of less than 1 per cent in Wiltshire between 1841 and 1851, the total population of five rural counties in the south and east fell, and the adult agricultural population fell in 17 counties. The exodus continued, more slowly, in the 1860s; it was largest from the grain-growing counties of the south and east and smallest from pastoral districts. The numbers of agricultural labourers, farm servants and shepherds in England at the censuses were:

1851	1,253,786
1861	1,188,786
1871	980,178

Even on the unlikely assumption that all casual labourers were employed in agriculture there would still have been a fall in the hired labour-force:

1851	1,578,370
1861	1,495,330
1871	1,489,634[20]

Since work was expanding in agriculture, a commentator on the 1861 census (to whose own Yorkshire parish supplementary Irish farm hands had to be brought in winter, whereas formerly the local labourers had been stood off at that season) could 'only conclude that the redundant agricultural population has been absorbed by manufacturing industry; and that those who remain are more

Q

efficient, better paid, and more fully employed than they were 10 years ago'.[21]

By the late 1850s the exodus was giving rise to serious apprehensions of a shortage which would be more permanent than the occasional embarrassment at haymaking and harvest. The impact was felt severely in the summer of 1859, when it was aggravated by a slackening in the annual immigration of Irishmen. The crops were gathered successfully but at an unprecedented cost. This shortage persisted beyond the summer. The following year the *Farmer's Magazine* drew incredulous attention to the first advertisements in Nottinghamshire and Sussex newspapers for ordinary farm hands, who were offered good wages and even cottages.[22]

IV

The threatened onset of a labour shortage had been accompanied by a chorus of declarations that the farm labourer deserved a better life, backed by action which dwarfed into insignificance earlier philanthropic efforts. The employing groups hastily adopted an attitude of enlightened self-interest so far as labour was concerned. Some parallel to this *volte-face* is to be seen in the interest which was shown in allotment schemes after the 1830 riots, which although it led to a substantial provision of allotments in eight counties had significantly faded once the threat of revolt receded and as the rural population continued unflaggingly to grow. With his new-found scarcity value from the 1850s the agricultural labourer was to find a renewed and less transient interest in his welfare.

This is not to take an over-cynical view of nineteenth-century welfare endeavours, for many Victorians unashamedly admitted their economic motive for improving the lot of their workmen. All-round betterment of labouring life came only with economic inducement—with the new belief that better-paid, better-fed, better-housed men were more profitable employees, and with the belief that concessions had to be made if the necessary labour force was to be held on the land. In Norfolk according to Miss Springall, 'at first farmers and landlords scarcely noticed the change in their labour supply, particularly if they could employ gangs, but by 1866 they were alarmed' and were complaining of the 'insubordination' which resulted from their competition for labour.[23] Where gangs were not customary the change was noticed earlier. 'Before we hear of a strike amongst agricultural labourers', the Lord Lieutenant of Herefordshire had implored the Agricultural Society of his county as early as 1853, 'let us do all we can to show them that we have their interest at heart—not screwing them down in wages, but allowing them to share in the prosperity that has dawned upon us; let us not be hard upon them now that prices are better (Hear, hear)', while a few months later the *Hereford Journal* thought it 'gratifying to find an increasing desire for ameliorating the wants and necessities of our labouring population extending itself through this county'.[24] Labour scarcity might bring some attempts to extract more work from the existing labour-force, but it seems that only in the presence of scarcity could the benefits which had formerly accrued, capriciously, to a few recipients of charity become part of the ordinary rewards of farm work for the many.

Whilst labour had been plentiful the landowner had often been held to be 'in duty bound to see as much labour employed on his estates as possible, without positive loss to himself or his tenants'.[25] Land improvement was much advocated as a means of creating employment for the poor. At that time the more thoughtful an observer was, the more pessimistic he was likely to be about such expedients. Thus in 1846 George Nicholls, the Poor Law commissioner, wrote, 'it may perhaps be said that the labourer's condition will depend upon the amount of his earnings, which in the long run will be governed by competition in the labour market... All our efforts for improving the condition of the working classes must be in subordination to this ruling principle, with the view of mitigating its intensity in particular instances, not of counteracting its general working.'[26] Writing in the gloomy first months of 1846 Nicholls thought that as the labouring population seemed continually to increase more intense competition for work would (and from his *laissez-faire* viewpoint should) force wages lower and lower. He was merely anxious that philanthropy should avert revolution. Individuals and agricultural societies were working in this direction, 'but what', T. D. Acland demanded of them in 1850, 'is a "coat, buttons, and framed testimonial of merit" in return for a life of labour? After all that palliatives can do, the questions remain, why are wages so low, and how are they to be raised? I know of only one answer—wages will rise when there is more work to be done or fewer hands in proportion to the work.'[27]

The relations between master and man, before Arch's unionism stirred up rancour and perquisites were cut in favour of a bigger wage in cash, were not uncommonly semi-patriarchal. Some farmers preferred to provide meals for their men rather than to raise cash wages when grain happened to be dear, and many paid their men during weather which made productive work impossible, or they kept the old men employed for more years than was strictly worth while. The intolerable aspect of this was that it depended on the employer's circumstances and whim and could not be relied on. Before the middle of the century the labourer might, too, if he were fortunately placed and sufficiently docile, receive a dole of soup, blankets, coal, and medical attention from the squire or his lady. The farmer who employed him might, or might not, propose that he receive a medal from the local agricultural society for a lifetime's work on the one farm or for raising a large family without recourse to public assistance. After mid-century, when the shortage of farm labour loomed, gestures of these kinds became more fashionable. The need for them became a common cry. After Archdeacon Freer had spoken at Hereford on the need to provide comfortable homes for labourers, for example, his seconder laid bare the motive: 'when labour was scarce the good workman would serve that master who took the greatest care of his moral and domestic comforts'. At Ledbury another speaker emphasized the need to make loyal subjects, good Christians—and better workmen.[28] The agricultural press became filled with expressions of this economic piety. At its most sophisticated the farmer's view was put by a speaker at the Norfolk Chamber of Agriculture who argued that young girls should not be employed as gang labourers since—'on principles of political economy'—the nation had an interest in their future well-being, just as it had in educating the farm hand well enough to keep accounts or to operate machinery.[29]

In some quarters the premises and measures of the benevolently inclined were resisted. Many farmers were enraged when Canon Girdlestone preached his sermon in March 1866 on the text 'behold the hand of the Lord is upon thy cattle', in which he pictured the cattle plague as divine retribution on the farmers of his north Devon parish for treating their men like the beasts of the field.[30] First-hand accounts of the employing class's attitude during the 1850s and 1860s are scarce, but A. G. Bradley, who could recall the 1860s, vividly claimed later that neither the most benevolent Liberal squire nor the most pious clergyman, and certainly no farmer, believed the prevailing low wages to be unreasonable. Bradley had automatically shared their view that farm wages should be unrelated to rent or profit levels and that a bare living wage, by the standards of the day, was all that the labourer had a right to expect. 'In short,' he wrote, 'they had to be kept in their place, though it wasn't always put so crudely as this, while the situation was, of course, mitigated by a vast amount of personal kindness and charity.'[31] But the rewards of labour were rising and despite resistance to their ultimate social and political implications so, too, attitudes to welfare were changing.

V

Much of the gradual shift in attitudes and in the arrangement of rewards for farm work becomes explicable in terms of the structure of the emerging labour scarcity. One of the commonest assumptions of agricultural history and agricultural policy is that industrialization most conveniently both initiates and requires a flow of labour from farm to factory. Industry needs this external source of hands; the level of earnings in agriculture depends on the scale of the exodus. Broadly speaking this analysis is reasonable, but the concept of an average annual surplus of labour in agriculture, involving gross changes in the supply and demand of labour over a period of years, can be most misleading. The outflow may create as well as resolve problems in the farm sector because the pronounced seasonality of farming operations requires for some months in the year a supply of hands which is vastly in excess of that which can be occupied the whole year through. A point will be reached beyond which labour can only be withdrawn seasonally if withdrawal is not to raise farm costs.[32]

The significance of this model for English agriculture during the 'Golden Age' should be apparent. Even during the first half of the century the resident labour-force had not been able to cope with peak season requirements. The long-term movement out of agriculture from the 1850s, while improving winter employment and earnings levels, was also accentuating the problems of scarcity at times of peak cultivation and crop-gathering. Thus in 1857 the chairman of the Herefordshire Agricultural Society actually remarked that labour was fortunately short at harvest since otherwise it would be superabundant in winter.[33] The growing seasonal deficiency was much greater than the supply now available from the Celtic countries could make good. Unless the remaining labour-force worked much harder or more efficiently, or unless capital were substituted for labour, output would suffer. Yet the demands on agricultural output were growing and in practice they were met.

One solution was for farmers to hire specialists in particular farm tasks from a distance. Joseph Arch himself travelled as a hedger as far from his Warwickshire home as Leominster in Herefordshire.[34] Another solution was mechanization. From 1815 to 1850 the abundance of cheap labour had militated against new technology. Bell's reaper, for instance, had lain dormant from its invention in 1826 until its manufacture under a new name by Crosskill in 1853. Welfare considerations had also impeded technological advance: as late as 1848 some Suffolk farmers were still obliged by their leases to thresh by flail instead of machine in order to maintain winter employment, while in Nottinghamshire leading landowners had deliberately delayed the introduction of threshing machines.[35] The seasonal pattern in the labour shortages of the 1850s induced farmers to mechanize mowing and reaping; according to the *Farmer's Magazine* this was 'the very age for the ready adoption of such a substitute', not least because American mowers and reapers had first been exhibited in this country at the Great Exhibition but also because the Irish Famine, the gold rushes, the Crimean war and industrial expansion were combining to cream off the itinerant haymakers and harvesters. Using machines these operations could be completed in the same time as hitherto, using only the regular farm staff and free therefore from the uncertain flow of travelling hands and of the strikes which they engineered whenever their number was few.[36] The permanent farm staff would not resist mechanization since some of them would be paid more to work the mowers and reapers. Similarly cultivation was mechanized and its work spread more evenly over the year. Steam-engines for a variety of farm jobs, steam threshing machines and ultimately steam ploughs were widely adopted.

An important consequence of mechanization was the creation of an élite of machine-minding labourers more skilled and better paid than their fellows, and a body of full-time machinery operators in the employ of agricultural contractors. Full-time machinery operators numbered 55 at the census of 1851, 1,441 (including 236 proprietors of machines) in 1861 and 2,160 in 1871. The number employed as specialists in land drainage was also rising, from 11 in 1851 to 1,761 in 1861.[37] There had always been great variety in the occupations of the countryside, but in the 1850s and 1860s the differentiation of farm hands into skilled and unskilled was on an entirely new plane.

The potential demand for skilled farm mechanics was apparently exaggerated at the time, but it helped to overcome the reluctance of the farmers to have their men schooled. Many cases were cited of clumsy labourers who repeatedly broke the machinery entrusted to them. Edwin Chadwick was told by a firm which hired out steam-engines to agriculturists that they were willing only to have them handled by their own employees, 'for they cannot trust their engines in such hands as are at present to be got amongst farm servants'.[38] It was generally agreed that the skill of the machine operator must command appreciably higher pay than ordinary farm work and in response to the demand there arose a generation of young steam labourers who were regarded by their fellows as 'a mild species of aristocracy'.[39] The problem, as employers saw it, was to train the operators to perform their tasks efficiently without allowing them to forget their station in life. As late as 1875 this was expressed in the terms, 'the rural Arcadia of which we can at present do little more than dream is one . . . in which education will make our peasants more intelligent workers while it will be too widely spread to make them look down on work'.[40] The demand for better-trained workers doubtless led to better attendances at village schools, which were surprisingly numerous, and helped to change rural attitudes in favour of the Education Act of 1870.

VI

Schooling and other social overheads ought, in fairness, to be considered part of the return to labour. As Richard Jefferies remarked in his letters to *The Times* in 1872 on the Wiltshire farm labourer, the farmer was 'expected to find the labourer, not only good cottages, allotments, schooling, good wages, but Heaven knows what besides'.[41] Cash wages were rising. A significant proportion of farm workers received over £100 per annum in cash and kind for the labour of their entire families in 1870, and even more received £70 or £80 per annum. Such men were able to deposit money in savings banks, but very few were able to move into the dealer and smallholder class. The growing proportion of labourers who could save demonstrates that the rise in money wages was not wholly wiped out by the rising cost of living.[42]

Fringe benefits and social overheads improved in step with the rise in cash wages and were less sensitive to erosion by the rising cost of living. Information on the value of perquisites during the 1850s and 1860s is hard to find and the enormous variation from farm to farm and season to season in any case prevents exact calculations. Nevertheless there are plenty of signs of a general improvement in conditions. Men who were hired by the year began to switch jobs more often. This was attributed to the desire of young wives to secure better cottages and seems to have spurred landowners to provide improved housing and to attach gardens to newly built cottages as an additional attraction.[43] Allotments spread. Labourers broke away in thousands from the Church of England and built Wesleyan and other chapels. Branches of the Oddfellows, the Foresters and other national friendly societies of a more reliable kind than had hitherto existed in rural areas sprang up, as well as some forms of co-operative society. The use of gang labour for cultivation work was dwindling before the Gangs Act of 1867 was passed, since the labour of wives and children was spontaneously withdrawn from the rougher field work as male earnings rose. The poaching gangs and presumably the urgent need and intense bitterness which had brought them into existence faded away. The cottage hospital movement began at Cranleigh, Surrey, in 1859 and spread to other rural districts. Some clergymen organized libraries and lectures which were extensively patronized by labourers; over 2,000 periodicals circulated in 40 Norfolk parishes in a single winter. In north Hampshire it was estimated in 1874 that 30 per cent more of the labourers could write than in 1850 and that most of the young people were now literate. In Herefordshire in 1865 eight landed proprietors and professional men founded the Hereford Cottage Improvement Society Ltd. to buy and build cottages to sell or let to labourers, and in 1867 they founded the Herefordshire Domestic and General Farm Servants Registration Society, which two years later had 260 employers and 323 servants on its books.[44] These improvements had their counterparts elsewhere. After the bleakness of life for the bulk of farm workers in the 1820s, 1830s and 1840s, these changes, slight as they may now appear, represented an immense bettering of conditions.

VII

The difficulties which beset the organizers of farm workers' unions are almost proverbial. This makes the more surprising the customary accounts of the rapid growth of Arch's union in 1872, accounts which suggest that farm labourers suddenly and spontaneously combined in a vast national organization to combat atrocious conditions which had persisted unchanged for scores of years. It has recently been observed that 'why discontent became articulate at precisely this period is not wholly clear'.[45] Any sign of labour organization which can be detected before 1872 may confirm the impression that bargaining power in the agricultural labour market had in fact begun earlier to shift from the employer's side, and at the same time may afford a more satisfactory account of the supposedly abrupt genesis of Arch's union.

At the end of the 1850s the shortage of hands at hay-time and harvest had emboldened the resident labourers of some districts to strike for higher pay. Already in the early 1850s there had been a short-lived union at Montacute, Somerset, and there are tantalizing hints of others which left no real trace. During the 1860s there were occasional strikes of hop-pickers in Kent and the Farnham district directed against individual growers, and a society which had been founded in mid-Kent to regulate the supply of pickers was engaging in strike-breaking activity. 'Wildcat' strikes like this, together with occasional stoppages of work in winter when higher provision prices and uncertain employment still threatened the slender gains of the 'Golden Age', took place throughout the 1860s, although they were mainly confined to one farm or parish. In 1866 mowers were so scarce in one west Midland county that even without resort to strike action the men so much held the upper hand that piece rates were advanced and they were conveyed to work by fly.[46]

Wages in agriculture began to rise steeply from the mid-1860s. More formal combinations to improve the pay and conditions of farm workers still further arose in widely scattered counties. For short periods they often attained their objects. By this time a generation had reached manhood which had no personal experience of the mass pauperism of the first half of the century, a generation familiar with the migrants from farm labour who had bettered their lot, a generation becoming accustomed to reading weekly newspapers and above all possessed of organizing experience acquired by running chapels and branches of friendly societies. The labour combination which followed began in England with the formation of an Agricultural Labourers' Protective Association in Kent in 1866. The next year a major strike at Gawcott in Buckinghamshire spread over into Hertfordshire and there were incipient combinations in Lincolnshire. From that time on there was rioting (precipitated by alterations in the administration of village charities by the Charity Commissioners and more immediately by enclosures of commons at Swaffham and Fakenham) and union activity in Norfolk, where an Association for the Defence of the Rights of the Poor, founded in 1870, grew into Flaxman's Eastern Counties'

Union. The combined number of offences against the game laws and cases of arson in the counties reached its peak in 1870, while between 1870 and 1872 labour unrest was widespread. It was generally agreed that the leaders of the snowballing unions of 1871–2 who were themselves farm workers (and many leaders were not) were men who had been able during the preceding years to rise a little above the mass, often local preachers. The widening range of earnings had, ironically, brought forth some of the movement's key men.

In 1871 the first large-scale, more than local, union was established by the vicar of Leintwardine, Herefordshire, and called the North Herefordshire and South Shropshire Agricultural Labourers' Improvement Society. This body sponsored a successful policy of migration to higher-paid districts, held a number of well-attended meetings to one of which Arch himself came, and rapidly gained approximately 30,000 members in six counties. The Society set its face, however, against strike action. In February 1872 a deputation of men who were apparently disturbed by a fall in the real wage invited Joseph Arch to address the famous meeting at Wellesbourne, Warwickshire. Nation-wide union activity followed throughout 1872, although some of the organizations, such as the first to be established in Oxfordshire (at Milton in April), seem to have started independently of the Wellesbourne movement.[47]

These instances show that strike action and unionism among farm workers were not so much a product of Arch's endeavour in the 1870s, important though that was in securing national action, but earlier and spontaneous reactions to the gradual shift in the balance of the labour market and perhaps finally to a check in the upward course of the standard of living. Legislation like the Union Chargeability Act of 1865 (which ended the closed parish system), the Royal Commission on the Employment of Children, Young Persons, and Women, of 1867 (which was followed by the Gangs Act) and the first Education Act (of 1870) reveal that a wind of change was already blowing in the 1860s.

The repercussions on the farmer's purse and attitudes were bound to be considerable. Labour costs per man rose just when farming could have absorbed more employees. Mechanization was part of the answer, the more forceful because the seasonal tasks which were most affected by labour scarcity were most amenable to machine work. According to the censuses the number of agricultural labourers, farm servants and shepherds in England in 1871 was 22 per cent smaller than it had been in 1851. Since more work was available the reduced labour-force was more efficiently employed and better rewarded. The farmer had been obliged to substitute capital for some of the labour he needed and this had its effect on the level of industrial inputs to agriculture, and hence on the prosperity of mid-Victorian industry.

VIII

The bewildering variety of local experience perplexes any attempt to generalize about the agricultural labour market. Nevertheless the basic supply and demand situation provides a scheme for descriptions and explanations of the level of return to labour which, although a simple enough device, has not been systematically used by historians. Certainly the notion of an unevenly felt shortage of farm labour during the 'Golden Age' may be used to organize the scattered indications of accompanying changes: changes in attitudes to labour's welfare, in wages, fringe benefits and social overheads, in the farmer's willingness to mechanize, and the transition to collective bargaining.

In summary, the salient features of the English agricultural labour market during the period 1793 to 1872 seem to have been these: during the inflation of the Revolutionary and Napoleonic wars the diminishing supply, rising demand and rising return to labour were interrupted only by the brief pause of the Peace of Amiens. Between Waterloo and the middle of the century, despite the long-run growth of demand, the continual burgeoning of the rural population produced a supply of farm labour which was usually excessive. The peak labour-force was reached as late as 1851 and neither the seasonal shortages of resident labour nor private charity were able to raise the total return to labour measurably.

The striking change came with the third quarter of the century when the expansion of demand for labour overtook (at some points more than others) a supply which was starting to contract. The only reversal of this new trend, whereby farm wages came to fluctuate with the volume of migration rather than with the price of flour, was in times of trade recession. In 1858, for example, there was a backwash of labour into Norfolk just when the demand for farm products was least, and there was in consequence a sharp, temporary drop in earnings.[48] Otherwise, during the 'Golden Age' as a whole, a shift in the attitudes of the well-to-do towards the labourer and a thin froth of welfare legislation followed the discovery that the labour supply was less than adequate. The shift in attitudes was almost mechanical. Social facilities were quickly extended by landowners and philanthropic associations. Farmers were obliged to pay higher wages and swung round, too, to express agreement that poorly paid labour was in the long run inefficient. Wages, fringe benefits and social overheads varied from one district, one type of farming and one year to another. They are amenable only to a makeshift assessment of the direction and magnitude of the changes. Such an assessment shows that it was during the 1850s, not the 1870s, that the balance of advantage in the agricultural labour market first favoured the employee, that this was recognized and that the return to labour was expanded beyond precedent.

NOTES TO CHAPTER 10

1. E. L. Jones, 'English Farming before and during the Nineteenth Century', *Economic History Review*, 2nd ser., xv (1962), 150–1.
2. *Reminiscences of Country Life* (1939), p. 121.
3. *General View of the Agriculture of ... Hereford* (1805), pp. 148–9.
4. Charles Hadfield, *The Canals of Southern England* (1955), pp. 77–8.
5. Jack Simmons (ed.), *Robert Southey: Letters from England* (1951), p. 42.
6. The most convenient source for the whole period dealt with in this paper is B. R. Mitchell and Phyllis Deane, *Abstract of British Historical Statistics* (Cambridge, 1962), pp. 348–50.
7. On Hampshire, E. L. Jones, 'Eighteenth-century Changes in Hampshire Chalkland Farming', *Agricultural History Review*, viii (1960), reprinted as Chapter 1 above; on Cumberland, William Dickinson, 'On the Farming of Cumberland', *Journ. Roy. Agric. Soc. Eng.*, xiii (1850), p. 233.
8. Agricultural Economics Research Institute, Oxford, Special Collection.
9. H. P. R. Finberg (ed.), *Gloucestershire Studies* (1957), p. 260; Jones, *loc. cit.* [Chapter 1 above]; F. Bamford (ed.), *An Eighteenth Century Correspondence* (1936), p. 222.
10. M. J. R. Healy and E. L. Jones, 'Wheat Yields in England, 1815–59', *Journal of the Royal Statistical Society*, Series A., 1962, Table 1 in Chapter 8 above; Phyllis Deane and W. A. Cole, *British Economic Growth* (Cambridge, 1962), table 31, p. 143.
11. John Arkwright to Richard Arkwright, 27 September 1831 (in possession of D. L. Arkwright); John Biddulph's Diary, 16 January 1833, Hereford City Library; J. D. Marshall, 'Nottinghamshire Labourers in the early nineteenth century', *Transactions of the Thoroton Society*, lxiv (1961), 66.
12. A. M. Colson, 'The Revolt of the Hampshire Agricultural Labourer', M.A. thesis, London University (1936).
13. E. Selley, *Village Trade Unions in Two Centuries* (1919), p. 24.
14. *Ibid.*, p. 32; R. Groves, *Sharpen the Sickle* (1949), pp. 26–7; Barbara Kerr, 'The Dorset Agricultural Labourer, 1750–1850', *Proc. Dorset Nat. Hist. and Arch. Soc.*, 84 (1962) n. 13.
15. *Hereford Journal*, 29 June 1842.
16. *Ibid.*, 29 July 1846.
17. J. D. Dent, 'The Present Condition of the English Agricultural Labourer, 1871', *Journ. Roy. Agric. Soc. Eng.*, 2nd ser., vii (1871), 347.
18. 'Recent Improvements in Norfolk Farming', *Journ. Roy. Agric. Soc. Eng.*, xix (1858), 292.
19. J. R. Bellerby, United Kingdom: Average of Industrial Wage Rates, Annual Series 1850–1947. A.E.R.I. Research Paper, typescript (n.d.), 7.

20. See F. Purdy, 'On the Decrease of the Agricultural Population of England and Wales, 1851–61', *Journ. Stat. Soc.*, XXVII (1864), 399, and 'Decrease of the Agricultural Population', *Farmer's Magazine*, 3rd ser., XXVI (1864), 283; Deane and Cole, *op. cit.*, p. 143; Mitchell and Deane, *op. cit.*, pp. 20, 60.

21. J. D. Dent, 'Agricultural Notes on the Census of 1861', *Journ. Roy. Agric. Soc. Eng.*, XXV (1864), 320.

22. See e.g. 'Scarcity of Labourers', *Farmer's Mag.*, 3rd ser., XVI (1859), 189; 'The Scarcity of Hands at Harvest', 3rd ser., XVI (1859), 313; 'Agricultural Labourers Wanted', 3rd ser., XVIII (1860), 354.

23. L. Marion Springall, *Labouring Life in Norfolk Villages, 1834–1914* (1936), p. 50.

24. *Hereford Journal*, 26 October 1853 and 18 January 1854.

25. B. Almack, 'On the Agriculture of Norfolk', *Journ. Roy. Agric. Soc. Eng.*, V (1845), 345.

26. 'On the Condition of the Agricultural Labourer', *Journ. Roy. Agric. Soc. Eng.*, VII (1847), 23–4.

27. 'On the Farming of Somersetshire', *Journ. Roy. Agric. Soc. Eng.*, XI (1850), 754.

28. 'The Agricultural Labourer: His Condition and Requirements—as considered at the recent agricultural meetings', *Farmer's Mag.*, 3rd ser., X (1856), 500–1.

29. 'The Employment of Women and Children in Agriculture', *Journal of Agriculture*, 3rd ser., III (1867), 47.

30. Selley, *op. cit.*, p. 33.

31. A. G. Bradley, *When Squires and Farmers Thrived* (1927), p. 120.

32. Cf. A. A. Pepelasis and P. A. Yotopoulos, *Surplus Labor in Greek Agriculture, 1953–1960* (Athens, 1962).

33. *Hereford Journal*, 21 October 1857.

34. Hampton Court Collection, Labourers' Wages Books, Herefs. R.O.

35. H. Raynbird, 'On the Farming of Suffolk', *Journ. Roy. Agric. Soc. Eng.*, VIII (1848), 284; Marshall, *loc. cit.*, p. 67.

36. See e.g. Buckman, *op. cit.*, p. 11; 'The Present Position of Agriculture', *Farmer's Mag.*, 3rd ser., XV (1859), 174; J. B. Spearing, 'On the Agriculture of Berkshire', *Journ. Roy. Agric. Soc. Eng.*, XXI (1860), 42–3, 45.

37. Dent (1871), *loc. cit.*, p. 393.

38. Edwin Chadwick, 'The Demand for more Intelligent Labour in Agriculture', *Journ. Stat. Soc.*, XXVII (1865), 32.

39. C. C. Spence, *God Speed the Plow* (1959), p. 116.

40. F. Clifford, 'The Labour Bill in Farming', *Journ. Roy. Agric. Soc. Eng.*, 2nd ser., XI (1875), 126.

41. Reprinted in *The Toilers of the Field* (1892), p. 246.

42. T. E. Kebbel, *The Agricultural Labourer* (1887), pp. 221–2.

43. Dent (1871), *loc. cit.*, p. 346.

44. Springall, *op. cit.*, p. 75; Joseph Stevens, *The Farm Labourer, at home, and in the field* (1874), no pagination; Memo. and Articles of Association of Hereford Cottage Improvement Society, 1865, and 'Farm Servants Registry', Hampton Court Collection, Herefs. R.O.

45. J. P. D. Dunbabin, 'The "Revolt of the Field": the Agricultural Labourers' Movement in the 1870s', *Past and Present*, 26 (1963), 71.

46. C. Cadle, 'The Agriculture of Worcestershire', *Journ. Roy. Agric. Soc. Eng.*, 2nd ser., III (1867), 449; see also 'Scarcity of Labourers', *loc. cit.*, p. 189; Spearing, *loc. cit.*, p. 45; 'A Strike of Farm Workers', *The Countryman*, LVI (1959), 622–4; George Sturt, *A Small Boy in the Sixties* (1927), p. 79; C.

Whitehead, 'On Recent Improvements in the Cultivation and Management of Hops', *Journ. Roy. Agric. Soc. Eng.*, 2nd ser., VI (1870), 360.
47. The sources on formal labour combinations are Selley, *op. cit.*, pp. 36–7; Groves, *op. cit.*, pp. 33–4; R. C. Russell, *The 'Revolt of the Field' in Lincolnshire* (n.d.), pp. 78–83; A. E. W. Salt, 'The Agricultural Labourer in Herefordshire', *Trans. Woolhope Club* (1947), pp. 98–9.
48. Springall, *op. cit.*, pp. 50, 79.